CW00751506

The Real Hawaii

THE REAL HAWAII

ITS HISTORY AND PRESENT CONDITION

INCLUDING

THE TRUE STORY OF THE REVOLUTION

(A Revised and Enlarged Edition of " The Boston at Hawaii ")

BY

LUCIEN YOUNG, U. S. N.

DOUBLEDAY & McCLURE
COMPANY : NEW YORK
MDCCCXCIX

Copyright, 1898, by
LUCIEN YOUNG.

———

Copyright, 1899, by the
DOUBLEDAY & McCLURE CO.

The Author dedicates this book to

J̇NO. L. STEVENS

and

G. C. WILTSE,

two as honorable, efficient, conscientious, and patriotic Americans as ever represented their country at home or abroad.

PREFACE.

During the period of seven months before and seven months after the overthrow of the Hawaiian monarchy, in 1892 and 1893, I was a Lieutenant on board of the U. S. S. Boston, stationed at Honolulu. The period was one of intense political activity and feeling in that city, and the development of republican sentiment, ending in the overthrow of Queen Liliuokalani, interested me greatly. The people of Honolulu, of all classes and nationalities, are hospitable, social, and communicative, to a greater degree than those of any other country I have ever visited. Within a few weeks after my arrival I was upon terms of more or less friendly intimacy with nearly all of the leading men of all parties. I was more particularly brought into personal contact with leading royalists, they frequently discussing their plans and projects, without reserve, in my presence. The evident transition state of the country, and the great importance, both from a commercial and a military standpoint, of Hawaii to the United States, caused me to study the people and the situation, as well as the past history of the country, most diligently, and to keep full current notes of the results of my observations and studies.

Upon my return to the United States in the fall of 1893, I wrote out these notes.

About this time the report of Commissioner Blount stating that the Hawaiian monarchy had been overthrown through the agency of the American Minister and the Boston, the letter of Secretary Gresham to President Cleveland recommending the restoration of ex-Queen Liliuokalani, and the attempts of the President to carry such recommendation into execution, became public.

Knowing of my own knowledge that much of the evidence upon which Mr. Blount based his report was utterly false and unreliable; that his conclusions were, if anything, more misleading than his evidence, and that a deadly wrong had been and was being done to the diplomatic and naval officers of the United States who were in Honolulu at the time of the revolution, I desired to immediately publish my manuscript, and in compliance with the regulations of the Navy Department, submitted it to the Honorable Secretary of the Navy for his inspection, and requested permission to have it printed. No reply was made to my request for two months, when I was forbidden to publish it.

Since the late change of administration I have revisited Hawaii, brought my statements up to date in some respects, and obtained the permission of Secretary Long to publish my manuscript.

I am aware that, in some respects, this is a contribution to by-gone history, and that popular interest in the subject-matter does not exist to the degree that it did when it was fresh in the public mind, but the rank injustice done to Minister Stevens and Captain Wiltse, the Commander of the Boston, both of whom are now dead, and their associates, and the wicked and malicious misrepresentation and criticism to which they have been subjected, have impelled me, as a duty to the living and the dead and to historical accuracy, as well as in defense of American good faith and the fair name of the Republic, to put on record the facts, which I know to be true from my personal observation and investigation.

LUCIEN YOUNG.

WASHINGTON, D. C.,
May 8, 1898.

CONTENTS.

LIST OF ILLUSTRATIONS.

CHAPTER I.

Prior to the bloodless revolution in the Hawaiian
Islands, on January 17th, 1893, resulting in the
overthrow of a semi-barbaric monarchy, a large
number of people in the United States hardly knew
of their existence, beyond a vague recollection of
having read of Captain Cook and the Sandwich
Islands in their school books. It was not an uncommon occurrence for the merchants of Honolulu
to receive letters directed to the "Hawaiian Islands,
West Indies." Such was the interest of the majority of the people of the United States, especially
in the eastern section, in regard to this most important group of islands in the North Pacific, destined in
the near future to become more important to the west
coast of the United States than the Ægean Islands
were to the commercial enterprises of the ancient
Phœnicians. The simple overthrow of the Hawaiian monarchy would have created but a mere ripple
of interest that would have soon merged into the
ordinary wave of human progress; but when the
resulting Provisional Government appealed for
political union with the United States, and the adherents of the defunct royalty accused the sailors of
the United States Cruiser Boston of having assisted
in their overthrow, the Hawaiian Islands became

1

well known through the press comments. But as
the general statements published at the time bore
the same relation to rumor and canard that bread
bore to liquor in Falstaff's tavern bill, I propose to
give an historical account of facts as obtained from
personal observation and various sources of information during a stay of fourteen months in the
islands on a man-of-war. The official documents
bearing upon the subject are so easily accessible
that I have not republished any of them, and from
the smallness of this volume I have not considered
it of sufficient importance to quote authorities. It
is sufficient to say that all statements of fact herein
contained are either of my own knowledge or the
result of careful and painstaking study and investigation conducted upon the ground.

The United States has for many years found it
necessary to maintain a constant naval force in the
waters of the Hawaiian Islands to protect its growing interests and defend its treaty rights against
political agitation and foreign intrigue. In pursu-
ance of this policy, the United States Cruiser Boston,
on which I was serving at the time as an officer,
was ordered, in August, 1892, to relieve the U. S.
S. San Francisco at Honolulu. The Boston is one
of the most formidable cruisers of the new navy, of
the superstructure class, of three thousand tons dis-
placement and a maximum speed of fifteen and a
half knots per hour. Her crew consisted of 280
officers and men, well organized and drilled. The
main battery consisted of two 8-inch central pivot

COCOA-NUT GROVE

COCOA-NUTS

MANGOES

BREAD-FRUIT

(From photographs loaned by the San Francisco Wave)

high-powered guns mounted in echelon, and six 6-inch high-powered guns mounted in broadside pivots. The secondary battery consisted of two 6-pounder, two 3-pounder, and 1-pounder rapid-fire guns; two 47mm., two 37mm. revolving cannon; Gatling guns, torpedo outfit, and small arms.

We passed through the Golden Gate, bound for the Hawaiian Islands, on the 10th of August, 1892. A short stop was made at Santa Cruz, and from there we took our parting look at the California coast, steering direct for the Island of Oahu. The occurrences on our voyage from Santa Cruz to Honolulu were, like the generality of modern sea trips, too trivial to be interesting, and too unvaried to afford amusement. No fables of the ancients were realized, and Neptune offered no resistance to our invasion of his watery empire; nor did we see the beautiful goddess Amphitrite skimming the surface of the deep, seated in her coral chariot, drawn by mermaids and surrounded by musical neriads. In fact, we encountered none of the adventures or wonders that surrounded the celebrated voyage of Æneas. We simply had a smooth sea, fine weather, a light northeasterly breeze, and an occasional sight of a passing sailing vessel; yet all on board were cheerful.

Early in the morning of the 24th of August we made out Koko Head, a novel and attractive landmark on the eastern extremity of the Island of Oahu. In a few hours thereafter we rounded picturesque Diamond Head, a lofty extinct volcano, which marks the entrance to a long roadstead on the south of the island. Steering along parallel with a coral reef that protects the shore from the ocean swell, we soon passed through a narrow entrance in the reef to the snug harbor of Honolulu, the capital of the island government.

The Island of Oahu, the most populous, although the third in size of the Hawaiian group, is about forty miles long and twenty-three wide, and in appearance remarkably picturesque. As viewed from Honolulu on the south, a chain of lofty mountains extends from back of Diamond Head the entire length of the island. The elevated plain of Ewa separates this range from another parallel mountain range lying west of Honolulu. The main range is seamed by deep, shady ravines, which spread out in rolling valleys until they join the plain upon which Honolulu is situated. The whole island is volcanic, and in many parts extinct craters of large dimensions may be seen ; but many ages have elapsed since any eruption took place. In fact, all the islands of the Hawaiian Archipelago are of volcanic origin, and are situated in the Northern Pacific Ocean, just within the limits of the tropics, extending for nearly four hundred miles in a direction from southeast to northwest, from 18° 50′ to 23° 05′ north latitude, and from 154° 40′ to 161° 50′ west longitude from Greenwich. They are some 2,100 miles from San Francisco, 3,800 miles from Auckland, 4,400 miles from Sydney, 3,400 miles from Yokohama, and 4,800 miles from Hongkong. They

consist of eight principal islands and several islets.
Of these only seven of the largest are inhabited,
namely: Hawaii, Maui, Oahu, Kauai, Molokai,
Lanai, and Niihau. The bulk of population and
the principal industrial and mercantile enterprises
are on the first five. The eight islands combined
have an area of 6,740 square miles, of which Hawaii, from which the group takes its name, contains 4,210 square miles; Maui, 760; Kauai 600
and Oahu about the same, and Molokai 270 square
miles.

This group of islands was first discovered in the
sixteenth century by Juan de Gatan, the navigator
of one of the Spanish expeditions in the Pacific
during the period when the flag of Spain dominated in the waters of that ocean. The name given
to this archipelago by Gatan was Islas de Mesa, or
Table Land. From the evidences to be found in
old documents and charts, corroborated by native
tradition, there are several other instances where
these islands, during a remote epoch, were visited
by white people, but they did not come into prom-
inence until rediscovered by Captain Cook in 1778,
nearly three hundred years after the time of Gatan.
Captain Cook was in command of an English expedition in search of a northern passage from the
Pacific to the Atlantic, and by accident came upon
these islands; and in honor of his patron, the Earl
of Sandwich, the first lord of the admiralty, he
gave them the name of The Sandwich Islands. From
that time on, and especially after the visit of Van-

couver, the islands became of great importance to
the maritime world, and a bone of contention to
the European powers for their possession.   The
officials of France and England took every advantage of the primitive simplicity of the people, who
had existed for ages, isolated and unknown to the
rest of the world.   They commenced a series of
petty annoyances and vexatious interferences with
the island government which on several occasions
gave the foreign representatives pretexts for action
with a view to the ultimate subversion of the native government and seizure of the islands.   Timely
interference and threatening demands of United
States officials, of U. S. men-of-war, and Ameri-
ican diplomacy were all that preserved the independence of the islands.

At the time of the discovery of the Hawaiian
Islands they were inhabited by a race of Polyne-
sians living under a social organization strikingly
similar to that of Europe in the tenth and eleventh
centuries.   They had kings, who were hereditary
suzerains, having under them a lot of vassal chiefs,
who were granted certain tenures in consideration
of military service, leaving the common people
the mere privileges of villains.   The power of
these petty sovereigns was limited only by the endurance of the subjects, while the priesthood exercised an unlimited authority in the " tabu," which
means " prohibited," or forbidden under the penalty
of death.   As might be expected, where so many
small kingdoms existed within such narrow limits,

war was of frequent occurrence, until a powerful
chief, from the Island of Hawaii, gradually conquered the whole of the island and then the entire
group, over which he ruled with great ability, wis-
dom, and good sense for a period of twenty four
years, under the title of Kamehameha I. It was
during this reign that the influence of the white
race began to assert itself and the whole social and
political condition of the people became revolution-
ized, the power of the heathen priests destroyed,
and the way paved for an easy introduction of
Christian civilization by the American missionaries,
who landed for the first time in 1820, the year following the death of Kamehameha I.

During this long and vigorous reign, in which
the chiefs remained in undisputed possession of
their lands, there was developed a sentiment favorable to permanent individual rights, which brought
about a remarkable change from feudal to hereditary succession ; followed ultimately by the buying
and selling of lands. White foreigners in consequence became land-owners. In 1833 Kamehameha
III came to the throne, and acting under the influences of the incoming tide of civilization and recognizing the defenceless condition of the common
people, he, a few years later, proclaimed a " Bill of
Rights," which at once transformed a feudal despotism into a constitutional monarchy. The Bill
of Rights was followed in 1845 to 1847 by the organization of an executive ministry, the creation of
a judiciary department, and the adoption of pro-

visions for an adjustment of land tenure; and in 1852 a constitution was promulgated forming the basis of others which followed. A legislative body was created, consisting of thirty nobles, appointed by the crown, and not less than twenty-four representatives elected by universal suffrage. This constitution was so modified in 1864 as to require both branches of the legislative body to sit and vote together in the same chamber, and the suffrage of the people was restricted by a property qualification and the ability to read and write; provisions which remained in force until 1887.

From the very first, and throughout the ninety-four years in which the Kamehamehas reigned over the islands, American influence dominated over that of all other foreign countries in Hawaiian affairs. American institutions were adopted, the American school system inaugurated, and American laws enacted and put in force, developing property interests, commercial associations and political education almost identical with those of any State within the American Union. To protect and foster these growing interests the United States, as early as 1820, established a commercial agency on the Hawaiian Islands, and, in 1823, Commodore Jones of the United States Navy negotiated a treaty of commerce and navigation, which, though it was not ratified at Washington, was the first treaty ever negotiated by the Hawaiians with any foreign power. From time to time thereafter naval vessels of the United States visited the islands, and on several occasions protected the autonomy of the native government against the English and French aggressions, based upon trumped-up claims of their respective consular agents. In 1842 the independence of the islands was practically recognized by the United States, the commercial agency was elevated to a diplomatic position by the appointment of a Commissioner, and in 1863 the rank of the United States diplomatic representative was again raised to that of Minister Resident.

During this entire period the continued and steady decrease of the native race, the creation of agricultural necessities and growing of sugar cane, importation of Oriental contract labor, together with the rapid growth of the foreign population, gradually developed a condition favorable to a political evolution calculated to disturb the internal affairs of the government, and injure those foreigners who had invested money in commercial enterprises in the islands. As long as the Kamehameha race of kings governed the islands, American interests were in no danger of being subverted, through internal intrigue, by those of any other foreign power; but in 1874, when the last of that dynasty, Kamehameha V, died, the political affiliations with the English intriguers became alarming and necessitated a renewed energy on the part of American residents and officials to maintain their commercial and political supremacy. Hence after a year's experience of political confusion and uneasy agitation under the elected King, Lunililo, David Kalakaua, supported by the American residents, was chosen, after a stormy election, by the legislature to fill the vacant throne, in opposition to Queen Emma, the widow of Kamehameha IV. Emma was thoroughly imbued with British sympathies and most hostile to the commercial interests of the United States, and her native followers, supported by the English and a lot of irresponsibles or refugees, bitterly contested the election. They organized a formidable riot and surrounded the Court-House and, when they saw they had lost by a large majority, attacked the building and assaulted the members, driving them from the legislative hall and killing several. Sailors and marines from the two American men-of-war in the harbor landed, and after suppressing the riot, maintained order in the city of Honolulu until Kalakaua was secure on the throne. An English warship also landed men, but they did not interfere.

Kalakaua was only a high chief, in no way related to the extinct royal family, and was reputed to be the illegitimate son of a negro cobbler who had emigrated to the islands from Boston. Before his elevation to the throne, he was a pettifogging police-court attorney. He had held subordinate positions under the government, from which he had been discharged for corruption and incompetence. He drank and gambled inordinately. The assumption of authority afforded him ample means of displaying his natural instincts—those of a Polynesian savage. At times he would disguise these instincts

under a social polish and the appearances of a
gentleman. He was superstitious, sensual, and
corrupt, and, with the assistance of a class of adventurers of the same type as himself for advisers,
it was not long before he committed overt acts in
opposition to the promises made to those who
placed him on the throne, and sowed the seeds of
discontent that ultimately led to the overthrow of
the monarchical form of government. His principal adviser and counsellor was an unscrupulous
ex-Mormon missionary who had apostasized from
and swindled that church, who aided him in
estranging the native element from the whites,
resulting in a theretofore unknown intense race
hatred. A secret society was established, in which
childish mysteries were combined with obscene
forms gathered from the ancient religion of the
Hawaiian Islands. Kalakaua became the head of
this society, and in the course of time undertook
the role of a god, and as such constituted himself
the divine guide to the native clergy, and impressed the native race with the fear of himself as
a " kahuna," a witch doctor, who assumes to pray
people to death or cure the sick at will. One of
the great privileges enjoined upon the head of this
polytheistic church was to appear among the be-
lievers, bereft of all attire, and perform unspeakable rites to prove himself fit for heathen worship.
On one occasion, as late as 1890, the King came
out upon a dais stripped to the skin, and, in the
presence of several hundred pagans, at a secluded

place near Honolulu, fully proved himself an adept
in all the filthy performances required by his native
followers—performances of such an indescribably
barbarous nature as can only be found among the
savages inhabiting the South Sea Islands.   He
would have songs chanted by the native women at
the great functions of the court, which were simply
exaltations of his powers to employ and gratify the
baser passions, and wherever he went his train of
attendants sang obscene songs and danced lewd
dances.   To afford a better opportunity for enter-
taining his favored courtiers and a few special
tourists who wished to witness the savage customs,
he caused to be built a large boat-house, in the
harbor of Honolulu, and the scenes enacted there
beggar description.   Gambling, lewd practices,
immoral exhibitions, drunken carousals, and the
abominations of the hula dance, all combined to
establish his reputation as a prince of good fellows
with his large retinue of dissipated dependents.
By wholesale bribery, the use of soldiers at the
polling places, and general debasement of the
electorate and the appointment of legislators to
lucrative offices while they still held their seats in
the legislature, he was enabled to carry through
pernicious and extravagant legislation against the
will of the people.   In short, he became absolute
ruler.

With such power unopposed it only required a
little flattery on the part of his various disreputable
counsellors to work the King's vanity and ego-

tism up to the point of aspiring to the " Primacy of
the Pacific." In consequence an old vessel was
purchased and fitted out at great expense, and in
command of a worthless, drunken, half-pay English naval officer, and manned by boys from the
reform school and a few low whites, she was dispatched as a man-of-war, with an embassy to
assume a protectorate over the Samoan Islands, as
a beginning. On December 26, 1886, an unworthy
half-caste by the name of Bush was sent as envoy,
accompanied by a secretary and other attachés, to
King Malietoa. Upon the arrival of the embassy
they became the object of hostile demonstrations by
the representatives of the German firm who had
instigated the revolution then existing in Samoa.
The embassy were driven from the hotel, and taking refuge in a Samoan house, gave themselves up
to dissipation. Bush gathered around him the
lowest kind of half-castes and beach-combers, and,
with a decided appetite for native beverages and
mixed drinks, he went on a protracted spree. He
was run out of the window at the hotel for insulting
remarks, and his disreputable, lewd, and intemper-
ate habits, together with an attempt to introduce
the hula, disgusted even that savage, Malietoa, who
asked for his recall, and thus ended the attempt at
the confederation of the Pacific. The riotous
drunkenness and mutinous conduct of the officers and
men of the man-of-war were such that a German
gunboat had to interfere, and the vessel was
ordered to return to Honolulu. The captain took

her, instead, to Pago Pago, where he exchanged her small arms for gin and had a month's debauch. Finally she was brought back, the captain dismissed and the vessel sold.

Failing to become Emperor of Polynesia, Kalakaua was not content with the mere title of King, so, after being on the throne for nine years, he determined upon a useless and expensive coronation, the ceremonies of which would convey to all nations evidence of his autocratic authority. Three years were consumed in preparing for this great pageant. Bombastic notices were sent to all the powers apprising them of the event and inviting their representatives to be present.

To gratify another of his whims and still further clothe his already overburdened egotism, his extravagant dependents caused to be celebrated, at great expense and legislative appropriation of a large sum, the fiftieth anniversary of his birth. The festivities were to extend over a fortnight but were somewhat curtailed by inclement weather. Receptions, presentation of costly gifts, torchlight illuminations, a great feast and grand ball were the general features of this birthday jubilee, winding up with a hula that was so obscene as to offend even some of his depraved associates. The printer who printed the programme of the dances, prepared by Kalakau himself, was fined for "publishing indecent literature."

These unpleasant details, which fall far short of the truth, are given merely to show the

King's utter. unfitness for his position. On his return from a trip around the world, where he had managed to deceive the high officials of each country he visited by a correct demeanor, modest dress and a knowledge of languages, his innate barbarism, escaping from the long imprisonment on this trip, again asserted itself in bolder relief. The rapidly increasing revenues occasioned by the treaty of reciprocity with the United States were not sufficient to support the expensive and puerile extravagances of Kalakaua, and to meet them he had recourse to exemption money from lepers, unlawful rental of government lands, abuse of the franking privileges, embezzlement of public funds, and gross official corruption, which hardships upon the people but hastened the inevitable. The financial benefits of the treaty of reciprocity with the United States had the effect of encouraging a spirit of forbearance towards him, but the patience of the respectable foreign element and progressive natives at last became exhausted when the King accepted a large bribe from a Chinaman for an opium license for which he had already taken a larger bribe from another Chinaman. A secret committee of safety was organized and quietly armed, and on the 30th of June, 1887, an enthusiastic mass-meeting passed resolutions to the effect that the administration of the Hawaiian government had ceased, through corruption and incompetence, to perform its legitimate functions and afford protection to person and property. A committee waited upon the King and exacted from him specific

pledges, within twenty-four hours, of future good
government on the basis of a new constitution.
Kalakaua appealed to the foreign diplomatic representatives to help him out of the dilemma, and they
not only refused but advised him to accept the
demands of the mass-meeting. Realizing his con-
summate guilt, and fearing the absolute loss of his
crown, the King, much to the surprise of the
revolutionists, who expected a fight, pusillani-
mously agreed to comply with all the demands of
the citizens. His most capricious and profligate
counsellor was removed from office and banished
the country, and a reform ministry appointed, one
that was in thorough sympathy with the people.
The King was compelled to sign a new constitution, which was subsequently ratified by a vote of
the people, in conformity with the demands of the
mass-meeting.

The general provisions of this constitution made
every male resident of Hawaii, of American or European descent, who had lived there a year and
taken an oath to support the constitution and laws
of Hawaii a legal voter, and distinctly enlarged the
measure of Hawaiian citizenship. The King was
deprived of the absolute right of veto, and the responsibility for the government was placed upon a
cabinet, subject to removal only by a vote of the
legislature elected by the people. Instead of the
nobles being appointed by the crown they were
chosen by a special electorate composed of citizens
possessed of an annual income of at least $600, or

unencumbered property to the value of $3,000, which practically gave to the whites the choice of one-half of the legislature. Another principal measure in the new constitution prohibited members of the legislature from holding any civil office. Emerging thus from an era of bombastic display, political corruption, and gross irregularities, the King was left as a mere figure-head. A large element of the population at first desired the total abolition of the monarchy ; but, after mature deliberation, they again exhibited their forbearance, and permitted the King to be tried once more, under the restrictions implied in the new order of administration. At the same time, it was explicitly understood and clearly foreseen that should the monarchy again fall into the hands of adventurers and repeat its imbecility and corruption, it would cease to exist, as it did on January the 17th, 1893. Kalakaua signed the new constitution under duress, and ever after he sought opportunities to regain his lost power. It is remarkable how patiently the foreign element endured and how considerate they were with this semi-barbaric monarchy. To a close observer, however, it was plainly apparent that the foundation of an ultimate abrogation of the monarchy had been laid, and the time was not far distant when it would cease to exist.

Princess Liliuokalani, a sister of the King, had been appointed heiress apparent. She strongly disapproved of her brother's assent to the reform constitution. In 1889 she joined what was known as the Wilcox plot for the overthrow of the new government and the establishment of herself on the throne. The entire plot was concocted in her home. Wilcox, a half-caste, who had been educated in Italy, at a military school, was to lead an armed revolt, which he did, the rendezvous and arming taking place at Liliuokalani's home. Wilcox succeeded in getting together a few natives and a band of disreputable loafers and surrounded the palace. The same people who brought Kalakaua to terms and enforced the reformations of 1887 reorganized and, after a small skirmish, drove the insurgents to cover, killed nine, and took the remainder prisoners. Upon the first fire the military ardor of Wilcox left him, and he immediately deserted his followers and took cowardly refuge in an old gasolene tank lying in the palace yard, where he remained, until the rest surrendered. The support thus given the King encouraged him in his efforts to recover his lost royal prerogatives, and he was able to find weak white judges to misinterpret the provisions of the new constitution and pervert its plain meanings in his favor. However, the principal constitutional limitations were maintained and the King up to his death remained simply the head of a constitutional government. The country became prosperous, taxes easy, internal improvements were carried on and the revenues were economically expended.

The once strong and athletic constitution of Kalakaua at last began to break down, under the influences of long and excessive dissipation, and in order to recruit his failing health the King visited California, in an American man-of-war. On the 20th of January, 1891, he died at the Palace Hotel, San Francisco. Upon the arrival of his remains at Honolulu, nine days later, his sister, Mrs. Dominis, who was acting as regent in the absence of the King, was proclaimed Queen under the title of Liliuokalani, and took the oath to support the constitution.

CHAPTER II.

The frequent attempts of Kalakaua to regain autocratic authority after the adoption of the new constitution led many whites and natives to believe that he would be the last Hawaiian monarch, and had it not been for the sudden surprise accompanying the tragic return of his remains, it is more than likely Liliuokalani would never have succeeded to the throne. It was a well-known fact that she had evinced on every occasion her disgust at her brother's acceptance of the new constitution, and her determination to re-establish the royal pretensions at the first opportunity was manifest. She had, on two occasions before her succession, entered into a conspiracy to supplant her brother even at the expense, if necessary, of walking over his dead body. The moment of her accession she fully intended to abrogate the constitution forced upon Kalakaua and proclaim one, instead, containing all the old prerogatives exercised by the Kamehamehas prior to the existence of a constitution. The cabinet of the late King, realizing the danger of such an act, promptly called upon the Queen in a body, and induced her to take the oath to support and maintain the existing constitution. Liliuokalani had greater courage and was more politic than her brother, but resembled him in superstition, selfish-

LILIUOKALANI.

ness, and savage ignorance, and, like him, was a hater of whites and a promoter of race prejudices. She was such a mistress of dissimulation as to convince many well-meaning people that she was a strict believer in the Christian religion, whereas she was an idolatress and worshipper of the old pagan superstitions of Hawaiian mythology. She kept continually around her kahunas and heathen sorcerers to counsel and assist her, and women of openly bad character were her constant personal attendants. She was addicted to the grossest social vices—in a word, she was the true sister of Kalakaua, and the attempt on her part to guide the destinies of not only her native subjects, but the thousands of Europeans in the Islands, was simply farcical. The course of affairs became evident at once. The Queen's first official act was a refusal to recognize the ministers of the late King, and they, upon the advice of the supreme court, resigned, and a ministry was appointed in their stead, composed of men she selected under promise, made in advance, that they would appoint her favorite paramour to the marshalship of the kingdom. This official had absolute command of the police force, and during the Queen's reign he was really vested with the powers of a dictator. His advice was paramount over that of the cabinet ministers, and it was not an uncommon procedure for him to openly, and in the presence of her ministers, oppose or nullify their contemplated acts.

Following the appointment of her ministry, the
Queen gradually began to interfere in the removal
of government officials, and to appoint incompetent
and irresponsible favorites in their stead.   She
stubbornly, but with more tact and diplomacy than
Kalakaua, usurped autocratic authority in all direc-
tions, yet with all her power and heathen practices
she was unable to obtain the fealty of her brown-
skinned subjects.   The reason for this was due
to the fact that Liliuokalani was not a Kamehameha, but only the sister of Kalakaua, both
of whom were the legitimate grandchildren of
the first man who was hanged for murder in
the Hawaiian Islands; and the occupancy of the
throne, established by Kamehameha, whom the
natives regarded as of divine origin, by this lowly
bred family, was keenly felt and bitterly opposed.
When she made a tour in state through her realm,
the natives received her with scant hospitality.
Her retainers could not even procure a supply of
food from the natives, much less presents, as was
the custom with ancient Hawaiian monarchs
travelling through the kingdom.   Fear and dissatisfaction on the part of some whites and many
natives led to a secret organization having for its
purpose the remedy of existing evils.   The Queen,
hearing of the formation of this conspiracy, at
first conceived the idea of using those engaged in
it in the promulgation of a new constitution, and
if unsuccessful in obtaining their co-operation, to
become familiar with their intents, so as to be able
at any moment to remove every possible danger of

disturbance in her contemplated *coup*. To this end she encouraged them in their designs, and diplomatically obtained at least a promise of their neutrality, if not their acquiescence. Then, relying upon the absolute support of the royal guard and the police force, she caused to be prepared a constitution granting her the powers which she craved, which she proposed to promulgate.

Everything was working well, when a large number of men, known to be hostile to her, were admitted to membership. In a feeling of unconcealed distrust, and fearing the legal opposition of the legislature recently chosen by the people, and soon to meet, she urged immediate action. Wilcox, who was one of the leaders, was sent for and given her ultimatum, that he and his colleagues must at once support her plans; and upon his refusal, she broke up the conspiracy, arrested him and a few others. They were brought to trial, and although the evidence was clear, she stopped the trial for fear the true facts would come out. Some of the conspirators fled the country, but others, including Wilcox, were elected to the legislature. This was in 1892. Before the Queen could do anything else in the way of changing the constitution, which she had, under mental reservation, taken an oath to support, the legislature met. The wire-pulling and political intrigue for a time were held in check through the approximately equal strength of three parties that composed the legislative body. The members were chosen at the biennial election in February, 1892, and in May following took their seats. They were divided into Reform, National Reform, and Liberal parties, and three or four independents. The Reform party was composed of the so-called missionary class, a term applied to all the progressive whites of American nationality or descent, Germans, and Portuguese. They had for their object the enactment of laws beneficial to commerce, the establishment of closer commercial relations with the United States, the construction of an ocean cable, and the development of agricultural interests based upon the minimum taxation for the support of the government. They supported all legislation that had for its object the internal improvements of the country, rigid segregation of lepers and contagious diseases, and were bitterly opposed to autocratic rule or personal power in the Queen.

The controlling power in the National Reform party was the English and Canadian whites, and those who had little or no property interests on the islands; among them were many adventurers who had immigrated to the islands for personal gain regardless of the methods of accomplishment. They favored English interests, and if possible an English protectorate as against American influences or commercial supremacy. The Liberal party was made up from the native members and lower class of whites and hangers-on at the palace. They had no policy and cared for none beyond the bribes or bargains they could obtain from the other two parties to vote in their interests. They were in favor

of universal suffrage and the absolute rule and au-
tocracy of the Queen. From the very first day on
which the members of the legislature took their
seats log-rolling, wire-pulling, and political corruption commenced. The Queen had this advantage :
her ministers could sit in the legislature and vote on
all subjects, except on a vote of want of confidence
or impeachment. They were of the National Reform party, that stood closer to the native branch
and strengthened the Queen's power in all legislation
tending to assist her in governmental interference.
The American Minister, realizing the situation, affiliated with the Reform party, and through them he
was enabled to check moves detrimental to the interests of the United States. On the other hand,
the English Minister was an active worker with the
National Reform party, and openly and in public
used every effort to support them and obtain any
advantage beneficial to his country. Having re-
sided in the country for many years and being the
head of a large family, some of whom had married
into Kanaka families, he had great influence with
the members of the National Reform and Liberal
parties. It was not an uncommon sight to see him
on the floor of the legislative hall, actually lobby-
ing for the passage of some measure detrimental to
American interests, or beneficial to British interference, openly expressing his approval or disapproval of current debate. With the assistance of
a simple, benighted, ritualistic English bishop, by
publicly sympathizing with the Queen and her min-

isters and privately advising both her and the
Liberal and National Reform leaders, he exerted a
powerful influence. But, from a want of tact and
diplomatic knowledge, he relied upon pompous demands and political intrigue with a class of political
intimates in the legislative body who would give his
secrets away.

The sagacious, well trained and experienced
diplomat of the United States, Mr. Jno. L. Stevens,
quietly sat in his legation, pulled the wires and
every time brought American interests to the front.
So well did he play his cards, resulting on every
occasion in success, that he became a subject of
personal abuse, and an object of intense hatred, by
the leaders of the National Reform and Liberal
parties. On the street and in public places they
would vilify and criticise even his personal and
private conduct, going so far as to attack his domestic way of living, and caused the arrest of his
domestic for some trumped-up offense of a minor
nature, which act was a violation of the national
sanctity of the United States legation. On one occasion a leader of the National Reform party, an
Englishman by birth, and a noble at the time in the
legislature, afterwards a minister of the cabinet, introduced a resolution in the legislature reflecting
upon the official acts of the American Minister, and
so offensive to the United States government that the
House voted to expunge it from the records. In
all these attacks the Queen appears to have aided
and abetted, but the power and activity of the

Reform members caused her much uneasiness and prevented her taking any decided steps towards carrying out her cherished plan of promulgating a new constitution. Therefore, in order to break the influence of the Reform party and that of the American Minister, while pretending to favor the most cordial relations with the representative of the United States, she conceived a plan of negotiating a loan in England upon a first mortgage of the port dues of Honolulu. A bill to that effect was subsequently introduced by one of her ministers, the same who had on a previous occasion offered the attack upon the American Minister, but it was promptly voted down. The English Minister, together with his wife, actively engaged on the floor of the legislature working for the support of this measure, all of which came under my personal observation while a visitor to the hall.

An English adventurer, a man of no principle but of fine education, was employed by the Queen on a stipulated salary to write articles, in support of her political course and against American interests, for a local paper owned by the Queen, using the name of her coachman as the author of these publications. A position was given to him as manager of the Hawaiian Hotel for his board, that he might, by his position as such, come in contact with tourists, win their sympathy, and fill them with misinformation concerning political conditions. In fact every means was used to further the Queen's ambitious designs, and the business depression, financial uneasiness, and national danger which naturally followed deterred any commercial agency or local corporation from negotiating any kind of loan from abroad or at home. Everything was in a chaotic state, with inevitable ruin apparrent on all sides. The large sugar interests that came into existence through the gratuity of the treaty of reciprocity with the United States were, in addition to the agitated condition of affairs, affected by the provisions of the McKinley tariff, and plainly foresaw that unless something was done towards establishing closer commercial relations with the United States they would suffer, and they therefore became more active in support of the Reform party, which was the party most strongly favoring American interests.

Such was the condition of affairs when the U. S. Cruiser Boston arrived in Honolulu. The U. S. Flagship San Francisco was relieved, and sailed for Mare Island Navy Yard, leaving the Boston to look after American interests and treaty obligations. The political agitation and uneasiness was so great that during the entire stay of the Boston in those waters it was impolitic for her to leave the harbor of Honolulu, except on two short occasions, and as a reminder of the force constantly present a battalion of troops was landed once a week and marched through the streets to the old base-ball grounds for drill.

The causes of the continued and increasing uneasiness and hostility to the Queen, and finally to the monarchy, were the stubborn efforts of the Queen to trample upon the constitution, and her persistent interference in politics, both directly and through her creatures in office, and by bribing native members in the legislature in order to secure illegal control of that body.

The executive members, or ministry, nobles and representatives sat and deliberated in one chamber presided over by a speaker elected by the whole body. As the Queen attempted to increase her arbitrary power over the legislative branch of the government, that body very soon asserted its constitutional prerogatives, and on August 30th, 1892, voted out the ministry that had consented to her maladministration. The Queen then, against the advice of the leading members of the legislature and the business men of the community, appointed, on the 12th of September, a ministry headed by E. C. Macfarlane, an Englishman by birth and sympathies, a naturalized American, and a domiciled Hawaiian. One of his first acts was to introduce and attempt to push through the legislature a bill authorizing a loan from England upon a first mortgage of the port dues of the port of Honolulu, a stepping-stone to a commercial protectorate by Great Britain, as was done in Egypt. Associated in this cabinet with Macfarlane were Sam. Parker, Paul Neumann, and Chas. T. Gulick, all of whom were of the National Reform party. In three days after they qualified an effort was made to vote them out, resulting in 24 for and 21 against their removal. The question was referred to the judges of the supreme court, who decided 25 votes were necessary to constitute a constitutional number to pass such a measure. Meanwhile, on the 4th of October, a special election was held in Honolulu to elect two nobles to fill the vacancies made by Macfarlane and Neumann when they resigned to accept positions in the cabinet. A native and a half-white, supported by the lottery and opium factions, were elected over two of the most respectable men in Honolulu, M. P. Robinson and H. Waterhouse. This election had a tendency to strengthen the National Reform party in the legislature, and realizing the danger of such a ministry remaining in office, some of the Liberal party coalesced with the Reform party and a few dissatisfied members of the National Reform party, and on the 17th of October voted to remove the Macfarlane cabinet. They carried the want of confidence by a large majority—32 to 15.

The Queen was obstinate, and knowing this, every irresponsible person in the legislature, and many out of it, urged their claims for a cabinet position, and failing to obtain their object turned upon her. In the little native paper, published by the notorious Bush, she was accused of ignoring the native claims. When the Queen, on November 1st, appointed a cabinet composed of men of no personal standing and representing no property interests, it was voted out in less than two hours by a vote of 26 to 15, being known as the " Nancy

Hanks cabinet," because it made the quickest time on record. By this time the patience of the members of the Reform party had become exhausted, and in caucus with their allies they passed a resolution calling upon the Queen to designate a leader, chosen by a majority of the legislature, to select a ministry.

A ministerial crisis was imminent and political agitation alarming; excitement was intense and business prospects gloomy, with every indication of a revolution. The Queen for the time being surrendered, and selected a cabinet on the 8th of November, known as the Wilcox-Jones ministry. This cabinet had the full confidence of the people and the country felt easy, but it was not long before the Queen began to dictate to them and to interfere with their line of policy, which was for retrenchment and moderate legislation.

It soon became known to the public that severe friction existed between the Queen and the ministry, and during the last of December it was the talk all over the town that there would be a vote of want of confidence against the cabinet. On the 4th of January, Bush introduced the resolution, and upon a vote it failed, 19 to 22. This failure to remove the Wilcox-Jones cabinet insured confidence, and encouraged the belief amongst the leading citizens, as well as the American Minister, that the Reform ministry had come to stay. The Queen, however, was not contented and did not mean to give up, but sent for the native members, and by bribes and

promises obtained their united support to pass the
lottery and opium bills, which every one supposed were dead, she having bargained with the
promoters of these measures, for their support in
return, to put the Wilcox cabinet out. Hopkins,
who was a half-white, and who was elected by the
lottery people, moved their consideration, and they
passed to the second reading, to the astonishment
of everybody, by a vote of 20 to 17; and on the
11th of January they were rushed through a third
reading on a vote of 23 to 20. This victory so
elated the Queen and her adherents that she took
advantage of the absence of members who had gone
home, and the following day, the 12th of January,
she induced a native member to introduce a vote
of want of confidence in the Wilcox-Jones cabinet,
and they were removed by a vote of 25 to 16.
Upon a canvass of the legislature by her native
followers, she discovered the fact that the vote of
one white man was necessary for a constitutional
majority. To obtain that the Queen sent for C. O.
Berger, and promised him that his father-in-law,
Widemann, should form a new cabinet if he would
vote with the natives. Berger took the bait, and
to the disgust of his friends voted that way, and the
Reform ministry went out. The Queen had no
intention of permitting Widemann to form a cabinet,
and when, in apparent compliance with her promise,
she sent for him and imposed obligations that
Colburn, a half-white and under a cloud, should
be named as one of the ministry, Widemann

demurred and he was dismissed. She had made up her mind to appoint a cabinet that would hold over during the interim of two years, in the absence of a legislative body, and be entirely subservient to her arbitrary whims. Colburn was sent for and instructed to form a cabinet of the persons she would name. The native members were instructed to remain away from the legislative hall on the 13th, so there would be no quorum on that day to vote the cabinet out, and the legislature would be prorogued the following day, at noon. Colburn, upon the request of the Queen, named as his associates, Parker, Cornwell, and Peterson. Colburn was a man of unsavory reputation in business matters, while all the rest were known to be zealous in their support of the Queen's misrule. The next morning, Saturday, the 14th of January, 1893, the ministry reported to the legislature that the Queen had signed the lottery and opium bills, and they became laws, by which the establishment of opium joints and the licensing of the sale of opium were to be given out, evidently to palace favorites. The exclusive franchise to conduct a lottery was given to a few men representing the Louisiana Lottery Company, which had just been evicted from Louisiana and was to remove its establishment from New Orleans to Honolulu, under a supposed obligation that the government was to receive $500,000 a year from that company. This annual revenue was, as a blind, to be devoted to internal improvements; and to secure the native votes of the legislature, promises were held out to them of lucrative offices, so dear to the Kanaka heart.

At noon the legislature was prorogued, and the Queen proceeded to the palace, the approaches to which were guarded by the government troops, and the grounds filled by a mob of natives brought from the other islands and fitted out with new suits of clothing to give coloring to a so-called petition, under which the Queen was now to perform her *coup d'état* by the proclamation of a new constitution. This caused her to lose her throne. During all this time the presence of the American Minister and of the United States ship Boston was a source of disquietude to the Queen and her supporters, as they feared interference by the American forces should any attempt be made to gain arbitrary power by force of arms which should result in injury to Americans or American property. On one occasion, when it was reported a boat had landed at Hilo from a wrecked American vessel, most villainous attacks were made by the royalist papers upon the American representatives, and it was while the Boston was away for target practice the Queen took her fatal step.

It will be seen from the foregoing that the political development of the Hawaiian Islands had been, in the early years of its transition, from a feudal and savage despotism into a free and civilized state, with only a few instances of foreign interference. Under the Kamehamehas the fundamental changes in the social and political organization were effected without disturbance or bloodshed, and armed resistance and revolutions were unthought of. The Hawaiian kings sought the counsel and service of able foreigners in the administration of the government, and there arose no occasion for foreigners to feel the need of suffrage rights to protect their interests. But with the failure of the Kamehameha line, Kalakaua set himself to work to undermine the confidence of natives in foreigners and injected into the elections the element of intense race hatred. In place of the diminished prerogatives of the sovereign and the increased privileges of the subject, by voluntary acts of preceding kings, there was manifested on the part of Kalakaua a disposition to extend his royal prerogatives and a return to absolutism. His acts inaugurated a series of revolutions that culminated in that of the 17th of January, 1893. The first was headed by the whites to secure responsible government through a representative cabinet, responsible to the people's elected representatives. Other revolutions were headed by the natives, instigated by Kalakaua and Liliuokalani, to regain their lost power, followed at last by a spontaneous uprising of the whites, who again asserted themselves in opposition to the revolutionary act of the Queen. They overthrew the ignorant, selfish, corrupt, and semi-barbarous monarchy and established instead a republican government, as will hereafter be detailed.

CHAPTER III.

The day following the first arrival of the Boston, the Flagship San Francisco gave a ball in honor of the officers of the former ship in order to afford an opportunity for them to meet the people of Honolulu and become familiar with the situation. To this ball all the leading white and native residents were invited, and it proved a most enjoyable affair. Cordial relations were established and invitations to social gatherings on shore were extended, which proved to be exceedingly pleasant and beneficial, reciprocated by frequent dinners, dances, and extensive receptions on board the Boston. At the first opportunity I went on shore to see the city and was escorted to the Pacific Club, where I met some old acquaintances whom I had known in the States and a number of most estimable gentlemen, with whom I took lunch. The club-house is well adapted for such a purpose in that climate, and is centrally located. Its membership is composed of the very best men in the city. In a stroll about I found Honolulu to be a city of about 25,000 inhabitants, having the appearance of a new England country town. It is situated on low ground with lofty hills behind and an untroubled sea in front; shaded by tropical trees, clothed with a variety of bloom and laden with the perfume of flowers.

The climate is that of a Washington city spring,
with an average temperature of 71°. Although as
far south as Havana, the heat is nothing to be compared to that of Key West and Cuba. Honolulu
is tempered by breezes that always blow, and by
rain that falls in intermittent showers. There are
a few broad avenues, but most of the streets are
narrow and go winding aimlessly through the town,
hardly wider than passing teams require and with
sidewalks where but two people can walk abreast.
The residence portion of the city has the appearance of a land of country villas, as each homestead
is surrounded by large yards, bótanical gardens,
and tropical trees, most of which have been transplanted from other countries and even improve
upon their native appearance when grown here.
The business portion of the town does not strike
one in an architectural sense, but the street scenes
are most interesting to the stranger. White duck
suits and panama hats give an equatorial glamour;
while the Kanaka in his nègligé suit, with floral circles hung about the shoulder, his feet unshod, and
his attitude extremely restful, presents a marked
contrast to the swarm of Orientals in their native
dress, sailors from the men-of-war in the harbor,
and tourists from every civilized country. The
female natives wear a Mother Hubbard gown, a
wreath of flowers called "leis," and go barefooted.
No one can accuse the female native of prudish-
ness, and her appetite for poi, raw fish, and the
hula dance is unappeasable, while her fondness for

gin, licentiousness, and kahuna doctors is a beset-
ting sin. She is an expert on horseback as she
gallops from place to place astride, with body erect
and firm as that of any cow-boy, her divided skirts
flapping to the breeze.

Frequently you meet with the offspring whose
nationality is hard to trace, produced by the inter-
marriages of Chinese and Kanakas, Japanese and
natives, Portuguese, whites, and half-castes—a sort
of composite issue which is often an improvement
on the mated types. The best class of white people
are as refined, polished, polite, and accomplished
as one will meet with in any city of the civilized
world, and their hospitality is unsurpassed. They
live in luxurious homes, fitted with the products of
American and European art, and are supporters
of every religious and moral movement. Though
largely of an admixture of the New England element, there are many whose ancestry came from
every section of the United States. There are excellent hotels, a large opera house and other places of
amusement; fine churches and magnificent schools
and hospitals. The sanitary condition of the
town is most excellent; there is a beautiful palace
and commodious government buildings, extensive water-works, majestic scenery, zestful sport,
glimpses of savage life, delightful homes, and all
the attributes of the most perfect state of advanced
civilization.

The town is lighted by a complete electrical
plant with an installation equal to that of any city,

NATIVE RIDING COSTUME.

and the telephone system is the best I have ever
seen, with a corps of operators that cannot be excelled in politeness. The telephone is the means
of communicating all manner of information, from
the market order to the arrival of a steamer or the
time of day. The stores are neat and filled with
all the articles of luxury as well as necessaries to
be found in those of the large cities on the continent. A system of street-car lines meanders
through the town, but these are mainly patronized
by the Chinese and lower class, there being a lot
of nice carriages that will take a person anywhere in the town for twenty-five cents. There
are foundries, workshops, and ship-yards, but no
manufactories. Down on the docks it will be
seen, from the character of the freight handled,
that Honolulu is the port of distribution of all
merchandise for the islands, and is dependent on
the industrial enterprises of the country. On the
wharves are bags of grain, cases of goods and machinery of all descriptions; furniture, bricks, and
cement, on which are marks showing that they
are from abroad. There are no metals or minerals
to be found on the islands, and the iron foundries
are wholly dependent upon the coal and iron
shipped from abroad in sufficient quantities to meet
the necessities of the country. The articles of export are rice, sugar, coffee, raw hides, bananas,
and pineapples.

To the rear of the central portion of the city is an
old extinct crater, called "Punch Bowl," that rises to

an elevation of five hundred feet above the sea-level. From the summit a fine bird's-eye view of Honolulu can be obtained. A fine roadway winds about the slopes that are dotted with the cottages of thrifty Portuguese. Back of Punch Bowl hill is the famous Tantalus Mountain, up which a splendid road enables one to obtain a view of surpassing beauty, from a height of 2,000 feet above the sea-level. Below is the city, immersed in a wealth of foliage, as though every quarter of the subtropical world had been laid under tribute, and beyond this the broad Pacific meets the gaze. To the west rise the beautiful Waianae Mountains, in front of which are the lowlands of innumerable rice fields and the Ewa plantation beyond the Pearl River locks. To the east rises the old extinct volcano called Diamond Head. On one side is the beautiful and historic Nuuanu Valley, and on the other side are the cocoanut-fringed shores of Waikiki. The hillsides are not under a state of cultivation as a rule, although the soil is fertile and covered with a rank growth of stiff grass possessing little or no nourishment for stock. Near the summit of Tantalus the ground has been covered with a thick growth of transplanted trees and laid out into villa sites. The land outside of this artificial forest is covered with the wild guava, which bears fruit as big as the lemon, and impassable patches of lantana, the seeds of which are scattered broadcast by an imported bird from India called the mynah.

One of the most beautiful sights in the vicinity of

NUUANU AVENUE—HONOLULU.

Honolulu is the trip to what is known as the Pali, a pass through the mountains to the windward side of the island, up Nuuanu Valley. The ascent is gradual for about four miles, through an avenue lined with handsome houses, set in grounds filled with rare trees and plants, over an excellent road to the apex of the pass, down which there is on the other side a sheer drop of nearly one thousand feet. It was over this cliff that Kamehameha the Great drove the remnants of the army of the Oahu chiefs when he conquered the island. A winding road down this cliff has been constructed for the convenience of descent. From the north side of this pass, and far below, the country spreads before the eye like a relief map, while on each side are sharp volcanic cones and mountain crags that pierce the clouds.

Another intensely interesting trip from the city is a ride on the railroad to Pearl Harbor and the Ewa sugar plantation. Near Pearl City is Reymond Grove with its large dancing pavilion, a favorite rendezvous for pleasure-seekers and picnic parties. The scenery on the road from Honolulu to Ewa is rather picturesque, with glimpses of mountain valleys on the one side and rice fields and the ocean on the other. Pearl Lochs is a favorite resort for aquatic sports, such as boat-racing and yacht-sailing. The drives about the city are smooth and picturesque. They run past groves of cocoanut trees and royal palms, taro patches, where the poi root is grown, banana plantations, and brackish ponds where fish are fattened for the market.

The favorite drive and bathing resort for the leisure class, white and tinted, is along the road to Waikiki. This place is four miles from the heart of the city, and is a curved shore line occupied by lovely villas. The ocean breaks on the coral reef several hundred yards from the beach, between which and the shore the water is still and transparent, affording most excellent bathing and fishing, in water with a uniform temperature of about seventy degrees the year round. The famous King's Cocoanut Grove is passed on the way, and just before reaching the beautiful Kapiolani Park is the little villa of Liliuokalani, close on the beach and shut in by a high board fence. This little villa has been the scene of many rather questionable festivities. Kapiolani Park is a government reservation, and in the center is the race-track, where some good sport is seen during the race season, especially on the eleventh of June, or Derby Day. Between this park and the beach is the Sans Souci Hotel and bathing houses, where one can lounge about in reclining chairs or hammocks on the large porches and enjoy the cool sea breeze, obtain a fine meal or refreshing draft. The great annoyances, however, are the insects, which, by the way, are of foreign importation. In the old times there were no mosquitoes here; in fact the name of them is not to be found in the Hawaiian language. The whaling ships brought the pests in their stagnant water-butts, and the residents even claim to know the very ship that brought the first consignment to

the islands. Be that as it may, the harpooning
gentry are of two kinds—those that trouble by day
and those that ravage by night. The two species
are quite distinct as to size and shape, as well as
habits. The day pest is noiseless and painful, while
the night prowler is noisy and poisonous, and
between the two they make life anything but
pleasant. The centipede and barbed scorpion have
also found their way to the islands, but from the
nature of their food and habits they are no more
poisonous than the honey-bee. The islands are
exempt from snakes, although a planter once imported some to kill the rats and mice in the cane
fields, but they were killed before they had time to
propagate and no more are allowed to come in.

In order to enjoy the beauties of the mountain
valleys that open out on the plains it is necessary
to go on horseback, as by so doing the head of each
valley can be reached without trouble. In the
Pauoa Valley the ride leads up to a point where, on
the right, the eye overlooks the whole of Manoa
Valley. The latter is closed in by high precipices,
down which slide numerous water-falls, one of
which forms at the base of the precipice a pool of
clear cold water, affording an opportunity for a refreshing bath. The next, or Palolo Valley, is most
interesting to a botanist, as high up in its encircling
peaks is a crater filled with peculiar vegetation,
delicate varieties of ferns and mosses, which are
elsewhere found in small bunches, but here they
entirely cover trunks of trees, and the further one

goes along the moist trail the greater is the variety to be found. Even those who have no special acquaintance with ferns will be struck by the variety and size of the specimens to be seen here. There are about one hundred and fifty varieties of ferns to be found on the Hawaiian Islands.

The paucity of crime is very noticeable, and it is an uncommon thing for the people to lock their houses. Such a thing as theft is very rare. The prison is built on a coral reef extending into the harbor and connected with the mainland by a narrow road. The prisoners are of many nationalities, and they do much of the hard labor in the streets of the city, working under overseers.

The city post-office is in the center of the business portion of the city, in close proximity to the steamboat landings and large warehouses. Through this office the mails from all parts of the world are distributed to the other islands, and upon the arrival of a mail steamer the scene in the vicinity is most interesting. The Hawaiian Hotel is situated in grounds comprising an entire square of about four acres. This large area affords ample room for a lawn and beautiful walks, which are laid out most artistically with flowers, plants, and tropical trees. There are a number of pretty cottages scattered about the inclosure, all under the hotel management, which afford accommodations for several hundred guests. The apartments open out on broad verandas from which a magnificent view of the mountains in the rear may be seen through the

THE PALACE—HONOLULU.

tropical foliage that surrounds the balconies. On the front lawn is an ornamental band-stand where musical concerts are given upon the arrival and departure of all foreign steamers. Across the street from the Hawaiian Hotel is the Central Union Church, but recently completed at a cost of $130,-000. It is built of volcanic rock and fashioned after the most modern church architecture, with a capacity of seating a thousand or more people.

Diagonally across to the southeast of the hotel grounds is by far the most attractive building in Honolulu, the new palace, built in 1880-'81, at a cost of over $300,000. It is a very modest piece of architecture, built of brick and covered with cement, and is surrounded by 11 acres of tropical park. The interior is finished with many kinds of native woods that take a high polish. The structure is two stories and a basement, with extensive balconies. The basement is divided into kitchens, servants' quarters, and store-rooms. On the first floor is a large hallway from which a broad stairway ascends. To the right of this hallway was the throne-room, a plain apartment in white, with two gilded chairs on a dais at one end and a round sofa in the center, with carved gilt chairs along the side of the room. Across the hall and at the front of the palace was the drawing-room, and off this, opening upon a tiled piazza, were the dining-room and royal council chamber. The second floor had three bed chambers, a library and parlor. About the various walls were hung oil paintings of the royal personages from Kamehameha the Great to Liliuokalani, royal orders and portraits of distinguished Europeans, and in all this array there was not the portrait of a single American. This palace, which had been the scene of court festivities and semi-savage orgies of Kalakaua and his sister, the ex-Queen, for a number of years, was taken by the Provisional Government as an executive building, and as such it is now used.

Just in front of this building, known as Iolani Palace, is the government building, or Aliiolani Hall, situated in a spacious ground. In this structure are the rooms of the supreme court, offices of the ministers and other executive offices, and the legislative hall. In front is an heroic statue of Kamehameha the Great. From the steps of this building the Provisional Government issued its proclamation abrogating the monarchy, and it was upon its tower that the United States flag was hoisted when the temporary protectorate was declared by the American Minister, and afterwards hauled down by the orders of the United States Commissioner. Another building of historic interest is the Oahu College for the education of foreign children. Through its educational advantages many distinguished men of the islands have taken their degrees from Harvard, Yale, and other American colleges.

Several charitable institutions ornament the city and have done much good. One of these is the Lunalilo Home, an attractive and comfortable place for indigent Hawaiians. The Queen's Hospital, partially endowed by the widow of Kamehameha IV and partly supported by the government, is centrally located in the midst of extensive grounds through which several avenues of rich palms mark the approaches to the building. In this building or institution the natives receive treatment free, and it is open to all nationalities. Just outside the western limits of the city is the hospital for the insane ;· it consists of a number of small cottages, and the inmates are of all nationalities. The next, and one of the finest institutions in the country, is the Kamehameha School, which was founded and endowed by Mrs. Bishop, a princess of high standing and great wealth. Since her death her husband has liberally donated monetary gifts until there has been more than $1,000,000 spent on its completion and endownment.

It comprises over thirty buildings in all, about two miles from town, on a beautiful location of high ground with the mountains in the rear and the sea in front, giving a cool and healthy breeze both night and day. The material from which the buildings are constructed is a dark gray volcanic rock, somewhat resembling coarse granite, and quarried in the vicinity. Connected with the school is an interesting museum containing Hawaiian antiquities, a collection which not only illustrates the ethnology of the islands, but every bird, fish, insect, shell, or plant, a collection which gives an accurate and scientific knowledge of the products of the islands in a remote past. It contains also an interesting collection of curiosities illustrating the condition of the Hawaiian people ages ago, and gives a most excellent idea of the advance in art made by the natives prior to the advent of the whites. The Kahilis, the insignia of royalty, are made of feathers, cylindrical plume-like ornaments, in the shape of a duster or fly-brush with long slender handles. On state occasions and royal processions there was a gorgeous display of these Kahilis, and the bearers were very close to the sovereign. A great variety of kapas or native cloth of different patterns, texture, and color is interesting, and as a manufacture most creditable to Hawaiian industry. From them one can trace the strip of bark through every process to the finished product of bark cloth. The handicraft of the Hawaiian fishermen is well shown here in many kinds of nets, fish traps and hooks of fine workmanship. Of the last some are made of human bones, or shells from a tiny size to the large shark hook that was frequently baited with human flesh. Wooden calabashes or bowls form another attractive sight, made from the wood of the Koa and Kou, resembling mahogany and rosewood in color and graining. Some are for the cooking of fish, or roasting pig and dog. Others are in size from the poi-bowl to the great trough in which the body of a chief was dissected and his bones cleaned, or for the great cannibal feast, although there was no cannibalism in Hawaii. The feather cloaks here preserved are works of art, of a bright yellow hue, and made from feathers taken from under the wings of tens of thousands of birds of a species now almost extinct, which makes their pecuniary value much greater than their intrinsic utility. Some of them are said to be worth more than $100,000.

The harbor of Honolulu is very spacious and stands as the highest foreign port in the world as to the amount of tonnage of American shipping visiting it. Improvements at the entrance have been made so that vessels of the deepest draught can now go alongside of the docks for handling freight.

Of late years a Bureau of Information has been established in Honolulu for the distribution of valuable Hawaiian information to the other countries of the world. This bureau has done much towards advancing the business prospects of the islands, and it will not be long, under the present system of responsible government, before Honolulu will become a great resort as well as commercial center.

CHAPTER IV.

As soon as the cruiser Boston was secure in the harbor of Honolulu, on the morning of the 24th of August, 1892, a national salute of twenty-one guns was exchanged with the Hawaiian battery on shore, and in the afternnoon of the same day formal calls were made on the officials of our own and the Hawaiian governments. The following day the Hawaiian Minister of Foreign Affairs, accompanied by three nobles of the realm, returned the calls and were received with customary honors and a salute of seventeen guns on leaving the ship. Officials of other nations paid visits of ceremony in the course of the few days following, and the quiet harbor of Honolulu was disturbed by an endless roar of cannon as these officials left the ship. On the afternoon of the 27th of August the flagship San Francisco got under way and left the harbor bound for San Francisco. Our men manned the rigging, and while the band played a few lively tunes they gave their parting friends three rousing cheers and God-speed on their homeward voyage. The San Francisco gone, the Boston settled down to the task of putting everything in shape for the protection of American interests on the islands, and in accordance with the custom on such occasions, and in maintenance of friendly relations, the commanding officer, through the United States Minister, made known to the Hawaiian Minister of Foreign Affairs his intention of calling upon the Queen with the officers of the Boston, and desired to know when it would be most agreeable and convenient. In reply to this request we were notified the Queen would be pleased to receive us at the palace at 10 A. M. on the 29th of August. Accordingly, the commanding and other officers who could be spared from the ship went on shore dressed in special full-dress uniform, and, escorted by the United States Minister Resident, proceeded in carriages to the palace entrance, where we were received by the royal guard drawn up in line at a present arms, with the band playing the national air of the United States. Ascending by the steps of the main entrance to the large hall, we were met at the door of the palace by the Minister of Foreign Affairs and the Chamberlain. After waiting a few minutes, the Chamberlain threw open a door on the left of the hall and announced that the Queen was prepared to receive us. Preceded by the Hawaiian Minister of Foreign Affairs and the United States Minister Resident, we followed in columns of two according to rank, and the presentation of each took place. The Queen was standing at the further end of the room. On her left stood four half-white ladies in waiting, and on her right were four aids, each in the regimentals of a colonel, and to her rear were the royal kahili-bearers. A few compliments were passed, and, after a short conversation with the attendants, we all, according to royal etiquette, backed out. The ceremony was rather stiff, and the head of the little semi-savage kingdom appeared to be up in all the customs of the most powerful monarchs. Queen Victoria was never more exacting in ceremonious requirements than this relic of barbarism.

The Queen was rather portly, of medium height, and plainly dressed. She was about 54 years of age, with a full, round face, broad across the cheeks, thick lips, rather dull expression, and a countenance indicative of a severe temper and strong determination. She was darker than the ordinary native, showing evident traces of negro blood.

With the exception of one, her maids of honor were beyond middle life, and were far from being attractive, either in appearance or intelligence, but they served the purpose of lending show.

The 2d of September was the Queen's birthday and we were given the first opportunity of seeing some of the surviving evidences of Hawaiian heathenism. The occasion was a great holiday, and during the day the Boston was dressed aloft, from stem to stern, with bunting, and a salute of twenty one-guns fired at sunrise and at sunset. The Queen gave a reception, "luau," or feast, and a hula in the palace grounds. The hula, while it did not possess all the abominable features of vulgarity associated with the ancient dance, was nevertheless hardly calculated to arouse in the audience any great reverence for the sovereign who made it a part of her formal reception to foreigners.   The word " hula " is a term applied to any dance which the natives used to accompany all forms of cere- mony from a dedication of a temple to the launch- ing of a canoe ; the nature of the ceremony implied the dance, and owing to its extreme vulgarity has been interdicted by law.   This was the last time the hula was ever placed on exhibition by royalty, and it is more than likely it will never again be. Natives came from all quarters to partake of the feast, and at Pearl River Lochs all kinds of aquatic sports were indulged in, such as swimming-matches, boat-races, and yacht-sailing, and in the surround- ing country the natives had luaus and hulas that did justice to the customs of past days of heathen- ish practices.

One of the ministers of the government, a noble of distinction in the legislature, took me at night across wet taro-patches to a secret grass house in the country, to see a hula as it was given before having been modified.   After witnessing this per- formance I was not surprised that its main features are interdicted by law.   None but those of the most depraved sensuality could enjoy its performance. Not far from the city, and off the road leading to Waikiki, is an old residence kept by a native and in this building the tourists were entertained with this royal sport.   A young man of no moral standing in the community and rather shady in his habits, but the keeper of a liquor establishment in Honolulu, a boon companion of the royal family, usually made the arrangements for the profits he

could make out of the sale of a few jugs of cheap
gin for the girls and a commission from the regular fees given by the visitors.   On these occasions
the police never interfered, and it was not an uncommon thing to see cabinet officials in attendance
giving countenance to the illegal dance.   Even in
the homes of some of the reputed respectable white
residents I have seen the ladies of the house indulge
in the dance, and though somewhat modified it was
still sensual.

The monotony of a long stay in one place was
broken in the latter part of September, when the
news cames that an American merchant vessel, the
William Campbell, had foundered at sea, and that
the first mate in charge of one of the boats, with
five others of the crew, had landed at Hilo, on the
Island of Hawaii.   He reported another boat, containing the captain with his wife and child and the
rest of the crew, as missing at sea, making their
way for Hawaii.   We got under way at half past
three on the afternoon of the 29th of September,
and stood to the southward and eastward in search
of this missing boat.   We passed the Island of
Maui at night, early the next morning sighted the
Island of Hawaii, and at 2 P. M. came to anchor
off Hilo, and sent a boat for the American Consular Agent, who came on board bringing the mate
of the unfortunate vessel.   From the information
obtained from the mate we got under way and
stood around to the southward of Hawaii, using
every effort to obtain some information of the miss-

ing boat. We steamed out to sea and then inshore, scanning the horizon and the beach with powerful field-glasses. During the night a signal light was made out which we supposed to be the long-looked-for captain of the Campbell. Guns were fired and rockets sent up to attract his attention, but it proved to be a native fisherman, and we gave up the search as hopeless and headed the Boston for Honolulu, arriving at our old anchorage on the afternoon of the 3d of October. The boat journey of the mate from the time he left the abandoned vessel to the time of arriving at Hilo was the longest ever known to have been made at sea in a little open boat, being 2,200 miles. The survivors were cared for and sent to the United States, but the captain was never heard from.

A few days after our return the keeper of one of the public institutions gave, in honor of his birthday, a grand luau, to which the Queen and all the leading natives were invited. An invitation was also sent to some of the officers of the Boston, myself included. It was given near the city limits and hundreds were in attendance, old and young. The reception was held in the house. When all was ready the spread was given under a thatched grass shed near by, and for the prominent guests was laid on a long table in the shape of three sides of a square, while the common people seated themselves about a spread on the ground. Facing the opening of the table were the inevitable and indispensable hula dancers, keeping time to the thumping on

calabashes by some old toothless hags in the rear.
On a raised platform in an alcove was perched the
Queen, and at the proper time she moved to the
table and took a seat, which was the signal for all
to follow. It fell to my lot to be seated between
two half-white damsels and opposite the Queen.
The dishes that were spread before us consisted of
all manner of native delicacies, poi in wooden bowls,
raw fish, roast dog, fowl, and pig, squid, live
shrimps, salted sea-weed, and other condiments of
a similar character. Each individual would thrust
the fingers into a common poi-bowl when a
mouthful was wanted, give a peculiar twist of the
hand, and hold aloft a round ball of the mushy
paste, and when through laughing and talking
push the morsel down the throat. Then he would
reach into a little calabash and pull out a raw fish,
which is considered a special delicacy. Live
shrimp were taken down in the same way. The
slimy squib, with a bad smell and an eye that stares
unhappily about, appeared to be a rare delicacy.
The guests would reach over and break off a tooth-
some tentacle, which, when it touched the native
palate, made him feel that the choicest part had not
been withheld. It took a strong nerve and stronger
stomach to sit by and see all this, much less eat
anything, and together with the sickening smell of
cocoanut-oil, with which my two neighbors as well
as others had smeared their hair, it made my meal
hardly pleasant. No one was permitted to rise, under
the rules of royal etiquette, until her Majesty had

finished her repast. Finally the Queen rose from the table, greatly to my relief.

The native luau is one of the leading characteristics of Hawaiian hospitality, and from its preparation to its consummation is exceedingly interesting. It is seldom given by a single individual, but several persons combine, each adding to the quality and variety of edibles. Thus one person will supply the poi, another the pig, dog or fowl, while others will furnish the fish, bananas and other fruit, and they will give their last fowl or pig for such occasions. When the great event is determined upon, depending upon the fattening of a certain pig or some noted occasion, they will all meet at the designated place and commence the preparations, which entail a great deal of work, the natives exhibiting an industrial spirit that is never witnessed on any other occasion. Some will go to the woods for ferns, ki-leaves, and other plants suitable for decoration; others will dig the oven in the ground and prepare the food for cooking, exercising great care in selecting stones that will not explode as they are heated. While the food is cooking they make a spread on the ground, consisting of ferns and ki-leaves laid out with much care. When the food is cooked it is taken out and put on the improvised table piping hot, and each one takes his place, squatting on the ground with his legs folded under the body, and the feast commences. No knives or forks are used, but each one eats with his fingers, and the greatest cordiality and good will prevails.

They will gorge themselves to such an extent that
for days after they are unfit for anything beyond a
lazy loitering about on the grass, never thinking of
the future. On all occasions like this both male
and female adorn themselves with wreaths of flowers called leis. One of the picturesque scenes in
Honolulu is a cluster of flower women seated about
on the sidewalk selling flower wreaths of their own
manufacture.

The monotony of every-day life was again broken
on the 28th of November by another Hawaiian
national holiday, known as the anniversary of recognition of Hawaiian independence by England and
France. Boat-racing, yacht-sailing, and the usual
luau and games to amuse the crowds were the
main features of the day. New Year, Christmas,
and the holidays of the United States and other
countries were observed with appropriate celebra-
tions. Washington's Birthday, Decoration Day,
and the Fourth of July were observed in such an
enthusiastic manner as to lead one to suppose that
for the time being he was in a typical American
town. The United States flag was exhibited on
every side, and the American patriotism displayed
equal to that of the most ardent supporters of the
free and liberal institutions of the great republic.
On Decoration Day, on the 31st of May, the local
G. A. R. post of 40 old veterans of the civil war in
the United States marched from their encampment
hall to their lot in the cemetery and paid homage
to the memory of their heroic dead by holding

literary exercises and garnishing anew the graves of their old comrades, of whom there are a number buried there. Appropriate speeches were delivered and the ceremonies were as imposing as would be found on a like occasion at any national cemetery in the United States, the government offices and business houses closing at noon and the local military as well as the U. S. naval forces participating in the parade.

The day on which the election of the President of the United States took place polling places were opened in Honolulu and as much enthusiasm displayed as though their votes were to be counted in the selection of the executive head of the republic. A great many votes were cast, Cleveland receiving a large majority over Harrison. When the steamer, bringing the news of the result in the States, hove in sight, the wharves and house-tops were covered with people anxious to hear the news. Just before the steamer arrived at the wharf some one on board formed with his bent arms a large C and it was at once known who was the successful candidate, the intelligence being received with cheer after cheer.

The local election for two nobles to fill vacancies occasioned in the legislature by resignations to accept cabinet positions was outwardly quiet and orderly. There was much bribery and wire-pulling among the natives, resulting in the choice of two candidates put up by the opium and lottery rings. The average native Hawaiian is a natural politician, likes to talk and is fond of discussion;

open to monetary considerations, defective in logic, and careful to turn every incident to his own advantage regardless of inconsistencies and with no regard for the future. His inherited instinct and intuition lead him to follow the dictates of the chief under whose rule he was servile, and he has little power to think for himself. This feeling of dependence was continued under the monarchy and fostered by some of the foreigners who perpetuated in some degree these relationships. The native is deficient as a legislator, possessing no originality or constructiveness, and when some pernicious measure was proposed in the legislature he readily fell a prey to demagogic arts. It was to this native weakness that a minority but aggressive party in the legislature was enabled, during the legislature of 1892, to vote out so many cabinets, and, until near the close of the session, to control legislation. Lobbyists and local politicians of a character fashioned after the "heelers" of the tough wards of New York or San Francisco, unscrupulous and ready at all times with proper gifts supplied by the bosses, vied with the Queen's agents in tempting the legislators to do their bidding, and the native members fond of office, unwilling to work, and with small salaries readily became willing tools.

On one occasion I had a very favorable opportunity to witness the methods of political corruption in Honolulu. I was invited by a supporter of a measure pending before the legislature to attend

a luau and drinking bout to be given that evening
to some of the native members of the legislature in
order to obtain their votes on the following day
for the passage of the act in question, which
was opposed by many of the white members.
About seven o'clock in the evening a little red-
headed Irishman and a friend of his, both of the
down-town gentry, called for me at the hotel in a
carriage, and informed me they had been instructed
to take me to the place of rendezvous. When I
was seated in the carriage they drove down town
by one of the drinking establishments and took in
a goodly supply of cheap gin and sour beer. They
then drove to a little shanty situated in the suburbs
of the city. We entered by a back door into a dark
room, and after stumbling over a few more boxes
of gin and beer that had been sent ahead, a door to
a larger room was opened by an old toothless hag,
who was the only female present, who appeared to
be on the most intimate terms with the little politician, as their greetings were of the most familiar
kind. In this large room were gathered many of
the native members of the legislature, and as we
entered they rose and shook hands, receiving us
with the most cordial salutations and alohas. The
degree of secrecy and manner of reception indicated
at once the methods of this little Irish politician, and
it was apparent that nothing was to be said or
known outside of this meeting until after the votes
were cast on the following day. Cheap gin was
immediately passed around, not in small glasses

but by the table-glassful, and many stone jugs
were soon empty. Nothing was said at the time
about the purposes of the gathering, but simple
good fellowship prevailed. In a short time we
were ushered into an adjoining room where, on the
floor, was the spread or feast in genuine Hawaiian
style, a bottle of beer and a stone jug of gin mark-
ing each man's place. The little Irishman took a
seat on the floor at the head of the spread, and his
companion at the foot, my place falling between a
full-blooded Kanaka and a half-caste Chinese and
native, the rest being seated around on the floor. .
The old female acted as hostess and waited on the
guests. Drinking and feasting commenced, and
as the legislators began to show indications of the
inner man being propitiated, the wily politician
began to unload his eloquent appeal for the passage
of the bill, and explaining the advantages each
would receive should the bill become a law. Personal flattery, and the legislative importance each
held in the legislative body, were dwelt upon with
much adroitness, and frequently he would hold his
glass on high and propose a toast to the measure,
which was echoed by each member as he would
drain his glass. Now and then, as the bacchanalian
festivities proceeded, the little Irishman and his
friend would pass around and drink toasts to each
individual, tipping glasses and dexterously dropping a coin into the hand as he passed along.
More gin was brought out, and the capacity of
these sons of the soil was beyond conception.

They emptied jug after jug, but finally the spell was broken and each exhibited evidences of intoxication, when the politician changed from argument to threats and demands. By midnight he had received written pledges from each to vote as directed on the following day. As a divergence, and in honor of my presence, a native would now and then fire off a series of word pyrotechnics to the health of America, and for fear I might not appreciate his love for the United States over and above that of his colleagues, he would take me into an adjoining room and explain that he was for America, and give me advice to beware of the others, all of whom were said to be sympathizers of Great Britain. By the time it was all over, every legislator in the party had inflicted me with the same dose. At midnight the party broke up, and as they separated to go to their respective homes they were informed by the little Irishman that if they broke their promises on the next day, he would see that his friends would no longer pay their board bills, to which an answer was given in a chorus of drunken shouts that disturbed the still night air. They all marched into the legislative hall the next day, and when the bill came up they voted for it to a man.

I knew repeatedly of legislative acts carried in this way, especially when the Jones-Wilcox cabinet was voted out and the opium and lottery bills passed. Such was the hold the common whites or National Reform party had with the native mem-

bers of the legislature, and it was no wonder that
the progressive people of the Reform party, representing the tax-payers and property-holders, became
so disgusted that they failed to put in an appearance in the legislative hall after the Jones-Wilcox
cabinet was voted out.

The average native Hawaiian is weak, not
wicked. He is naturally conservative. Under the
Kamehamehas, and now again under the Republic
he responds to honest leadership. The House of
Representatives under the Republic consists of a
majority of natives, who in the absence of the degrading influence of the crown and the National
Reform party, which has been disintegrated and
absorbed in the ultra royalist faction, have done
good work. The worst enemies of the native Hawaiian have been the Kalakaua family. He and his
sister, Liliuokalani, ever since their family came
into power, have constantly been the center of a
baleful, degrading influence, exalting immorality,
drunkenness, heathenism, and race hatred, for their
own personal, selfish ends. But for this the native
government and the monarchy could have retained
power indefinitely, without interference or opposition from the whites.

The downfall of the monarchy was the direct
and inevitable result of an attempt to arbitrarily
subjugate men of the Anglo-Saxon race, whose
homes and property were at stake, by illegal
means.

Another important Hawaiian holiday was the
31st of July, known as Restoration Day, the anni-

versary of the restoration of Hawaiian independence by the English admiral after the islands had been seized by the captain of one of the vessels of his fleet upon trumped-up claims by the consul of Great Britain. The friction arising from national prejudicies between the American and English residents on the islands led to severe troubles between the Hawaiian government and the foreign powers, which culminated in 1843, when the British consul, in a false statement of facts, urged Captain Paulet to demand redress for imaginary wrongs sustained by his countrymen. Captain Paulet, taking advantage of the occasion, made most unjust demands, evincing a determination to accept nothing short of the cession of the islands as redress. This demand was eventually complied with under protest. During the negotiations national feeling ran high between the American and English residents. Singular as it may seem, there was lying in the waters of the harbor at the time an American sloop of war named Boston, which came to the rescue, as the other United States Cruiser Boston appeared on the scene of the final overthrow of the monarchy. In order to enforce his demands, Paulet threatened to bombard the town, but Captain Long of the Boston notified the English captain that if any damage should be done to American property he would immediately open fire upon him from the Boston, and in support of this threat he immediately cleared ship for action and placed his vessel in position for a raking fire of the English ship. Shortly afterward the United States Frigate

Constellation, under command of Captain **Kearney,**
came into the harbor. When made acquainted
with the state of affairs, Kearney showed his disapproval of the English flag flying over the islands
by inviting the Governor and princes on board, and
with the Hawaiian flag at the mainmast-head fired
a salute, and made every effort to show his sympathy for the native people, much to the discom-
fiture of Captain Paulet. As soon as Admiral
Thomas, then at Valparaiso, Chili, heard of the
cession of the islands, he made sail in his flagship
for Honolulu and restored the rights and prerogatives of the King; the English flag was hauled
down and the Hawaiian flag resumed its place.
The square in the city where the ceremonies took
place is now one of the most attractive garden
spots in Honolulu, and is named after the Admiral,
" Thomas Square."

On this day the usual amusements, luaus, hulas,
and festivities were indulged in. The arrival and
departure of steamers from and to the United States,
the Orient and the colonies afforded another diver-
sion to the dull every-day life of Honolulu, as on
all such occasions the rank, wealth, and beauty of the
city are on hand to decorate their departing friends
with leis and chaplets of flowers until some of them
are so covered up that it looks as though they must
suffocate. The royal band was always in attendance upon such occasions, giving selections of
national and operatic airs. At night a band concert in the grounds of the Hawaiian Hotel or at
Emma Square two or three times a week is another

NATIVE FLOWER SELLERS—HONOLULU.

feature distinctly Hawaiian in its lavish hospitality.

One of the disturbing influences in the community during our stay in Honolulu was a church scandal occasioned by the Anglican bishop making an effort to coerce the American contingent of the Episcopal church into recognition of his supreme will. The Americans, together with a number of the more liberal members of the congregation, refused to accept such authority on the part of the bishop, whereupon, although the former had contributed nearly all the funds, nearly a hundred thousand dollars, with which to build the new cathedral, the bishop attempted to close the doors to all except those who agreed with him. It was finally settled by the bishop taking one part of the day for his services, his opponents holding separate services. The bishop was a ritualistic, orthodox bigot, possessing a strong aversion for Americans and a warm admiration for royalty, whereas the pastor was a man of strong intellect and liberal views, exceedingly popular, and a fine pulpit orator. The result was that the bishop remained as a figurehead with a skeleton congregation, while the pastor did the work, and carried the congregation with him.

According to the last census, the different religious denominations claim 30,000 Protestants and about 20,000 Catholics. The Protestants as a rule are in sympathy with American interests on the islands, whereas the Catholics are favorably disposed to native rule, notwithstanding the teachers in the Catholic schools are mostly Americans.

CHAPTER V.

The population of the Hawaiian Islands is decidedly mixed. By the census of 1896 it numbered 109,020 persons. Of these the natives numbered 31,019 ; part Hawaiian, 8,485 ; Chinese, 21,616 ; Japanese, 24,407 ; Portuguese, 15,191. The rest were Americans or Europeans. Those of American birth or descent constitute the most intelligent, influential, and largest property-holders of the community.

There are a number of very respectable English residents, of good character and abilities, but the majority of them are imbued with a sense of superiority, and seem to entertain the opinion that Americans have obtained advantages which should have gone to England. They feel deeply aggrieved at seeing the Yankee assert himself in Hawaii. Though not given to any genuine consideration of the sovereign rights and claims of the aboriginal race, they are nevertheless, with few exceptions, sympathizers with the corrupt royalty, and constantly intriguing against American influences. This is especially the case with Theo. H. Davies, the self-constituted guardian and champion of Princess Kaiulani, whom he took to England and educated there. He has become wealthy through the reciprocity treaty with the United States, but is most bitterly hostile to everything American. He was for many years English consul, a position now held by his partner, Mr. Walker. Mr. Davies now spends a large part of his time in England, but returns to Honolulu every year, where he poses as the friend of the natives, proclaims his willingness to protect them from the wicked Americans, makes long speeches and prayers in the native churches, and incidentally sows a crop of domestic discord and race prejudice. Whatever may be the policy of the British government toward Hawaii, the clique which trains with her consular representatives in Honolulu are responsible for nearly all the anti-American feeling in Hawaii, as they feel it an insupportable grievance that the Hawaiian Islands have not become a British stronghold in the North Pacific.

With very few exceptions, the Germans, Scandinavians, and other Europeans are supporters of the republic and opposed to the monarchy. The Portuguese are a desirable class of laborers and make good citizens. They are of European descent, but were originally brought from the Azores and Madeira by the Hawaiian government as laborers on the plantations. Over 7,000 Portuguese children have been born in the islands. The Hawaiian-born white population numbers 14,000. Upon the subsequent introduction of cheap Oriental contract labor, the Portuguese became the leading mechanical and expert workmen on the various internal improvements. They are very strong in their opinions and sympathies with the United

States. In the exercise of their rights of suffrage they form an important adjunct to the strength of the Reform party, and co-operate with the most responsible men of the community.

In the summer of 1865, under arrangements for the importation of laborers made by the Hawaiian Bureau of Immigration, 500 Chinese were brought to the islands as contract laborers, and these were followed by others in great numbers until their immigration was checked in 1886. They are a patient and industrious people, and in the struggle for existence have crowded the improvident natives from the rich bottoms and taro-fields. On every hand can be seen their rice-fields and taro-patches, truck-farms, and poultry-yards, giving evidence of their thriftiness. Some of them have become very rich. Coming as they did to the islands in large bodies composed almost exclusively of men, they soon began to intermarry with the natives, and a mixed race is the result, but of an improved type, in many instances, to the mated pair. However, the distribution throughout the islands of a large number of wifeless Chinese, in close contact with the natives, has had a pernicious influence upon the social life of the Hawaiians, necessarily destructive to the purity of native families.

The Japanese began to come to the islands in 1868, but it was not until 1884 that the consent of the Japanese government was obtained for the systematic immigration of its subjects; and then only as contract laborers. Early in the following

year they commenced to arrive in great numbers.
From that time to the present the Japanese have
been coming, many returning as their three-year
contracts expired. At first they consisted of a very
low caste of Japanese, gathered from the riffraff of
the cities, but later they were gathered from the
interior and were a better class. They are a
combative set, ignorant, mulish, and mutinous,
and are likely to give great trouble to the government as their numbers increase. Under the terms
of their contracts they are partially held in check.
If the laborer is idle he is docked a portion of the
day, and if he refuses to obey orders or to work he
is arrested and tried by the civil courts, and, if
found to be in fault, is ordered to return to work ;
on repetition of the offense he is punished with a
light fine, which is taken from his wages. If he
persists in a refusal to work, or is mutinous in conduct, he is given a term of imprisonment.

The native race is thriftless and indolent but
amiable and attractive, physically strong, cordial,
and generous. They are in general above the
middle stature, well formed, with fine muscular
limbs, open countenances and features, frequently
resembling those of Europeans. The higher class,
or remnants of the chiefs, are tall and stout and
their personal appearance is so much superior to
that of the common people that they look like a
distinct race. Their hair is black or brown, strong
and frequently curly. Their complexion is neither
yellow nor red, but a kind of olive, and sometimes

reddish brown. The question of their origin is merely speculative, but it is pretty well settled by native tradition that their ancestors migrated from one of the Samoan Islands, which was the chief center of dispersion for the Polynesian race. The Phœnicians, who were of Hamitic origin, originally came from the shores of the Persian gulf, and carried with them the nautical traditions and commercial customs of the most ancient times. As they were in the habit of using the Ægean Islands for a port of call and distribution, and as a means of keeping secret their communications with the rich countries of the west, it is more than likely the Chaldean navigators in a remote period had a similar custom in the use of the Samoan Islands to preserve their knowledge of the existence of the rich islands of the Pacific Ocean and of the American continent. From this it would appear the earliest inhabitants of the Hawaiian Islands originally came from Southwestern Asia, a conjecture that is borne out by the fact that domestic animals of Asiatic origin were found among them. They had dogs, the common hens and chickens and pigs, which are certainly of Asiatic origin.

The ancient Hawaiians were very bold and skillful navigators, and often made voyages of great length to the Polynesian islands to the south. They had a knowledge of astronomy, knew the planets and had names for the brighter stars. Their year was 365 days. They practiced agriculture and constructed immense canals for irriga-

tion. Accustomed to the water, they were wonderfully expert fishermen and built large fish-ponds
for rearing select varieties. Situated as they were,
thousands of miles from the discord and anarchy
that convulsed the archipelagoes of the south, as
they grew dense in population, struggling for individual supremacy, the Hawaiians developed into
comparative peace and prosperity, and settled down
to the task of working out a destiny in advance of
the aborigines of the other Pacific islands.

They were in a state that admitted of a rapid
transition to civilization without war. This easy
transition from barbarism to civilization, and sudden adoption of the Christian religion in place of
superstition and idolatry, has been regarded as a
signal instance of the triumph of Protestant prop-
agandism. But it is a mistake to cherish the idea
of their having become thoroughly Christianized
or enlightened, as the greater part of the natives,
from Liliuokalani down, are more or less tinctured
with their ancient superstitions and idolatrous worship, practicing the old forms, and in secret pray-
ing to their old-time gods. The idols have been
destroyed or hid away, yet in secret haunts, concealed from the public gaze, the natives still practice their incantations and believe in the mysteries
of their time-honored religion. Liliuokalani supported heathen sorcerers, with whom she was on
terms of intimacy, making them her secret confidential advisers. Her Christianity was but a
mask. Some of the native pastors are worshippers

of the old gods, and heathen at heart. Civilized doctors have great difficulty in alleviating pain or destroying the germs of disease owing to the prevalent heathenism of the patients and their faith in the kahunas, or native " medicine men," who teach that diseases are due to some offended deity that must be propitiated.

The natives believe that an individual who possesses the means of employing a kahuna may afflict with painful disease, and even death, any person against whom he has feelings of hatred or revenge. They also believe that these sorcerers by certain incantations can discover the author of the disease. A great many natives are brought to their death by the pretensions of these ignorant medicine-men, whose influence is so great upon the minds of the people that in all manner of distress or disease their spirtitual aid is sought for relief. A pig or a fowl for sacrifice is at all times necessary for the ceremony, and the fees to the kahuna are regulated according to the wealth or standing of the employer. The kahuna who is supposed to have most influence with the gods is most frequently employed, and derives the greatest emoluments from his profession. The offerings on such an occasion are accompanied with heathenish ceremonies and sacrifices, and are not lacking in mesmeric or hypnotic phenomena. Violent sweatings and purgings, as well as other great physical severities, are frequently used to promote the expulsion of the demon, and, from the anxiety and dread, the mental apprehen-

sion is so great that the victim often dies when no
disease originally existed. The sufferer is told that
a kahuna is at work against him; he at once
sickens, becomes prostrated, aud frequently dies.
Very recently the sister of Liliuokalani, Princess
Likelike, mother of the heiress apparent, Kaiulani,
died from the effects of this heathen superstition.
Human sacrifices were in vogue up to 1820, but
ceased then.

The Hawaiian religion was the embodiment of
beastiality and malignity, that frequently lapsed
into crimes of lust and revenge. The various legends of their gods abound in attributes of the most
excessive animalism and cruelty. Lewdness, prostitution, and indecency were exalted into virtues.
One of the most foul practices intimately connected
with Hawaiian idolatry, and forming an essential
part of its services, was the hula dance. The chief
posturings are illustrated and varied with elaborate
art, accompanied with chants of unspeakable foul-
ness of diction and description, elaborated with foul
wit and jest and extolling impurity. The motive
of the dance is grossly sensual. Sometimes it is
performed to the music of the orchestra, but usually
the accompaniment is the thumping of calabashes
and a weird song, in the Hawaiian dialect, unfit for
civilized print. The dances commence by the
appearance of the performers in the middle of a
ring. Seated on the ground behind them are the
musicians. The hula girls wear a short frock over
the loins, their legs bare to the knees, and around

their ankles are circles of grass fringe. Their
heads and shoulders are ornamented with circlets
of flowers called " leis." A weird chant from
among the squatted musicians, accompanied by the
thumping on the calabashes, starts the dance, at
first slow, but as it proceeds the music grows
louder and more discordant. Each hula dancer,
keeping time to the music, gives an exhibition
of indecent pantomime. With body erect and
shoulders motionless, they keep up a constant
gesticulation with the arms and hands and nervous
stamping of the feet as the hips are made to rotate
about as though they were pivoted to the small of
the back and knees. The performers at times join
in the strident chant. The dance is exceedingly
tiresome and seldom lasts more than ten or fifteen
minutes, when the performers pause to refresh
themselves with cheap gin, and the next act
commences. A dancing debauch usually lasts all
night, and as a rule ends in a promiscuous drunk.

The hula was Kalakaua's favorite pastime, and
he kept a dancing troupe of his own for the amusement of not only himself, but to entertain his favorite courtiers and special tourists at the boat-house.
The dance requires years of training, and cannot
be acquired by an adult any more than an acrobat
can be developed from an old man. The extreme
vulgarity of the hula has been interdicted by law,
but in secret it is carried on with the same lewdness
and obscenity as in the olden times.

It must not be forgotten, however, that it has

TARO PATCH

TARO PLANT, SHOWING THE
ROOT FROM WHICH "POI"
IS MADE

A TAMARIND BRANCH,
SHOWING LEAVES
AND FRUIT

(From photographs loaned by the San Francisco Wave)

only been seventy years since these people commenced to receive Christian civilization, and for
the past twenty years the entire tendency and influence of the reigning family has been of the most
degrading character, so that it is small wonder that
the retrogression of the common people is so in
evidence. Relieved from this blighting influence,
there is already an upward tendency in the native
moral tone. Unfortunately, the native population
is rapidly decreasing, and ultimate extinction
threatens the race. From a period prior to the advent of the white race they have continued to
steadily decrease. At the time of the discovery of
the islands by Captain Cook, in 1774, there was,
upon a moderate estimate, a population of 250,000,
which has dwindled down to less than 30,000 pure
natives at the present date. This decrease was
greatly augmented by contact with the whites, but
prior to their coming the elements of decay were
already in operation, owing to the entire absence of
morality. Chastity had no recognition in the social
organism, and, unlike other races, the female was
aggressive in solicitation. A woman who withheld
herself was considered sour and ungracious, and it
was a matter of good form that all proposals should
come from her. It was the universal practice for
the mother to place her hands on the hips of the
infant female as soon as it could stand up, and by
careful manipulations teach it the sensual and abominable movements of the hula, that upon arriving
at maturity she might, with that accomplishment,

attract the favor of some influential chief. Hospitality was thought to be neglected if the host did not supply his visitor during his sojourn with the women of his family, and there was no more impropriety attaching to it than in the free life of animals.

This condition of society naturally led to wholesale infanticide, which was practiced by all ranks of the people. However numerous the children were, parents seldom reared more than two or three, and many spared only one. All the others were destroyed, sometimes after birth, and the infant living a week, a month, or even a year, was still insecure. The method of destruction was usually by strangulation, frequently by burying them alive, often in the floor of the house, within a few yards of the bed, and the spot where the mother took her meals. The principal motive for this crime was idleness and the trouble of bringing up children. Every effort has been made to check this criminal practice, and infanticide is not now more common than elsewhere.

The diseases brought by the contact with the whites have done much towards decimating the race. For instance, on two occasions the ravages of small-pox were terrible, and the measles made sad havoc among their ranks.

Other infectious and epidemic diseases largely added to the destruction of the population, but venereal diseases were the chief agent of depopulation. From the very first intercourse with the crew of Captain Cook, the amiable and social nature of the Hawaiians caused to be introduced these scorching and withering diseases that ran like wildfire through the nation. When a portion of the United States Army took their station at Honolulu, the First New York Volunteers were the means of introducing the last epidemic. They did not seem to have any idea of how to take care of themselves, and although typhoid fever is almost an unknown disease in Hawaii, a large number of these troops died, and in some companies the percentage of numbers on the sick list ran as high as fifty per cent., and when they were recalled a large number were still sick. That this pernicious disease was caused by the carelessness of the First New York Volunteers is shown by the fact that the regulars and the engineers who were camped side by side with the volunteers had almost no sickness. Fortunately the health conditions here arising from the fate of the New York Volunteers were eliminated by their timely recall and subsequent hygienic regulations. It is true that typhoid fever did not get much headway, but its appearance did much injury to the favorable health reports of the islands.

One of the most loathsome and incurable diseases is leprosy. This disease was first discovered in the islands in 1853, and was introduced from China. Since then it has claimed about 4,000 victims. It very rarely occurs among the whites. Scientific and medical experts from all over the world have been employed by the Hawaiian government to study the disease, and, if possible, to find some cure. So far, it has baffled the medical fraternity. Some have reported it to be the outcome of too much fish food and improper diet; yet if such was the case, why did the natives not develop it before, as from all ages they have been a fish-eating people? Others lay its origin to the want of cleanliness, yet, personally, there is not a cleanlier person in the world than the Kanaka. He not only bathes frequently, but is almost amphibious. Again, it is asserted that the disease is an aggravated form of tertiary syphilis in a race virgin to the disease, and this is more likely the case. The disease is but slightly contagious, and heroic doses of iodide of potassium seem to give relief. Its general appearance is of the constitutional and not the ulcerated form, and the period of incubation of the germ after once implanted in the body is probably from two to five years, and death occurs in from four to seven more years.

In an experiment by inoculation a convict who was sentenced to be hanged submitted to leprous inoculation on condition of sparing his life. Two years after inoculation the disease made its appearance, and in less than four more he died. The efficacy of the experiment was destroyed, however, by the fact that there was leprosy in his family, from whom he might have caught it. Inoculation of animals has produced no perceptible result. The contagiousness of the disease is so slight that the doctors and attendants at the hospitals and settlement never contract it. In one instance a native woman was married three times. Each of her husbands contracted the disease and died from its effects, yet frequent medical examinations developed no trace of the disease in the woman. Again, a pronounced leper has for years lived and cohabited with his wife, and she has not contracted the disease; and of some sixty children born of leprous parents who have been cared for by the government, only two or three have developed the disease. In the absence of knowledge as to the method by which the disease is communicated, and in view of the fact that it was spreading rapidly among the natives, who have no fears of the disease and mingle freely with lepers in the most intimate daily intercourse, an act was passed, in 1865, segregating all lepers and providing a hospital and isolated establishment for them at government expense. A site was selected on the north side of the Island of Molokai, about 50 miles from Honolulu. The site so selected is situated on a narrow peninsula, comprising about 5,000 acres, surrounded by the ocean in front and shut in on the rear by a precipice from two to three thousand feet in height. To this location the government in 1866 commenced to segregate the lepers, sending 140 that year. The number receiving treatment there at present is about 1,100. Several lovely villages of these poor creatures have grown up, and all means that governmental aid and popular charity can devise have been

taken to alleviate their sufferings. They are provided with hospitals, a Y. M. C. A. hall, a public
library and concert and lecture hall, provided with
a piano, organ, seats, &c. There are three
churches—Roman Catholic, Congregational, and
Mormon—and a boy's and a girl's home, each built
by donations from wealthy white residents of Honolulu, which are presided over and managed by
Catholic sisters—all Americans, from a sisterhood
having its headquarters at Syracuse, New York.
There are about 800 horses in the settlement, and
horse-racing is one of the holiday amusements.
Wives and husbands are permitted to accompany
each other into this exile. A band of music plays
in the public park several days in the week, and
medical treatment is administered by efficient spe-
cialists, the whole being under the supervision of
the government board of health. No nation in the
world provides more liberally for its afflicted than
does Hawaii.

Prior to the exiling of patients to this settlement
an examination is made at the Kalihi hospital, near
Honolulu, and not until they are beyond all doubt
suffering from the disease are they sent to Molokai.
The natives regard this segregation of their leprous
relatives as a cruel and uncalled-for hardship, and
Kalakaua practically permitted the law to lapse in
his efforts to control native influence; but now it is
so rigidly enforced that but few lepers are at large.
Either from segregation or because the disease has
run its course, the number of lepers is gradually
decreasing, and ultimate extinction is hoped for.

Another great curse to the native race is their natural fondness for stimulants. Even before the arrival of the whites a narcotic called "awa" was a favorite beverage, and when taken in excess has a tendency to waste and paralyze the system. A liquid was also made from fermented sweet potatoes, but the strongest alcoholic beverage was concocted from the macerated and fermented ki-root. With the introduction of the foreigner came the products of the still, and this craving appetite knew no bounds. The previous mild orgies were transformed into a carnival of excess and contributed largely to depopulation. The narcotic influences of opium took with the natives under the tuition of the Chinese, whose smoking joints are exceedingly numerous. Importation of opium is prohibited by law, but the quantity smuggled is very large. Some idea of the quantity sold on the islands may be obtained from the fact that two Chinamen paid Kalakaua bribes, one $75,000 and the other $80,000, for the privilege of securing a license, for which $25,000 a year was paid, to sell it. This fondness for alcoholic stimulants and narcotics, with its resultant exposure, is one cause for the decrease of the Hawaiians.

The native Hawaiian race is doomed to extinction. They cannot compete with other races, and as new conditions are evolved, and a possible overcrowding of the islands by thrifty and capable classes in the near future takes place, the little remnant of natives will soon disappear as an im-

portant element in the population of the country.
Like all semi-savages, they are poetical, eloquent,
and fond of holding office; but the Hawaiian, with
his superficial civilization and inexperience in
practical government, is incapable of governing or
controlling the stronger races, which now outnum-
ber him three to one. He has already passed from
the stage as a controlling factor in Hawaiian government, although under firm and capable leadership he does not make a bad citizen.

CHAPTER VI.

The native Hawaiians are natural sportsmen, and some of their games would favorably compare with those of civilized races. One of their most popular and delightful sports was surf-riding. Familiar with the sea from birth, they have no dread of it, and are as much at home in the water as on dry land. On these occasions they use a board generally six to ten feet long and rather more than a foot wide, sometimes flat, but more frequently convex on both sides. The natives choose a place where the deep water reaches to the beach and where the surf breaks violently. They take their boards and pushing them ahead swim perhaps a quarter of a mile or more to sea, dodging the billows or diving under them as they roll towards the shore. Arriving far enough out, they adjust themselves on the rear end of the board, lying flat on their faces, and upon the approach of the largest billow, paddle with their hands and feet toward the shore. The breaker catches up with them, and by skillful manipulation it is made to bear the board forward upon its face at an angle of 30 or 40 degrees, with the speed of an express train, to within a few yards of the beach, when, by a quick movement, they slide off the board, and grasping it in the middle dive under the water while the wave

breaks on the shore. Sometimes the swimmer assumes a sitting or standing position on the board in
the midst of the foam, balancing himself in a way
that would prove fatal to even the best American
swimmer. The larger the waves, in their opinion,
the better the sport. They have a variety of games,
and gambol as fearlessly in the water as the children of the United States do on their playgrounds.
Occasionally a light canoe, holding from one to
half a dozen people, is used instead of a board.
This is less difficult than board-riding, and is one
of the favorite amusements afforded tourists at the
Waikiki beach, a few miles from Honolulu. In
the olden times all ranks and ages were equally
fond of this sport, but when the king or queen or
any high chiefs were playing in the surf none of the
common people were allowed to approach the
place.

Another favorite amusement with the common
people was the throwing of a blunt dart, varying in
length from two to five feet, and thickest about six
inches from the point, after which it tapered gradually to the other end. These darts were made with
great care and ingenuity, of a hard wood and highly
polished. They were thrown with great force and
exactness along the level ground previously prepared for the game. The ground was laid off into
a court about fifty or sixty yards long, upon which
two or more darts were laid down at a certain distance, three or four inches apart. The excellence
of the play consisted in the dexterity with which

SURF-RIDING—WAIKIKI, HONOLULU.

the dart was thrown. He who in a given number
of times threw his dart most frequently between the
stationary darts without striking either of them
won the game. Again, the play was a mere trial
of strength. A mark was made in the ground from
which the player must throw his dart. He bal-
anced the dart in the hand, retreated a few yards
from the starting point, and then sprang forward to
the mark and threw it along the ground with great
force. All the darts were left wherever they stopped
until all were thrown, when each player ran forward to the other end of the course to see who had
made the most successful throws.

In throwing darts, casting spears, and dodging
them the Hawaiians were great experts.

A game somewhat similar to the dart-throwing
was bowling, and the skill with which the native
Hawaiian could handle the ball would compare
with the most expert ten-pin player of to-day with
all his knowledge of how to make the spare, strike,
lighthouse break, or Dutchman's bridge. The native game consisted in bowling a highly polished
stone disk, three or four inches in diameter and an
inch thick, with a slight convexity from the edges
to the center. They were made of compact lava,
or of a white alluvial rock, and were highly valued
and carefully preserved, being always oiled and
wrapped up in native cloth after having been used.
A narrow course about half a mile in length was made
on the ground, similar to that made for dart-throwing, and at one end, about thirty or forty yards from

the starting mark, two sticks were stuck in the
ground only a few inches apart, and between these
the parties at play strove to throw the stone without
striking either of the stakes. At other times the
play was to see who could throw the disk farthest
along the course. Sometimes the inhabitants of a
district, believing they had the champion, would
challenge the other people of the whole island to
bring a man to compete with their favorite. This
game required great bodily exertion, yet the natives
would play it for hours with restless avidity and
untiring effort.

In athletic sports boxing was a favorite national
game, was regulated by fixed rules, and presided
over by umpires. The usual contestants were the
chiefs of different districts. When they entered the
ring they were usually attended by a large crowd
of partisans. The fight was severe and determined,
and when a knock-down occurred or blood was
drawn, the partisans of the victor indulged in deaf-
ening yells, danced and beat drums, while the
champion would strut around the ring with an air
of a John L. Sullivan, challenging others to the
contest, until he finally met his match. It was not
uncommon for several of the contestants to be left
dead on the field during one of these games.
Wrestling and foot-racing were much practiced, as
well as jumping the rope and kite-flying.

Another popular sport was sliding down hill on
a long narrow sledge. The runners were from
twelve to fourteen feet long, and two or three

inches deep, made of hard wood, highly polished, and curved at the forward end. They were set up about four inches apart and fastened together by a lot of cross-pieces, on which two long tough sticks were fastened and connected by wicker-work. A smooth narrow track was made of cobble-stones or dry grass down the side of a steep hill, extending to a great distance over the adjoining plain. The performer would grab the sledge about the middle, run a few yards to the starting place, and, with a good start, would throw himself upon it and shoot head foremost down the hill, going sometimes half a mile before stopping. In all these games the natives indulged in various kinds of gambling. Scarcely any individual resorted to a source of amusement but for the purpose of gambling; and at those periods they exhibited all the excitement, anxiety, and rage which such pursuits invariably produce. These feelings were not only visible in every countenance, but were fully acted out, and all the malignant passions which gambling engenders were indulged without restraint. The female would hazard her beads, cloth, beating mallet, and every piece of clothing she possessed, except what she actually had on. The male would risk his implements of husbandry, his hatchets and adzes, and even the mat on which he slept. All were eager to stake every article they possessed on the success of their favorite player, and when they lost all, would become frantic with rage and tear their hair from their heads. These scenes frequently ended in quarrels, sometimes of a serious nature.

A complicated game like our checkers was played with black and white pebbles upon a board divided into numerous squares. One of the favorite gambling plays consisted in hiding a small stone under one of several pieces of native tapa or cloth, so as to prevent the spectators from discovering under which piece it was hid. The parties at play squatted on the ground, each one holding in his right hand a small elastic rod about three feet long and highly polished. The small end of the stick had a narrow slit in it through which was drawn a tuft of hair or piece of ti-leaf. The players were usually divided into two parties of five persons each, and the pieces of tapa were placed between the two parties. One person was selected on each side to hide the stone. In doing this the stone was taken in the right hand and passed along several times underneath each piece of tapa and finally left under one of them. All this time the other side was closely watching to see where it was deposited. The stone deposited and hand withdrawn, the opposite party would then point with the sticks to the piece of tapa under which they guessed it to be concealed. The cloth was instantly lifted up, and should the stone be under it that side had won the hiding, and the side that guessed right the greater number times won the game.

As almost all the men were taught the use of various weapons employed in battle, they frequently engaged in martial exercises or warlike games. One of these exercises consisted in throwing stones with a sling at a mark, and it was remarkable with what precision and accuracy they would, with great force, strike a small stick fifty yards away, rarely ever missing it.

The throwing of a javelin and catching and returning it, or warding it off to avoid receiving any injury, was another game. This feat was one of Kamehameha I's greatest accomplishments, in which he excelled to an astonishing degree. He was known to have six men throw their javelins at him at one time, three of which he caught and returned to his assailants, two he parried, and one he dodged.

Wrestling was an athletic practice of the youths as a preparation for the single combats usual in almost every one of their battles. Sham battles were frequently indulged in, when large numbers would take part. Divided into parties they would advance and retreat, attack and defend each other, and engage in all the manœuvres employed in actual warfare. They took great delight in these gymnastic and warlike exercises, and spent a great deal of time in their practice. In actual hostilities it was not an uncommon occurrence for the result to be decided in a single combat. A boastful warrior would advance beyond the line of his companions and in opprobrious terms challenge his enemies to mortal combat. A warrior from the army of the other side would come out to meet him, and the duel would be continued until one or the other was disabled or slain.

Although actual warfare may not be considered one of their games of amusement, yet their mode of carrying on war was the result of their national character and training, and some account of their system of military tactics and methods of fighting will probably be acceptable in this place. The native traditions are full of accounts of plundering expeditions of one island against another, or the murderous battles between the various independent chiefs of different parts of the same island. No pretext was wanted to commence the fight. It was simply started by one party who thought themselves powerful enough to invade with success the domains of their neighbors and plunder their property. Not until the introduction of fire-arms and the subjugation of the whole group by Kamehameha I. did this custom cease. Whenever war was in contemplation sacrifices were offered, and advice sought from the war gods through the appearance of the entrails of a hog or fowl that was sacrificed, or by the interpretation of dreams. If the expedition was of great magnitude or threatened imminent danger, human sacrifices were offered to the war gods. These victims of sacrifice were either captives or individuals who had broken tabu or made themselves obnoxious to the chiefs. The number offered at one time varied according to the importance of the enterprise. War was never declared without the approbation of the gods made known through the priests, having due regard to the views agreed upon in a public meeting of the

chiefs and their warriors. As soon as they were
ready, the chiefs and priests fixed upon the time
and place for commencing and the manner of carrying it on. Messengers were sent to all the districts
under their authority to require the attendance of a
sufficient number of men provided with their
weapons, kukui nuts for torches, calabashes and
portable provisions. If the circumstances justified
it, all persons capable of bearing arms were summoned, and any one failing to obey had his ears slit
and was led to the camp by a rope. This slit was
ever afterwards a mark of cowardice, and was so
humiliating that very few ever lingered behind.
When all had assembled at the place of rendezvous
a general muster was held by the inferior chiefs,
and the number present reported to the commander-
in-chief. They then went into camp on some plain,
or near the banks of a river, or in a deep ravine
secured from sudden attack, and threw out pickets.
Near by they usually constructed a fortress, including a spring, for the protection of the women and
children. The field chosen for battle was generally
on some uneven or broken ground or rugged tracts
of lava, and from the elevated positions they fought
with slings and stones, and repelled the assaults
with spears and clubs. When compelled to fight
in the open plain, their tactics were of a superior
kind. They advanced in the form of a crescent, with
the wings thrown back, center considerably in advance and reserve to the rear. A line of skirmishers
was formed along the entire front, composed of the

slingers and javelin-throwers. The high chief led
the center. In passing a defile, or when engaging
in a narrow pass, the wings were massed to the
rear and the center led, deploying by divisions after
emerging from the defile. The priests kept to the
rear, and just before the engagement commenced
were consulted by the chiefs, and if the auspices
were favorable they brought out the images of the
war gods and placed them near the head chief.
Prayers were offered and speeches of encouragement made to the assembled warriors, when the
signal was given and the onslaught commenced.
As the fight progressed the priests bore near each
chief the image of his particular war god. After
the fight was over it was the duty of the priests to
sacrifice a certain number of prisoners in honor of
the gods.

The usual mode of fighting was by a succession
of skirmishes, but at times the whole army would
engage except the reserve, which was used with
much skill when required.

Sometimes their disputes were settled in a great
naval engagement, and fleets of hundreds of canoes
were opposed to each other with a skill equal to
those of the flotilla engagements of the ancient
Phœnicians. They went into the fight with
boastful shouts and confusing noise. The first
victim slain was treated with barbarity : his hair
cut or torn from the top of his forehead, his ornaments stripped off and his body dragged to and
mutilated on the altar as the first blood to the war

god. When routed in the field they fled to some sacred enclosure, and if successful in reaching that place of refuge they were preserved, but if intercepted they were slain. If they took to the mountains they were pursued for weeks and months, and if discovered were cruelly massacred. If taken prisoners they were taken before the high chief, who passed judgment, by which they were either slain or spared. If spared, their persons became the property of the captor as slaves. The victors usually buried their dead, but the bodies of the vanquished were left on the field to be devoured by hogs and dogs, or suffered to rot. When completely routed, the country of the vanquished was portioned off to the chiefs of the victorious army, and the wives and children of the defeated were made slaves and treated with great cruelty. If the battle was a draw, a flag of truce, or messenger with a plantain tree or branch of the ki-plant, was sent by one side with proposals, and if agreed to they were ratified in the temple by sacrifices, feasting, dances, and public games, and a wreath of a particular plant was deposited in the temple as a record of the treaty.

With the introduction of the whites the ancient games almost ceased, those of the new-comers were adopted instead, in which the natives have proven themselves exceedingly expert. They have several base-ball clubs in Honolulu, and in the frequent matches against clubs composed of whites they are often the victors. There is a centrally located and spacious base-ball ground, amphitheatre, and all accommodations for the public in Honolulu. Great enthusiasm is shown for the sport, and on occasions of a match game the élite of Honolulu turns out.

In boating, the natives take to the long narrow shell with as much skill as they did in their old time-honored canoe, and in the many regattas at Pearl river and Honolulu harbor they are frequently victorious over their white competitors.

Rifle-shooting and target practice come in for their share as an amusement, and the natives have a team that has made a good record for disfiguring the bull's-eye at short and long range.

One of their favorite sports of to-day is the " tug of war," which consists in a certain number of men on one side matched against an equal number on the other. Each side, taking the most favorable position for bringing all its strength into play, holds on to one end of a rope and pulls against the other until the mark in the middle of the rope is drawn across the limits of the field, when the game is decided. The test requires not only strength, but judgment, knack, and endurance. Sometimes they will tug at the rope for hours before either side wins. The bowling-alley has superseded the old disk-rolling floor, and in this modern game the native is also an expert.

With the introduction of fire-arms, and the moral superiority of the white inhabitants, the natives have become exceedingly docile and a remarkably peaceful race of people.

Horse-racing is a favorite sport. On nearly all the islands there is a well-regulated track, and at the regular meets the races are hotly contested, with good exhibitions of speed.

In the field the sport is magnificent. Quail have been imported from California, and though they will not remain on the lee side of the islands, do well on the windward side, which makes the sport a little more difficult. Japanese and Chinese pheasants have also been imported and do well, having multiplied in sufficient numbers to permit shooting them. Domestic turkeys became so plentiful that the surplus took to the woods and went wild, and turkey-hunting has become quite a sport as well as a means of supplying food. In the mountains there are wild geese, most delicious in flavor, but as they occupy the higher regions of the mountains they are difficult to reach by the sportsmen. During the winter months, or what is known as the rainy season, the marshy ponds around the lowlands of the islands are filled with many species of wild ducks and fowl, and the sport is extremely fine. Numerous ducking clubs and preserves have been formed and it is not unusual for a few gentlemen from Honolulu in two days' outing to bag as many as one hundred ducks. On the northern side of the Island of Oahu there is a series of marshy ponds, near which is the most popular club on the islands, its membership being composed of many of the leading gentlemen of Honolulu. In the winter months also a kind of upland plover make their way to the islands from their breeding ground to the

north. The great distance to this breeding ground
is shown by the impoverished condition the plover
are in upon arrival on the islands, but only a
week or so after landing they become so fat as to
be dull and slow in flight compared with their
rapid movement at first. They are a most deli-
ciously flavored bird, and the sport in shooting them
exceeds that of any other of a similar nature on the
islands. They feed along the beach and marshes
or outlying points, and the sportsman simply takes
a stand on one of the projecting reefs while a dog
is sent around to flush them, or in the absence of a
dog an attendant is sent the rounds. As they fly
from one place to another they nearly always cross
the spit, and a good shot is obtained. Three
sportsmen and two attendants bagged over
five hundred in three days on the western end of
the island where the field was not so frequently
shot over. As the birds fly across the little water
indentations to cross the reef or spit they are very
likely to fall in the water when shot. It is therefore necessary to have a good retriever, of which
there are many fine ones in Honolulu.

At other times during the year dove-shooting is
the favorite sport in the field. These doves are a
little larger than the ordinary dove of the United
States and somewhat smaller than a pigeon, having
a wreath of white mottled feathers on the top of
the head. They fly with a swiftness equal to that
of a blue-rock pigeon, and when coming towards a
person are hard to kill. They feed along the rich
rice bottoms and cultivated fields, and when flushed

fly singly towards a certain cover of woods. Hence to enjoy the sport the marksman takes a stand, as much concealed as possible, near some opening through which the birds usually fly. Early in the morning they leave their roost, and late in the afternoon are again on the move, but in the middle of the day one person goes to a favorable spot on one side of the fields, and another to one on the opposite side, so that as the one fires he drives the birds to the other, and *vice versa*. The sport is very fine and not too much work, and unless the wind is blowing hard can be indulged the entire day.

Of the large game, the little spotted deer have been introduced on the Island of Molokai, and become so numerous as to be an injury to the forests. In the mountains, however, there are a great number of wild cattle and wild hogs on five of the islands, and the sport in chasing them, joined with the danger accompanying the hunt, is highly exciting and very interesting. The hunt is made on horseback, and the weapon is the rifle, hence it takes a good shot and cool judgment to be successful. A wounded bull is no insignificant foe, for he will attack man or beast when in that condition.

There are great numbers of wild goats in the mountains of all the islands, which are much hunted for sport. They are very destructive to vegetation, and in some places men are hired to exterminate them. The skins used to be exported, but the price is now so low that this is only done on a small scale.

CHAPTER VII.

The description of a race of people is incomplete without an account of their religion. The religion of a people has always been considered to have an immense formative power over them. For instance, the religion of Egypt and Chaldea, of Greece and Rome, by its exaltation of the higher elements of character, laid a foundation upon which advanced civilization became possible, while all those nations which worshipped evil gods became corroded and poisoned in their social and political life. The Hawaiian religion was of the latter kind, polytheistic and idolatrous, coupled with oppressive restrictions, superstitious exactions and human sacrifices. It was impure and malignant, evil and unclean, possessing strong tendencies to animalism and cruelty, lust and revenge.

This diabolical religion drew its greatest strength from idolatry and sorcery which brought their evil gods down to living, active powers, interposing in all circumstances of life, and holding the people in habitual fear of the powerful gods and their subordinate demons. Their lives were constantly threatened by them, and every illness, however slight, was the deadly touch of a god. In fact the people were held in abject slavery to the gods and their priests who represented them. The high chiefs even bowed in submission to their rules and dictates and dreaded their vengeance. Their highest gods were absolute embodiments of beastiality and malignity, and their various legends abound in attributes of loathsome filthiness incapable of being printed without extensive expurgation. Yoked to such unclean beings the people lost all sentiments of morality, and lewdness, prostitution and indecency were exalted into virtues. In the construction of their idols or images of the gods, an effort was made to depict their lineaments in as revolting and horrible a manner as their imaginations could conceive. They peopled the sea and air, the sky and heavenly bodies, as well as the valleys and volcanoes, with vindictive and malignant spirits who were subservient to the arts of the haughty and powerful kahunas, or priests.

While believing in a future life, the Hawaiians recognized a distinction in the lot of the dead. They divided the future realm into four separate and distinct regions. The heaven beyond the clouds was reserved for the departed spirits of the noble chiefs. For the souls of the great heroes there was a hidden land or fairy island in the distant west which was said to have been seen sometimes by the mariners in the far-off horizon, covered with cocoanut-trees and rich foliage, and beautiful to behold, but as they approached, it receded before them like a mirage. For the select few of the common people who, through life, had been scrupulous in observing the religious rites and

the laws of tabu there was an upper region of the
lower world where quiet, peace, and comparative
comfort existed, which was presided over by the
great god Wakea, the reputed ancestor of the race.
The last, or terrible inferno, where the majority of
the dead were conducted, was the lower region of
the world, filled with misery and woe, noise and
disorder. It was presided over by the notorious
and wicked god Milu, a former chief of Hawaii,
who was given this power for his excessive evils
during lifetime. From each of these spiritual
dwelling-places the souls of the departed were
permitted to emerge in company with some particular god, who would conduct them back to earth,
where they were not only supposed to watch over
the destinies of their survivors, but at times their
bodies would become reanimated and youthful,
and the existing generation would see and know
their parents and ancestors. In time all who had
died would be restored to life and resume the same
position and authority originally held before death.

The means by which the various legends and religious rites were transmitted was through the
kahunas, or priests, who were divided into several
hereditary orders. It was their special duty to commit to memory and teach their children the long
prayers used in the temple service, and the gene-
alogies and tales of prowess of the chiefs and their
ancestors. They were the learned class, who kept
alive the knowledge and handed down the traditions of what was known of astronomy, history, or

medicine. They selected and executed the victims for human sacrifice. The lever by which the chiefs and priests compelled implicit obedience to their will was the tabu, a complete system which covered the entire daily life of the people with a vast network of regulations and penalties. The people were, at no period of their existence, exempt from its influences, and no circumstance in life could excuse their disobedience to its demands. The death penalty was often inflicted on those who violated the tabu. It was not only a legal requirement, but a religious ordinance ; hence its violation broke both divine and human laws. It was divided into many kinds, some permanent and others special and temporary. Those relating to the chiefs, the idols, and the temples were permanent, while others belonged to particular times, or were imposed arbitrarily by the king.

During a common tabu, the men were only required to abstain from their usual avocations and attend at the temple when prayers were offered, every morning and evening. During the strict tabu the requirements were most oppressive and the prohibitions strictly enforced, and every breach of them was punished with death. For days the strictest silence was observed ; every fire and light in the district was extinguished ; no canoe could be launched, no person could bathe, no tapa be beaten, or poi pounded ; no dog could bark, pig squeal, or cock crow. On these occasions the dogs and pigs were muzzled, and the fowls put under large calabashes.

All the common people prostrated themselves, with their faces touching the ground, before the sacred chiefs when they walked abroad. It was tabu for men and women to eat together, or have their food cooked in the same oven, and it was death for a woman to enter the chapel for the family idols or the men's eating-house. The best kinds of food, such as pork, bananas, cocoanuts, turtles, and certain kinds of fish, were tabued to the women on pain of death.

During each month there were four tabu periods of two nights and one day each, dedicated severally to each of four gods. These four tabus were so sacred that the king spent the time in the temple in prayer with the priests, while the congregation stood with uplifted arms for quite awhile, at the beginning and ending of the prayer. Sacrifices were offered and profound silence was observed. Tabu was sometimes laid on places and things by affixing certain marks, the purport of which was well understood. When the fish of a certain locality were tabued, a small pole was fixed in the rocks on the coast, in the center of the place, to which was tied a bunch of bamboo-leaves or a piece of white cloth. A cocoanut-leaf was tied to the stem of a tree when the fruit was tabued. If the chief wanted any portion of a tenant's crop he simply caused a pole to be placed in the patch, and from that time on it was tabued, and it was death for the tenant, . who had raised it, to use any of it. In collecting taxes the assessor went his rounds carrying with him a certain idol and preceded by a man who, upon arriving at the boundary of a land, set up a pole which placed the land under tabu, and no one could leave it until the taxes were paid in full. If anything was to be exempt from use for a certain period of time a tabu was placed upon it. For instance, a certain kind of fish had a sacred character, and was tabued during certain periods of the year. When cattle were first introduced on the islands they were tabued for ten years.

The ceremonies by which the people worshipped their gods were elaborate and complicated. From the building of a canoe to the dedication of a temple all enterprises were attended with prayers, offerings, and sacrifices. In addition to the worship of the four principal gods the people in every avocation in life had their patron gods, who had to be propitiated, and innumerable omens had to be observed. The dedication of a temple was the most laborious of their religious services. Many days were occupied in the preliminary rites of purification. A religious procession was formed, and headed by a man personating the god and accompanied by a priest, made a tour of the district levying contributions from the tenants. They managed to complete this tour on the evening of the new moon, when a responsive service was held in the temple, before the whole population, and the priests sprinkled the people with holy water, prepared for the occasion. A tree was selected in the forest from which the principal idol was to be made, and a great procession was formed and marched to the spot, headed by the chief and priest with a crowd of attendants carrying idols and various offerings and leading a human victim. Upon arrival at the tree the priest recited the ritual and the chief offered prayer and killed a hog. If no sound of man or beast, insect or fowl, had been heard, it was a good omen, and the doomed man was then brought forward and offered to the god, after which his body was buried at the foot of the tree. The consecrated hog was baked in an oven on the spot while the tree was being cut down. A feast was then held, and the procession re-formed with the feather gods in front, the rear men carrying the new idol and yelling at the top of their voices. It was death for any of the inhabitants to meet this procession, and when it returned to the temple the images were finally deposited in their places amid the shoutings of the people and the beating of drums. The final ceremonies were then held in the temple, where for days the entire multitude took part. Prayers were offered by the priests amid various evolutions of the people and the image-bearers. Finally a hole was dug near the altar, in which another human victim was buried and the image erected over the dead body. Other and subsequent ceremonies, sacrifices, and offerings were performed before the temple was finally dedicated.

The temples differed much in variety of plan and construction. The priesthood were divided

into several orders, some of which were more
severe and exclusive in their ritual than the others.
Other temples formed places of refuge and were
inviolable sanctuaries in time of war, or for any
fugitive who had broken tabu or committed any
sort of crime. The gates were always open and
any one pursuing a fugitive to within the walls of
the sacred inclosure was put to death. After remaining a few days in the temple the refugee could
return unmolested to his home.

In every avocation in life the native Hawaiian
had some form of ceremony, incantation, and offerings to the tutelar deities. A man could not even
build a canoe or use a new fishing-rod without
prayer and sacrifice to his patron god. The building of a house was in accordance with superstitious
rules, even to the arrangement of the sticks, and in
the case of a chief's house human sacrifices were
required. In the building of a canoe an idol was
brought out, the tree selected, the flight of birds
noted, and offerings made. After it was finished
a final sacrifice was offered, and in the launching,
if the silence was broken, the canoe would not be
safe. About the only act in life that was not accompanied with prayers and sacrifices to the gods or
with religious ceremonies was marriage. In the case
of marriage not even the favor of departed ancestors was invoked, and the husband could dismiss
or kill his wife without ceremony or cause. When
a male child was born, offerings were made to the
priests and prayers made to the gods. When he

reached four or five years of age he was permitted
to partake of tabu food, and forbidden to eat with
women, a sacrifice was offered and a feast given, and
he was circumcised. But the female child was
left to its chances and suffered the same restrictions under the tabu as were imposed upon matured
women. The female child was not even allowed
to be fed with a particle of food that had been kept
in the father's dish or cooked at his fire.

✳ (With regard to the dead, their interments were
conducted in great secrecy and without ceremony,
and took place in the night. The people had a
superstitious dread respecting the places where the
dead were deposited. They were exceedingly
superstitious about ghosts and haunted places.)
During the first few days after death, the spectres
of the deceased haunted the sepulchre and endeavored to strangle their enemies, often inflicting
death, but they grew weaker and weaker day by
day. The remains of the chiefs were secreted in
the most inaccessible caverns, and frequently the
bones of the legs and arms, and sometimes the
skull of the king and principal chiefs, who were
supposed to have descended from the gods, or were
to be deified, were preserved, and either deposited
in the temples for adoration or distributed among
the immediate relatives, who carried them wherever they went. The other parts of the body were
either burned or buried. The bodies of the priests
and chiefs of inferior rank were laid out straight,
wrapped in tapa and buried in that posture; the

priests within the precincts of the temple. A pile of stones or a circle of high poles marked the place of their interment.

The common people committed their dead to the earth in shallow graves, and the bodies were placed in them in a sitting posture. The upper part of the body was raised and the face bent forward to the knees, with the hands put under the hams and passed up between the knees, the whole bound together with a cord and then wrapped in a coarse mat and buried.

Sometimes the inhabitants of a village deposited their dead in one large cavern.

The fishermen, after wrapping their dead in red native cloth, cast them into the sea to be eaten by the sharks, in the belief that the sharks would be animated by the spirit of the dead and never devour the survivors. The bodies of human sacrifices, and those who broke tabu, were left to rot, after which the bones were piled up in the temple. The method of killing was by strangulation or by striking with a club or stone, within the precincts of the temple, or the victim was decoyed into the bush by cries of help and knocked in the head. The next morning after burial, it was necessary for those persons who were defiled by handling the dead to bathe in fresh water and seat themselves in a row at the door of the house, when the priest would come along with a calabash of holy water, pronounce the form of purification, and they became clean.

Although the funeral rites were not attended by any ceremony, the death of a great chief was accompanied by human sacrifices and with paroxysms of grief so violent that the people lost all reason. They would knock out their front teeth, shave one side of the head, and tattoo their tongues. The whole community would exhibit a scene of confusion and cruelty that the most barbarous condition could devise. The people would run to and fro without clothing, acting more like demons than human beings. Every vice was practiced and every species of crime perpetrated. Houses were burned, property plundered, murders committed, every base and savage feeling gratified without restraint, and long forgotten injuries revenged with unrelenting cruelty.

If the service in the temples, idolatry, and the restrictions of the tabu imposed such great severities on the people, they did not have the debasing influences that sorcery had. The basis of sorcery was a kind of spiritualism, hypnotism, and faith cure, with a belief that all forms of sickness and disease were caused by evil spirits, with whom communication could only be held through the sorcerers. There were many omens by which the sorcerer judged whether the patient would recover or not. In addition to prayers and sacrifices, herbs and hygienic treatment were also used. They had, through their arts, powerful agencies of death, and were great experts in the knowledge and use of poisons. Some of these sorcerers were so expert in their profession that superstitious fear of them was often sufficient to make the victim give up all hope and pine away until he died. They were frequently employed to use their black art to gratify personal revenge upon an enemy, after which the speedy death of the unsuspecting victim was sure to follow. To accomplish his purpose it was supposed to be necessary for the sorcerer to secure something connected with the person of his intended victim, such as the parings of the nails, a lock of the hair, and the like. For this reason the chiefs always kept their most faithful servants around them, who carefully buried everything of the kind or sunk it out at sea.

The more respectable class of sorcerers were the astrologers, soothsayers, and prophets. They were comparatively harmless persons, attached to the high chiefs as counselors. They helped to keep alive the knowledge of astronomy and navigation and kept up a continual study of the heavens, predicted future events and changes in the weather.

The Hawaiians believed that each individual was possessed of two souls, one of which occasionally left the body in trances and dreams and returned again. The sorcerer was believed to have not only the faculty of seeing the souls of living beings, but of catching them. If he desired, he could either squeeze them to death or imprison them, whereupon the owner of the soul would be terrified and willing to do anything that the sorcerer required.

Kamehameha II, in order to ameliorate the

condition of his wives, and women in general, whom
the tabu had sunk into a state of extreme wretched-
ness and degradation, and to destroy the power of
the priests, abolished idolatry and the tabu system
by which it was upheld, a few months prior to the
advent of the missionaries. One of his first acts
upon coming to the throne was to commit several
violations of the tabu, especially the tabu which
prohibited men and women from eating together.
The abolition of idolatry was the immediate occasion
of war. The high priest acquiesced in the acts of
the King; but some of the subordinate priests and
chiefs took up arms, and in a decisive battle, in
December, 1819, the rebels were completely overthrown, their leader killed, and forces scattered.
This resulted in the destruction of their idols, the
abolition of the system of the tabu and of human
sacrifices. The people were thus left without a
religion, opening the way for American missionaries, who arrived and commenced their labors early
in 1820. The devotees of the ancient cult, with its
cruel and bloody ceremonies, though cowed by the
changed condition, were not exterminated, but continued to exercise powerful influences. There
have always been those who have clung to the faith
of their fathers, who in secret have kept up the
worship of their ancestral gods and the superstitions relating to sorcery, and the influence of this
faith is destined to survive for generations to come.
Under the royal favor and sanction of Kalakaua and
his sister, Queen Liliuokalani, the heathen doc-

trines of the past were publicly revived, and the influence of the kahunas over the people encouraged ; the King even securing the passage as late as 1884, by a subservient legislature, of an act authorizing the licensing of kahunas. This determined spirit of retrogression is what finally wrought the downfall of the monarchy.

CHAPTER VIII.

RESOURCES, PAST AND PRESENT.

At the time of the discovery of the Hawaiian Islands by the whites, the industrial resources of the country were of a nature to support only a barbarous race of people. The sea supplied a great portion of their wants, and as fishermen the Hawaiians were unsurpassed. They used a great variety of hooks, lines, nets, and other apparatus, fishing in the shallows, on the reefs, and even going miles out to sea in frail canoes and catching fish from depths as great as a hundred fathoms. All kinds of superstition attended success in their fishing, and the hook made from the shinbone of some noted chief was of incalculable value. Such was the importance attached to particular hooks of this kind that different tribes have gone to war for the possession of one, and to avoid the use of their bones for that purpose it was the custom for faithful attendants to hide the remains of their chiefs in some secret cavern or bury them at sea.

Sharks were caught for sport, and eaten to some extent. Shark hooks were very large, and were frequently baited with human flesh. One method of catching these monsters was to carry pointed sticks which were thrust between the jaws of the shark or into his vital parts. Men would perch themselves upon some outlying rock or swim around in the clear warm water, until they caught a glimpse of a shark, and then jump or dive under the big fish and attack it as it would turn on its back to bite. As a rule the fight would result favorably to the man, but sometimes he was worsted. In the shoaler waters and inside the reefs, large schools of rare edible fish run, and were caught in great quantities by the natives, in various forms of nets. Certain kinds were placed in the large ponds to fatten. These ponds are large and shallow, made by the construction of long sea walls, requiring much time and labor. Sluices and gates are provided to permit the flow of the tide and the admission of spawn. When once in, the fish cannot get out, and can be easily caught as needed.

The importance attached to the supply of fish food caused canoe-making to be one of their greatest industries, which, like all other works of a similar nature, was accompanied by superstitious incantations and ceremonies. When completed the canoe was christened, not by the breaking of a bottle of wine over the bow, but by sacrifices to a particular god of the sea. In the case of a large canoe for some noted chief a human sacrifice was necessary to insure its safety and lucky voyages. These canoes were low, narrow and light, drawing but little water and made out of a single tree. Some of them were upwards of fifty feet long, one or two feet wide, and sometimes more than three feet deep. The body of the canoe was generally covered with a black paint, made of various

earthy and vegetable materials, in which the bark
and oil of the kukui tree were the principal
ingredients. On the upper edge of the gunwales
was neatly sewed a wash-board or small strip of
hard white wood about six inches wide. These
wash-boards met and closed over stem and stern.
The tackling was very simple, consisting of a stub
mast supporting a sail made of mats in the shape
of a sprit. The paddles were large and strong,
with an oval-shaped blade and round handle, and
were made of the same hard wood employed in
building the canoe. Neither the canoe nor paddles
were carved or ornamented, but were nevertheless
very neat. To give the canoe greater stability and
steadiness, curved outriggers extended to one side
and supported a narrow float, giving the whole
the appearance of a catamaran. In these canoes
the natives would go through any kind of surf,
with a velocity that would excite the apprehension
of any man-of-war's-man, were he even in a good
whale-boat. Should they capsize, the natives swim
around, right the canoe, and get in as though no
accident had occurred.

The wonderful productiveness of the Hawaiian
Islands made it easy for the natives to obtain a liveli-
hood on shore, and had it not been for the system of
tabus and traditions, by which the common people were held in subjection and their privileges
confined to a practical serfdom, life would have
been one continual pursuit of pleasure. Bananas,
yams, and other edible plants grew wild in all the

valleys of the wooded districts ; while bread-fruit, cocoanuts, and a wild apple constituted the indigenous fruits of the islands. The most important of all the vegetable supply for food was the taro, and the cultivation of this plant occupied all the farming abilities of the native Hawaiian. It consists of two kinds, the upland and the lowland. The former grows on the hillsides, in dry ground, whereas the latter, or more important staple, is propagated, like rice, under water. Long irrigating ditches were constructed to supply the water, and great skill was required in preparing the bed, to obtain a good crop. The ground was leveled off and enclosed by a low wall impervious to water. The floor of the patch was made as rich and as free from clods as possible, and the tops cut from the ripe roots set out in hills several feet apart. The water was let in upon them, to remain until the crop was ripe, usually about twelve months. The only labor required was to keep the weeds out, and keep a depth of about six inches of running water. The climate permits planting at any time, so that a continuous supply of ripe taro can be insured. No other plant yields more food to a given space. The root of the taro is oblong, from three inches to a foot in length, and three or four inches in diameter. The substance of the root is somewhat like that of a yam, but more fibrous. Before it is cooked the taste is exceedingly pungent and acrid. The young leaves of this plant are cooked either separately or with meats, making a delicious green,

known as " luau." The method of preparing the
root by the natives is by cooking it in a stone oven
or pit in the ground. The stones are first heated
red-hot and then, after brushing off the dust and
ashes at the bottom, the taro is laid in the oven till
it is full, and a few leaves spread on top. Hot
stones are then placed on these leaves, and a covering of leaves and earth over the whole. In this
state the taro is steamed or baked about half an
hour.

Potatoes, yams, fish, and meats are cooked in the
same manner. From the baked taro poi is made.
This is the national dish of the Hawaiian people.
The baked root is pounded into a moist paste and
thinned down by the addition of water, when the
mixture is allowed to ferment. To a stranger it
appears to be almost tasteless, but upon use it becomes very palatable. It is very nutritious, easily
digested, and can be retained on the stomach of an
invalid when no other food can be. When thinned
down to a thick liquid, by either the addition of
water or milk, it is called a poi cocktail, and is
most soothing to the stomach and highly beneficial
to an invalid. A pudding called "kulolo" is made
by the natives by mixing poi with the grated meat
and milk of the cocoanut, which is sweetened and
baked. Cocoanut mixed with sweet potato, and
baked, forms a compound called " poi-palau." In
no case does poi ever induce dyspepsia and its kin-
dred afflictions. With poi the natives usually eat
the roasted kukui nuts salted with a coarse salt,

which is regarded as a great condiment. Limu, a kind of sea-moss, is also eaten with relish by the natives.

Another very important plant much used by the natives is the ti. It is a slow-growing plant with a large oblong root, which, when first dug from the ground, is hard and fibrous, almost tasteless, and of a white or yellow color. The leaves are of a lively, shining green. The natives bake the root in large ovens under ground. After baking, it appears like a different substance, and is of a yellow-ish-brown color, soft though fibrous, and saturated with a highly saccharine juice. It is sweet and pleasant to the taste, and much of it is eaten in this state. It is used to make an intoxicating drink by bruising the roots with a stone and steeping the mass with water until it ferments. The liquor is then drawn off and drunk without any further preparation. Since the introduction of the still by the whites the fermented mass is distilled, making a powerful liquor called "okolehao." It is an excellent antiscorbutic, and as such became very useful to the whaling ships on their long voyages. The leaves are the best provender obtainable on the islands for stock taken to sea. The ti-leaves were woven together and formed a short cloak which the natives sometimes wore. They are also universally used to the present day to tie up meat, fish, and other articles in the markets, and in which to wrap meats which are to be cooked under ground, imparting a delicate flavor thereto.

The kukui (candle) nut, a heart-shaped nut about the size of a walnut, was used by the natives for many purposes. The tree furnished a gum used in preparing varnish for their tapa; and when burned to a charcoal and pulverized, was used for tattooing the skin, or for making paint. The hard shells of the nuts were removed and the kernels slightly baked in an oven, when they were strung on the center rib of a cocoanut leaf and burned as a torch, giving a tolerably good light. The nuts were also baked or roasted, and eaten with a coarse salt.

The meat supply of the natives was exceedingly limited. The only indigenous quadrupeds consisted of a small species of hog, with long head and small erect ears; dogs, lizards, and a small animal between the mouse and a rat. In the mountains there were several varieties of birds and wild geese, and near the lagoons or ponds in the vicinity of the seashore there were great numbers of wild ducks and other aquatic birds, and plover. The domestic fowl was raised as an article of food. Fish were eaten raw, dried, or baked. Pigs, dogs, and fowls were killed, dressed and baked in the oven. In this way the flavor was much improved over that of the other methods of cooking. No labor was required to raise hogs and fowls; they were simply permitted to roam about. The dogs used for food were of a breed that was rather small in size, something like our terrier, and when raised for food were exclusively fed on vegetables and poi. From experience I can say the flesh is sweeter than that of the pig, and much more palatable than that of goats or kids.

With the introduction of the whites, the abolition of the tabu system, and the distribution of lands, the industrial conditions underwent great changes. For several years after the discovery of the islands by Captain Cook, very few vessels communicated with them; but later on, when Vancouver and other navigators made public the accounts of their voyages, nearly every vessel employed in the Pacific visited the country. Hence in the course of time a regular market was established for the sale of the products of the islands, and the harbor of Honolulu soon became crowded with ships of all nations. The discovery of sandal-wood in the mountains opened a profitable channel of commerce, and from 1810 to 1825 its sale became a source of great revenue to the islands. Adventurers, chiefly from the United States, opened an advantageous trade by collecting it from the natives. They found a ready market for it in China, and the goods from that country were brought in return, laying the foundation of an extensive trade. The chiefs became very rich and accumulated large treasures from the supply of this precious wood, by means of which they were enabled to purchase guns, ammunition, liquors, and vessels, and the luxuries of life. They indulged in all manner of extravagances and created extensive establishments, the maintenance of which soon exhausted their means. Dissipation, ruinous purchases, and expensive ideas combined to leave them in a worse condition than they were before this boom.

The sandal-wood requires many years to arrive at a fit state for the market, and there being no cultivation of a fresh supply it soon became exhausted. The common natives were forced to exceedingly severe labor and suffered increased oppression, being obliged to remain for months at a time in the mountains, searching for the trees, felling them and bringing the wood down on their backs to the royal warehouses. The odor of sandal-wood is very strong and is retained for years after the tree is cut. The wood was extensively used by the Chinese for the manufacture of fancy articles and ornaments and to burn as incense in their joss-houses. With the failure of a supply of sandal-wood, the profits arising from the sale of salt, and from the port dues from merchant vessels visiting the islands, were not adequate to meet the expenses of the government, much less liquidate the debts of the chiefs.

Attempts were made to manufacture sugar from the cane, which grew very abundantly and in great luxuriance. Tobacco, coffee, and spices were introduced, and an attempt made to raise cotton, which was tolerably successful the first year, but by neglect the crop was not gathered and it rotted in the pod.

In exchange for an immense quantity of vegetables, hogs, and native presents, Vancouver, on his second and third voyages to the islands in 1793-'94, landed some live stock, consisting of cattle and sheep, and a tabu was laid upon them for ten years. In consequence of this tabu they increased very rapidly, until now there are not only large cattle ranches on the islands, but the mountains are full of wild herds. Later on, in 1803, Captain Cleaveland, on his way from California to China, touched at the islands and landed a few horses, which soon multiplied, and the natives became expert horsemen, making excellent cow-boys.

The principal receipts of the islands for a long while were from the sale of supplies to the whale-ships, of which a great number made their head-quarters at Lahaina or Honolulu. This source of revenue continued up to the civil war in the United States, when the whaling fleet suffered so much that the industry never recovered.

At first the cultivation of sugar-cane and manufacture of sugar met with many obstacles, in consequence of the lack and great cost of the proper machinery and plant. The first sugar plantation was started on the Island of Kauai in 1835, under a concession, signed by the king, to Ladd & Co., an American company, by which certain lands were leased for the purpose of agricultural development. A start was made, and though labor was cheap the methods were so crude and wasteful that but little progress was made, and the company failed. With the importation of laborers from abroad, and the hope of reciprocity with the United States, the sugar industry revived, but it never amounted to much until 1876, when a treaty of commercial reciprocity with the United States went into effect. Under the provisions of this treaty an era of unexpected prosperity set in and the production of sugar and rice increased more than was ever dreamed of. Not only the rich valleys that were well watered were planted in cane, but large tracts of previously barren land were brought under cultivation by extensive irrigation. Canals were constructed for that purpose. Artesian wells were bored, and the water pumped to heights of four and five hundred feet. Great mills were erected at enormous cost, and sugar became the chief product of the islands.

Although the rainfall on parts of the islands is sufficient to supply the growing wants of vegetation, in other parts everything requires irrigation, as the soil is disintegrated lava, frequently over beds of porous coral. Some of the irrigation ditches are forty miles in length, through dense woods, tunneled through solid rock, and spanning wide canons by means of substantial iron bridges, wooden fluming or steel piping. The Ewa plantation, near Honolulu, one of the largest, was originally a worthless and unproductive area of land, unsuitable even for pasturage; but by means of artesian wells and enormous pumps the water is pumped through pipes to an elevation of several hundred feet to irrigate the cane. It is now one of the finest plantations on the islands. There are about sixty sugar plantations on the islands, covering about 90,000 acres of land, employing about 20,000 laborers, with a yield per annum of about 225,000 tons of sugar. It requires an average of eighteen months for a crop to mature, and the ordinary yield is about three and a half tons per acre; yet on specially rich alluvial soil the yield is sometimes as great as nine tons to the acre. Steam plows, the latest improved cultivators, and the most modern, elaborate, and perfected machinery are used. Both the diffusion and crushing methods are used to extract the sugar from the cane.

The cane is cut and stripped in the field and by means of portable railways is transported to the mills. It is then run between several sets of large rollers, steam being applied to the crushed material between each set of rollers to extract the juice; or if the diffusion method is used the cane is cut into thin slices by means of revolving knives, and the juice soaked out in tanks of hot water, under hydraulic and steam pressure. After the juice is extracted it passes through filters into clarifiers, where it is heated and skimmed, passing thence into the boilers, where it is boiled down into syrup. From these boilers the syrup passes into a vacuum pan, where it is boiled to granulation, passing thence through centrifugals, where it is freed of all molasses or syrup, the dried sugar dropping into bins for bagging and shipment. The molasses is boiled, granulated, and passed again through the centrifugals, making a lower grade of sugar.

The market for the sugar produced in the Hawaiian Islands is the Pacific Coast of the United States and Canada. For a number of years the entire crop has been purchased by the American Sugar Trust, but this year (1898) about two-thirds of the crop has been sold to rival refineries in New York and San Francisco.

The passage of the McKinley bill giving a bounty on domestic sugar, and the cultivation of beet sugar in California and the northwest, and placing imported sugars on the free list, lowered the price of Hawaiian sugar so much that the value of Hawaiian sugar property was materially lowered. It became apparent that the country could not exist on a single industry that was liable to fluctuations by every modification of the American tariff laws; hence the cultivation of new products on the large extent of country unsuited for the culture of sugar or rice was commenced.

Rice, which is also admitted free of duty to the United States under the provisions of the reciprocity treaty, is extensively cultivated. Its culture is principally carried on by the Chinese, and in the markets of San Francisco it grades with the best shipped from China. The ground is plowed and well harrowed and the field then submerged and the water allowed to stand until the crop ripens, when it is drawn off. The method of cultivating rice is crude and primitive. On a small field the Chinaman thickly sows the seed. When the plants are about six inches high they are pulled up and taken in great bales on the backs of men to the field for planting. The plants are set out in the mud by hand, in rows about eight inches apart. As the crop begins to ripen it takes about all the time of one man to about ten acres to scare off the small birds that devour the crop. When matured the water is run off for the ripening of the straw, and the crop is harvested with hand-sickles. It is spread on the ground to dry, and then bundled and carried to the threshing-floor. The grain is separated from the straw while on the floor by walking a lot of horses or Chinese cattle over it, and by beating the straw with hand-flails, the straw being then carefully raked off and the chaff separated by fans. The rice is then milled. Very little of it is shipped to the United States as paddy.

Coffee cultivation has been begun with most flattering prospects. Hawaiian, or Kona coffee, as it is called, takes a high place among the best coffees in the world. The trees are grown anywhere from the sea-level to 3,800 feet above the sea. In three years from the time of setting out, the plantation will yield expenses, and in five years commence to pay well. One of the greatest difficulties in coffee-growing is the blight, but by the introduction of peculiar parasites and lady-bugs for each kind of pest the various blights have been very nearly eradicated.

The cultivation of tea has met with good results. It grows to better advantage on the higher elevations than in the lower sections. The high price of labor has prevented its extensive cultivation.

Hemp has been experimented with, and the samples grown were pronounced by experts to be of good length, clean, strong, and fairly bright. The plant is free from enemies among the insect tribe, and it is not injured by rain or storms nor by drought. The expense of cultivation is almost nothing, and the yield per acre was found to be at the rate of thirteen and one-half tons of clean fiber.

Ramie, or vegetable silk, grows luxuriantly, but the want of proper machinery to prepare its fiber for the market has prevented development of the industry.

Tobacco has been produced of a quality that compares favorably with the best manila wrappers. There is no question but that the raising of tobacco in the islands can be made a paying industry.

The soil and climate of Hawaii cannot be excelled for the production of tropical and subtropical fruits, and their introduction has added largely to the industrial enterprises of the islands, especially so in the case of semi-tropical fruits, such as the avocado pear, banana, pineapple, orange, lime, and lemon. The avocado pear is common to the West Indies and Mexico, and of different varieties, varying in size and color, the largest being about six inches long and weighing upwards of three pounds. The trees grow to a large size in the Hawaiian Islands, and the fruit is of a superior quality. It is of a butter-like consistency, with a nutty flavor, and makes a delicious dressing for salads. The mango grows in great profusion, and several varieties are used for making chutney. The best qualities of mangoes were imported from Jamaica and India, and, for eating, their flavor is exceedingly fine. The mango tree is an evergreen, with small glossy leaves, makes a good shade-tree, and the gum which exudes from the trunk is used in medicine. It is very prolific, and bears fruit which ripens during several months of the year. Frequently trees are found with ripe fruit on one side and blossoms on the other.

Cocoanuts, which grow along the shore where nothing else will, are now very little cultivated. If attended to they will, after about ten years from planting, bear steadily for generations. Not only the nut, but the husks or fibrous covering and the leaves furnish valuable marketable material.

The sapodilla, soursop, cherimoya, custard-apple, jack-fruit, pomelo, papia, citron, mammy apple, water-lemon, granadila, pomegranate, and tamarind are some of the desirable exotic fruits that do well in the islands.

Vegetables of all descriptions are raised the year round, and watermelons and cantaloupes are superior to those grown in most countries.

Pineapples were introduced in the islands by some of the early navigators. They grow wild on all the islands, but the later introduction of a superior quality, and recent revival of the industry, have developed quite an export of this fruit. There are some twenty-five varieties, known by different names in the various localities from which they are obtained. Near Pearl City is quite a plantation where a most excellent variety is cultivated. They have good shipping qualities and grow to a good size, some reaching the extreme weight of seventeen pounds for a single fruit. though a fair average is from six to ten pounds. The season of pineapples is from the middle of May to the middle of August, although some varieties bear fruit throughout the year. In the year 1893 no less than 60,000 pineapples were shipped from the islands.

The banana business has of late become of great importance. At present bananas are raised in very small patches. yet in the year 1892 there were $175.000 worth of bananas shipped from the islands. There is a great market for bananas on the western coast of the United States, and the cost of raising them is very small.

Along the mountain ranges is a most luxuriant growth of trees and vines, large forests of magnificent trees whose wood is beautifully marked and takes a high polish that would place them in competition with the best walnut or mahogany for the manufacture of ornamental furniture. All that interfered with an exceedingly rapid development of the industries of the country was the uncertainty of the political future, for capital is ever wary of investment in a country in which political stability does not exist. The Republic of Hawaii was honest, able, and progressive, but the intelligent leaders had every reason for anxiety and future

PACKING PINEAPPLES—PEARL HARBOR.

uncertainty, as they fully recognized the fact that there did not exist the elements, in sufficient numbers, to maintain a stable independent government. Now that the Hawaiian Islands have become an integral part of the United States, development will proceed with giant strides. Since the annexation of the Islands to the Great Republic of North America a desirable class of people have begun to look about for both large and small investments. With American industry and American thrift and American emigration, with the present conditions considered, the future industrial outlook of the Hawaiian Islands is very flattering, and as soon as the large leaseholds shall expire and the government lands taken up and developed, there will be a great increase in the production, manufactures will spring up, and great shipping industries established.

CHAPTER IX.

One of the most important features of Hawaiian evolution is the system of land tenure, past and present, by which the soil was distributed and is now held by the present owners. At first, during the time of the earliest native occupation of the islands, there were land and water enough for all, and possessions were based upon use only. Industrial enterprises were commenced; canoe-building was developed; the manufacture of native cloth flourished. Great engineering feats were undertaken, such as irrigating ditches and sea walls, inclosing bays and reefs for fish-ponds; and implements of stone and wood for mechanical and industrial works were invented and improved upon. As the different communities began to crowd the limited areas of the valleys, and the population grew until the whole group was stocked with people, the principles of land tenure developed from the patriarchal system into one of tribal or communal ownership. The improved condition of the lands by irrigation led to strict rules for the distribution of the water supply, and the developed localities acquired a special value. As the population continued to increase, and the best lands became occupied, an increasing demand gave them a market value, giving rise to disputes over boundaries, and gradually developing a feudal system of land tenure. The head men acquired the rank of chiefs, and class distinction became very marked, by which the people were divided into a nobility, comprising the kings and chiefs ; the religious order, including priests, sorcerers, and doctors ; and the common people or laborers.

Internal wars were frequent, and the ambition of the chiefs for political power and personal aggrandizement led to their increased importance, which was prejudicial to the rights of the common people, who were oppressively taxed in support of the wars and in defence of their chiefs from the attacks of ambitious rivals. Necessity for the protection of life and property caused the people to become closely attached to some chief, who afforded protection in consideration of service and a portion of the produce of the soil. The chiefs assumed not only political power, but also that of a sacred and religious character, claiming to be of divine origin and in close alliance with the invisible rulers, and they were looked upon with superstitious awe by the common people, who became separated from them by a wide and permanent distinction. When they went abroad all the common people prostrated themselves upon the ground, face down. Death even became the penalty for the slightest breach of etiquette. It was death for a common man to remain standing in the presence of the King, or even at the mention of his name, or when the King's food, drinking water, or wearing apparel was carried by; to enter his inclosure or house without permission, or even to cross his shadow or the shadow of his house; to touch his head or occupy a position above it. It was the custom for any one approaching the King's presence to crawl on the ground and leave in the same manner. No one but a chief could wear the red or yellow feather cloak and helmet or ivory clasp, and his canoe and sails alone were allowed to be painted red. Wherever he went he was surrounded by a retinue of attendants, some of whom carried the royal kahilis (feather ornaments); others took charge of his spittoon, while others were always at hand to knead and shampoo him whenever he desired. There were also in attendance priests, sorcerers, bards, and story-tellers, with dancers, drummers, and buffoons. With a growing power like this the chiefs became not only the owners of the soil, but of all the products that grew out of it, as well as of the time and labor of the people. The constant wars between the rival chiefs resulted in the smaller or weaker of their number allying themselves to some one of the more powerful warrior chiefs, until each island was under the control of its high chief, when finally the whole group passed under the sovereignty of Kamehameha I, about 1790, and the feudal system was complete. Each of these smaller chiefs divided his territory among an inferior order of petty chiefs, who owed to him the same service and obedience that he owed to the high chief. In this way the land was subdivided again and again, down to the serfs who tilled the soil. The common people received not more than one-third of the products of their industry, while the other two-thirds were divided between the chiefs of different grades. The taxes were paid in articles of food, vegetables, fruit, hogs, dogs, fowls, and fish, ku-kui nuts for light, kapa, nets, calabashes, and feathers, besides personal labor on certain days of every moon, which consisted chiefly in working the taro-patches of the chief. They were made to work on all public works, such as building and repairing the temples, fish-ponds, houses, and canoes of the chiefs.

Whenever the chief travelled about, his horde of retainers were supported entirely by the contributions of the people, and if sufficient quantity was not forthcoming, the people were plundered of almost everything they had. Upon the death of a chief, or the accession of a new one, either by inheritance or conquest, it was the custom to redivide and distribute all the lands among his adherents. The only redress the common people had was the privilege of moving from one land to another and joining the forces of a new landlord, becoming in each case merely tenants at will and liable to be dispossessed at any time, subject to the personal whim of the ruling chief. Thousands of unoffending people would in this way be sent houseless and homeless to find a resting-place in some other section of the country. This redistribution of lands was carried out with great severity, and especially so if the chief came into power as the result of war. When the islands were conquered by Kamehameha I, the fullest and severest application of this custom was carried out. He divided the lands among his principal warriors and chiefs, retaining a portion to be cultivated by his own immediate servants or attendants. Each principal chief divided his lands anew and gave them out to an inferior order of chiefs, by whom they were again and again subdivided, passing through the hands of five or six persons, from the king down to the lowest tenants. Each island was divided into several districts, and each district was subdivided into long strips extending, as a rule, from the sea to the mountains, so that each chief should have his share of all the products of the mountain regions, the intermediate cultivated land and the sea. These strips were again subdivided into smaller holdings, which in turn were divided into patches. Each division had a carefully defined boundary and a name.

During the long reign of Kamehameha, affairs became settled, and the long and undisturbed possession of the lands by the chiefs developed a sentiment favorable to permanent individual rights in land, which finally crystallized into law. Upon the death of Kamehameha I, his son came to the throne, and it was his desire to redistribute the lands according to custom, but the united opposition was so strong that beyond a few assignments among his intimate friends he relinquished his purpose, and from that time on until the year 1839 the chiefs remained in possession of their lands. In that and the following year laws were passed to prevent evictions without cause and the wanton seizure of the property of the tenants. This increased security of tenure led to activity in land transactions. Chiefs transferred lands to others, they became a marketable commodity, and incited speculation in buying and selling. The King even gave away and sold some of his personal lands, and foreigners became land-owners. But these sales carried with them no permanent title to the lands, as the act of the chiefs was simply an expression of an opinion, and not a binding law. Nevertheless, purchasers felt a degree of security in their holdings through a public sentiment favoring permanent occupation and hereditary succession. Besides, the possession of lands by foreigners with strong governments back of them, and zealous consuls to insist upon their claims, supported by men-of-war in the harbor, rendered their occupation secure.

When Kamehameha III came to the throne the unsatisfactory status of land tenures was pressed upon his attention, and realizing the defenceless and wretched condition of his people, he became deeply interested. The increasing demand of the foreigners for the right to buy and hold land finally brought about a national crisis forcing the King to decided action. He thereupon consulted the chiefs and conferred with the whites on the subject, the result being the proclamation of a Bill of

Rights on the 7th of June, 1839, by which protection was secured to the persons of all the people, together with their lands and their property, while they conformed to the laws of the kingdom. Although the Bill of Rights did much towards defining the rights in lands granted by it, the feudal right of controlling transfers of land was still retained by the King, and all lands forfeited for non-payment of taxes reverted to him personally. His consent was necessary for any transfer of real estate in the kingdom, for real mortgages, and for the seizure of land for debt. Upon the adoption of the constitution of 1840, the question of the proportionate interests of the King, the chiefs, and the common people in the lands of the kingdom was one of great difficulty, and the necessity of an organized government, separate from the person of the King, became apparent even to the chiefs. This was carried out by three comprehensive acts in 1845, 1846, and 1847. The King retained all his private lands as his own individual property, subject only to the rights of the tenants. Other lands were designated by him, about one-third of the lands of the country, to maintain the royal state, since known as " crown lands." One-third of the lands were set apart as the property of the Hawaiian government, subject to the control of the sovereign as pointed out by the constitution and laws; and one-third to the chiefs, and common people, each receiving what he was actually in possession of. The division in nowise interfered with the lands that had been or might be granted by the King or his predecessors in fee simple to any Hawaiian subject or foreigner, nor with unexpired leases. It was left optional with any chief, holding lands in which the government held a share, to pay into the treasury one-third of the unimproved value of said lands, or surrender portions of land in lieu thereof, which payment or surrender extinguished all claims of the government to them. The division between the King, chiefs, and the people was carried out in 1848. Laws were also passed providing for the purchase of land from the government by private land-holders. A record of the division and sales by the government is contained in books of registry of land titles, deposited in the office of the Minister of the Interior.

In 1850 most of the chiefs ceded a third part of their lands to the government in lieu of paying for the government interest therein, receiving allodial title for the remainder, this being accepted by the privy council. By these cessions the crown lands received their designation from the King's donation, and much of the government land was derived from the chiefs. In all the awards of each of the divisions the rights of the tenants were reserved, and the acts of 1850 and 1851 protected the common people in the right to take wood, water and fish from the sea appurtenant to the land, but gave them no right to pasturage on the lands of the chiefs.

By the act organizing the Executive Department a Board of Royal Commissioners to quiet land titles was created. The Land Commission began its work in 1846, and made great progress in adjudicating the claims of the common people, but its powers were not adequate to dispose of the still unsettled questions between the King, the chiefs, and government. As the chiefs and tenants alike were required to make proofs of ownership to the lands they occupied, and failing to do so their rights were barred, the result was that the ignorant natives failed in many instances to comply, and so lost their property. The division between the King and the chiefs was effected through partition deeds signed by both parties. The chiefs then went before the commission and received awards for the lands partitioned off to them.

Kamehameha III and his immediate successors dealt with the crown lands as their private property, selling, leasing, or mortgaging them at pleasure, until 1864, when the supreme court decided they should descend to the successors to the throne. The following year the legislature passed an act to relieve the royal domain from encumbrances and to render the same inalienable. It provided for the redemption of the mortgages on the estate which had been incurred by the kings, by the issue of exchequer bonds not to exceed $30,000, and enacted that the lands reserved by the act of 1848—*i. e.*, the crown lands—should be henceforth inalienable and descend to the heirs and successors of the Hawaiian crown forever; also that it should not be lawful to execute any lease for a term exceeding thirty years.

A board of commissioners of the crown lands was created consisting of three persons appointed by the King, two of whom were to be appointed from among the cabinet ministers. The King thereupon, in consideration of the payment by the legislature of the debts with which the estate had become encumbered, and of the income rents, renounced all personal claim to the lands which were set apart for the successors to the throne, instead of being governed by the general laws of inheritance. Since that time the government has exercised control over them, and the legislature has passed various acts relating to their disposition. The courts have also, by several decisions, drawn the distinction between these lands and the private lands of the Kamehamehas and their heirs. Now that the Hawaiian royalty has ceased to exist, the republican government claims title to these lands as the " successor " to the kingdom, and is selling the lands to actual settlers.

On the death of Kamehameha V, the last of the old line of kings, his half-sister, Princess Ruth, inherited his private lands. The boom in sugar, under the reciprocity treaty with the United States, had its effect about this time and Claus Spreckles made his appearance on the islands. He was desirous of obtaining a fee-simple title for a sugar company of certain rich crown lands on the Island of Maui, and secured from Ruth a quitclaim of all her interest or claim in and to the crown lands for the small sum of $10,000. These lands are now worth millions. This conveyance was disputed, but the Prime Minister of Kalakaua compromised the claim without taking it to the courts, an act was carried through the legislature to authorize the commissioners to transfer to Spreckles 24,000 acres, more or less, in fee simple, worth some $500,000, and a royal patent was issued to that effect. Spreckles then applied for a perpetual monopoly of the water for irrigating this tract, and upon refusal by the cabinet to grant it, he made an effort to secure the removal of the cabinet by a vote of the legislature of want of confidence. Failing in this, he made a bargain with the King by which the latter sent messengers at 2 o'clock in the morning demanding the resignation of each member of the cabinet. This was one of Kalakaua's first arbitrary and despotic acts, for which Mr. Spreckles was directly responsible. He then appointed a new ministry, who granted to Spreckles the water privilege for thirty years at a small annual rental.

The crown lands until recently were generally leased to corporations for cane culture and grazing, at very low rentals, for long terms of years. Legislative efforts were made to have them divided up (some 876,000 acres) into small farms for the settlement of industrious and thrifty farmers. The monarchy prevented this, but it is now being rapidly done under the republic. Between the years 1850 and 1860, most of the desirable government lands were sold, generally to natives, but in consequence of their thriftless dispositions they soon sold out, and the natives have become largely landless. Subsequently the natives purchased government lands under an act providing for the sale of residence lots from one to fifty acres each.

In 1850, one-twentieth of the lands belonging to the government was set apart for the purpose of education. Another large tract, known as the Bishop estate, a gift from a native, Mrs. Bishop, is devoted to educational purposes.

The chiefs generally were extravagant, got into debt, and, as they obtained title to their lands, these debts were mostly paid with lands which have become a part of the plantations. The distribution of the lands at present is about 830,000 acres of government lands, about 876,000 acres crown lands, and about 1,850,000 acres of private lands. Of these, in 1892, Europeans and Americans owned nearly 1,060,000 acres; natives, 257,-000; half-castes, 530,000; Chinese, 12,000, and Japanese, 200 acres.

Many of the old surveys made under the orders of the commission are full of defects. Some of the surveys are recorded which were made with a ship's compass or a pocket needle, with no allowance for variation. Very little attention was paid to local marks or topographical features of the country. This has resulted in many overlaps and gaps. General maps of districts or tracts giving the location of claims were scarcely thought of. Portions of government lands, sold to private parties, were surveyed at the expense of the purchaser. The pieces sold were of all sizes and shapes, and were surveyed without reference to previous surveys of adjoining land, frequently cutting across each other, leaving the worthless and unsalable portions after the rest had been sold. An efficient government survey bureau has been engaged for many years, however, in straightening out this tangle, and has now reduced the system to comparative certainty. A most careful and exact trigonometrical survey of the country has been made, and the details of most of the districts filled in. The late President of the Hawaiian Republic is an able lawyer, thoroughly posted on the landed system of the islands, and under an act drafted by him government lands with good and sound titles can be purchased.

CHAPTER X.

A failure to remove the Jones-Wilcox cabinet by a vote of want of confidence exhibited a strength in the cabinet, revived business interest, elicited expressions of satisfaction amongst the people, and indicated a final settlement of the political crisis, which made it justifiable for the Boston to leave the harbor for a long-needed target practice. The Boston got under way on the 4th of January, 1893, with the United States Minister and his daughter on board as passengers and proceeded to Hilo, situated on the Island of Hawaii, about 250 miles from Honolulu.

Just prior to leaving Honolulu I drove about town in a carriage with the ex-Minister of Foreign Affairs, and in listening to his talk with a number of the native members of the legislature, and their answers, I became convinced that a movement was under way to oust the cabinet, and that the chances were in favor of its accomplishment. In a conversation with the United States Minister, Mr. Stevens, shortly after, I remarked that I believed that the cabinet would be voted out before the adjournment of the legislature, and from what I had heard from reliable royalist sources, the Queen had no intention of permitting them to remain in office until the meeting of the next legislature; that she was using the lottery and opium bills as a leverage to induce the natives to vote solidly for the removal of the cabinet. The Minister replied that the Wilcox cabinet had come to stay; that he was pleased to know all was at last settled in Honolulu to America's interest, and expressed satisfaction at being able to have peace and quiet during the rest of his stay on the islands, and time to devote to some literary work. He was talking confidentially and with manifest sincerity, for he was an aged, frail man, in no condition to seek or endure the excitement of political strife attendant upon the overthrow of the monarchy, which did, in fact, hasten his death, that occurred a little over a year after.

This is extremely important, in view of the cruelly unjust charges since made by political opponents of Mr. Stevens that the overthrow of the monarchy was the result of a scheme of the American Minister.

On the way to Hilo it was not long before the Boston was abreast of the Island of Molokai, which is mountainous and thinly settled. The northern side is, to a limited extent, cultivated near the sea, and is the home of the lepers. The southern and eastern portions have rich valleys and plains that only await capital and irrigation. On the right was the Island of Lanai, a small, barren islet, wholly given up to sheep-raising. It has rich lands, only needing irrigation to bring them into cultivation. We next came to the Island of Maui, the second largest island of the group. It is about 48 miles

long and 30 miles wide. It is famous in ancient
Hawaiian military history, and is now the scene of
great enterprise and industry. At a distance it appears like two distinct islands, but on nearer approach, a low, narrow isthmus is seen to unite the
two peninsulas. These two peninsulas were probably produced by the action of two adjacent volcanoes. The southern peninsula, which is the
larger, is 10,000 feet high and frequently covered
with snow. The hills are steep and rugged, and
frequently marked with extinct craters or ancient
streams of lava. In places where the volcanic
matter has undergone decomposition, the ground
is covered with trees. The northern slope of the
island and the isthmus is well watered and in a high
state of cultivation. On the western half of the
island the mountains are 6,000 feet high and con-
tain a large valley of great beauty. On the summit of the eastern half of the island is Haleakala
(the house of the sun), the largest extinct volcano
in the world, the crater of which is 19 miles in circumference, with walls upwards of 2,000 feet high.

From the steamer-landing at Kahului, on the
northern side of the island, is a railroad to Wailuku,
and to and beyond Spreckelsville through the great
sugar-plantations. Lahaina, on the western side
of the northern peninsula, is the old capital of the
kingdom. At one time it was a most beautiful town,
composed of lovely homes and attractive public
buildings. It was the great port of call and
rendezvous for the whaling fleets of the Pacific in

days gone by, but is now simply a dilapidated
village of ancient buildings and abandoned houses,
scattered about beneath a thick foliage of shade-
trees and cocoanut-palms. Through these trees a
glimpse of cane fields can be seen running up to
the foot of immense hills in the rear, that are cut
by deep ravines between rugged bluffs.

Leaving Maui, we were in a few hours off the
north coast of Hawaii, the largest island of the
group. The scenery along the northern or windward side of the island is both grand and beautiful.
The land terminates in cliffs, varying from 200 to
2,000 feet in height, plunging down almost verti-
cally into the Pacific. The long, heavy swell or
the ocean, driven for several thousand miles before
the trade-winds, breaks with great force against
these bluffs, throwing spray high into the air and
decorating the walls with innumerable small rain-
bows, produced by the soft rays of the morning
sun. These bluffs are frequently cut by deep
ravines, canons, and narrow gorges, through which
copious streams discharge their waters in magnificent waterfalls and foaming cataracts, tumbling
into the sea, giving an additional splendor to the
scene. Above these bluffs, the surface slopes
upwards towards the mountainous interior, at first
with a gentle acclivity, then steeper, until at length
it is almost precipitous, culminating in the snow-
capped mountains of Mauna Kea and Mauna Loa,
upwards of 14,000 feet high.

All along the coast-line can be seen the rich cane-

RAINBOW FALLS—HILO.

fields, sugar-mills, and plantation-houses, little
villages, school-houses, and church-spires, while
in the valleys and ravines and on the face of the
bluff there is a luxurious growth of ferns, vines,
and tropical vegetation. About three miles inland
from the cliff-bound shore is a forest some ten to
fifteen miles in depth, so dense that it can hardly
be penetrated. Higher up, the sides are clothed
with bushes, ferns, and mountain plants, while still
beyond, the summits are composed of dark lava,
partly decomposed, and entirely destitute of every
kind of verdure, snow lying there throughout the
year.

Finally we let go an anchor in the Bay of Hilo,
from which a black sandy beach rises gently to the
pretty little town of Hilo, situated at the mouth of
the Wailuku river. Nature has been prodigal in
her gifts of beauty to this town by the sea. On
either side of the streets are merry bubbling
streams, and every little nook and hillside is banked
with masses of ferns and plants. Stately trees are
in leaf, and roses and lilies bloom the year round.
It is difficult to imagine any scenery more lovely
than that which borders the Wailuku river, which
has its source on the slope of Mauna Kea, and in
its course dashes in foaming cataracts over cliffs,
through dense tropical forests, and past the rich
lowlands into the Bay at Hilo. Along its banks
are scattered houses, and the lands adjoining are
very fertile, producing all the tropical fruits in
profusion. Just across the bay from Hilo is

Cocoanut Island, with a delightful white-beached bathing-place, where picnics are held. The people of the town gave us a grand reception there one afternoon. This island was the legendary scene of one of the greatest exploits of the last of the heroic kings of Oahu. To obtain the daughter of the great Kamehameha, the chief of Oahu quietly stole ashore here, abducted the sleeping princess and carried her from the magic shore across the moonlit waves in safety to his home, and as the picnickers while away the time on the wave-lapped beach, beneath the clustering cocoanut-trees, they still feel that Love treads the bleaching sands, a willing captive.

Hawaii is the largest and most southern island of the group, and resembles in shape an equilateral triangle, somewhat less than 300 miles in circumference. Nowhere else can the results of the interior forces of the earth be seen to better advantage than in Hawaii. The bulk of the island has been estimated to be 2,600 cubic miles of lava rock above sea-level, and it is remarkable that the soundings around the island show that less than four miles from shore there is a water depth of three and a half miles. The Pacific, if laid bare, would show these islands as a number of mountains, 32,000 feet high, with truncated tops, and presenting an appearance just the reverse of the mountains we see on shore. Instead of their being covered with vegetation at their bases, while their tops are barren, or covered with snow, they would be perfectly bare at their bases, and all around their tops they would be covered with beautiful vegetation and coral polypus. Unlike other volcanic piles of the world, which are covered with cinder cones, the lava of the great volcanoes of Hawaii flows out evenly in enormous deluges, running sometimes for months, or even a whole year, with little or no explosive action, except at the point of exit, which gives to the colossal piles an exceptional form—a great dome with a nearly flat summit—in the center of which is a sunken pit, two and a half to three miles in width, and upwards of a thousand feet in depth. At intervals an outbreak of lava occurs through huge fissures which open in the side of the mountain. The lava spouts out in gigantic fountains from 200 to 1,000 feet high, collecting into a river of fire from a mile to two and a half miles in width, which flows toward the sea, varying its velocity according to the slope. Sometimes it runs ten miles an hour, and at others it spreads out into great lakes and fields, making little progress for days. As the flow descends, small rivulets are shot out on the sides, which soon blacken and harden, only to be covered by another and another stream. As the surface cools it remains hot within, and beneath the hardened covering the liquid river flows on, advancing sometimes less than a hundred yards a day, leaving in its train fragmental products from which are formed, by explosions, steep conical hills. These flows are destructive of everything within their path. In 1880 the flow stopped within half a

mile of the beautiful little town of Hilo. So mild
in action are these flows, as a rule, that an observer
may stand a few feet to the windward of one, so
near that the heat will make the face tingle, yet
without danger. The people flock to witness the
sublime spectacle, and display as much eagerness
to approach the scene as the people of other countries show to get away from one. These lava-
flows have crossed and recrossed one another in a
confused network, in the paths of which desolation
is complete. The more recent ones are black
masses of lava, covering many thousands of acres of
valuable land. The great central valley between
Mauna Loa and Mauna Kea is a vast tangled wil-
derness of lava-flows, which sometimes extend
down the mountain-side for miles without a break.

The last great flow occurred in 1887. A stream
of molten lava broke through a fissure in the side
of Mauna Loa, nearly 7,000 feet above the sea-level,
and in three days it reached the coast, a distance of
20 miles. The most extensive flow of recent years
took place in 1880, and came near destroying the
town of Hilo. The lava stream burst forth from
the eastern slope of Mauna Loa, 11,000 feet above
the level of the sea, and continued to flow for nine
months. Along the entire upper line of its advance, it was one crash of rolling, sliding, and
tumbling mass of red-hot slag, from 10 to 30 feet
in height, accompanied by tremendous roaring and
incessant explosions. Its progress was from the
interior plain down through dark forests and dense

jungles, toppling over mammoth trees, filling up
streams, and driving before its lurid glare every
species of beast or fowl, until finally ceasing to
flow, within a half-mile of Hilo. Some of these
eruptions are attended by a preliminary series of
earthquake shocks and destructive tidal waves.
Others are accompanied by no such phenomena.

After a few days off Hilo, engaged in great gun
target-practice, a fellow officer and myself were
given an opportunity to visit the greatest active
volcano in the world, the volcano of Kilauea. We
made arrangements the evening before with parties
on shore for a conveyance, horses, and guide, and
early in the morning started out in a light buggy
over an excellent macadamized road being built by
the government to the volcano, but not then completed. The road took us through cultivated fields
and avenues of rich tropical jungle and foliage up
a gradual incline until we reached the lower slopes
of the majestic Mauna Loa on our right, with a
beautiful vista of rich fields, fern-forests, and the
broad Pacific on our left. Arriving about noon at
a small tavern on the side of the road known as
the Half-Way House, we stopped for refreshments,
and then drove on until we reached a point near
the terminal of the finished road, about 25 miles
from Hilo. There we met our guide with saddle-
horses, and a man to take care of the buggy.
In the saddle, and preceded by the guide, we
entered a narrow trail leading through an intensely
thick and marshy fern-forest. The horses were

protected from sinking by a corduroy of fern logs. For about three miles we were in this forest, emerging into an open, covered with tough grass and shrubs, between great lumps of lava-rock, and the trail became easier. For six miles more our way lay over rough and desolate tracts of lava occasionally covered with a thin layer of soil on which grew, here and there, a green tuft of grass, a straggling shrub or creeping vine. In every direction we could see little conical hills of lava in distorted forms, resembling small extinct craters.

Late in the afternoon the welcome Volcano House hove in sight, and all about were to be seen jets of steam rising from the ground in every direction. The Volcano House stands but a few feet from the edge of the great crater. Its close proximity to the crater subjects it to frequent shocks of earthquake, and it looks as though it might be insecure, yet no accident has occurred since its erection. The vicinity is marked by fissures, cracks, and steam-holes. Over some of these fissures and holes are deposits of sulphur, and from these pipes are led into the hotel, forming natural steam and sulphur baths, highly beneficial upon a return from the tedious trip to the crater. From the front of the hotel we could look down into the great crater, which is nine miles in circumference and 600 feet deep, with perpendicular walls, stretching out like a great plateau. In this crater and about three miles distant is the active lake of molten lava, the smoke from which could be distinctly seen.

So soon as we had rested a little, our impatience to see the lake before dark caused us to arrange at once for the descent. Fresh and experienced horses were secured, and with a crater guide we set out once more. Just in front of the hotel we descended into the great crater by means of a steep zigzag road. The floor of this vast pit is covered with black lava hills in gigantic convolutions, fantastic forms and irregular shapes, piled up in endless confusion, while the level portion is crossed by many cracks and fissures, from which jets of hot steam and sulphuric vapors are constantly arising. This glistening surface crackles under foot like a thin icy crust on snow, but is firm underneath, except in some places, where the brittle covering treacherously conceals a fissure or cavity. Myriads of thread-like filaments of lava resembling twisted hair are seen floating in the air or deposited here and there, the products of volcanic fires—a product similar to blown glass. This is known as "Pele's hair," Pele being the mythical fire goddess of the lake. Over this great waste a trail has been constructed to within a short distance of the final pit, in which is situated the burning lake. At the end of the trail there was a paddock, where the horses were left, and we went the remainder of the distance on foot. We arrived in time to view the scene by daylight, and to make the descent about 300 feet into the inner pit, to within a few feet of the molten mass.

In this great bed we saw a volume of liquid fire,

like molten iron, moving to and fro, surging and hissing like a sea in a storm. Conducted by the guide, I went across a thin shell of lava, burning to the soles of the feet, and over crevices through which the livid fire could be seen only a few inches down, until I came to the edge of the cone-shaped wall that confined the liquid mass of some twenty acres or more. Ascending to the top of this cone, I stood within a few feet of the boiling lake, and with a stick stirred its surface. The heat was intense, as the lake of fire, boiling like a caldron, covered in places with hardened crust, separated by great lanes of fire, surged and rolled its heavy surf against its enclosing walls. The whole surface was constantly changing, fountains were playing at many points, and liquid tongues of fire would leap up as the congealed surfaces would meet with a crash, and new lanes form, sometimes opening clear across the lake. One of the fountains broke out just in front of me, and threw its clots of melted stone over the wall close to my right. I immediately climbed down the cone and made for the bluff in a straight line, against the advice of the guide. One of my feet broke through into a crevice and the whole sole of the shoe was burned off. In less than an hour the cone on which I had been standing fell in and the lava overflowed several acres.

After that I followed the guide, and reaching the top of the bluff surrounding the pit, we sat down and waited for darkness to set in, that we might

LAKE OF MOLTEN LAVA—KILAUEA

get a good view of the lake by night. As daylight
faded away, the walls of the pit began to glow with
the reflection of the lurid volcanic fire, and the
heavy gases hung in clouds, like reflectors in the
star-lit sky. As the darkness deepened, the light
from the lava grew brighter, while the jets and
surges of molten fire continued without intermis-
sion, fountains of liquid fire shooting up some
thirty feet. The peculiar sullen or angry roar of
the fiery surf was distinctly heard, sometimes like
the noise of cannon or rattling fire of musketry.
The crust, which by daylight appeared to be uniformly black, now showed a network of cracks and
fissures, through which the light of the molten mass
could be seen. All of a sudden the fiery flood on
the left rose above its embankment, and in an in-
stant a lava stream began to flow, and soon became
a river of living fire, covering a large space on that
side of the pit. The effect was grand and suggestive
of the great hidden force within the bowels of the
earth. We sat for hours looking down on the boiling mass, entranced and fascinated. At last fatigue
and hunger reminded us of the lateness of the hour,
and we retraced our steps to the hotel. Arrangements had been made beforehand, so that we had
dinner served immediately on our return. After
dinner came a chat in the cosy room, by a cheerful
fire, over what we had just observed, a quiet smoke,
an exhilarating sulphur bath, and a good night's
rest in comfortable spring beds.

One of the very interesting objects in the hotel,

and over which a number of pleasant hours can be spent, is the register in which the various people who have visited the volcano have written their impressions, and sketches have been drawn of the lake at different stages. The tourist may find a different scene in the great pit of Kilauea upon each visit. Sometimes the lava will overflow and fill the entire pit, and then without warning suddenly drop out of sight, hundreds of feet, as though the bottom had fallen out; then again rise to the surface.

A couple of years before my visit, the lake disappeared down a pit a thousand feet deep, into an unknown abyss. When I was there it had risen again to within 300 feet of the surface of the inner pit. This was a repetition of what must have happened on a grander scale, when the crater was formed, for the entire floor of the great crater, three miles in diameter, was formed by one of these great "break downs." The lake continued its upward tendency until it completely filled again the great inner pit, overflowing all over the floor of the main crater, until it again fell in, in July, 1894. The inner pit is now (April, 1898,) about 1,500 feet across and 500 feet deep, an inaccessible well with hot lava at the bottom. After two days' pleasant enjoyment of the cool crisp weather of this altitude, 4,000 feet above the level of the sea, we turned our faces toward Hilo and arrived in due time.

Upon our return to Hilo a plunge in one of the

large stone bathing pools for which the place is famous had the effect of removing the soreness and fatigue caused by the long horseback ride.

The next morning we returned to the ship, and the Boston got under way and steamed to Lahaina, where we engaged in target practice in the roadstead, with the secondary battery. This being completed, orders were given on the evening of the 13th of January to have steam up and all preparations made for getting under way at midnight for the return to Honolulu.

Shortly before that time, the inter-island steamer from Honolulu came into port and anchored near the Boston. The purser, who was an intimate friend, came on board, bringing the Honolulu papers, and stated that the Wilcox ministry had been voted out the preceding afternoon, and another one appointed in their stead. I immediately informed Captain Wiltse and the American Minister; they both expressed much surprise and asked which of the white members of the legislature had joined in the vote, which information could not then be obtained.

The Boston got under way at midnight and steamed slowly back to Honolulu. When off Diamond Head a pet dog fell overboard, and the ship steamed around the spot looking for him for over an hour. Not finding the dog, the Boston was once more headed for port, and about 10 o'clock in the forenoon of the 14th of January she was moored in her old berth in the harbor of Honolulu.

CHAPTER XI.

As soon as the Boston came to anchor I was sent for by the commanding officer, who read to me an invitation from the Minister of Foreign Affairs to be present at the prorogation of the legislature on that day, January 14th, at noon. The Captain, in compliance with this invitation, instructed me to put on special full-dress uniform, and in company with the American Consul-General proceed to the government building as the representative of the ship on that occasion. After having dressed myself as directed, I went on shore and met the Consul-General at the consulate, and we took a carriage and drove to the government building. Upon arrival, and before entering the hall, I was informed by a very prominent citizen that the Queen, immediately after the adjournment of the legislature, was going to proclaim a new constitution from the palace—a constitution that would abrogate the rights and privileges of all foreigners in favor of native rule and autocratic power; that danger was imminent, and he wished I would return to the ship at once and inform Captain Wiltse. I laughed at the matter, and in reply said I placed no credence in the report, to which he said he had the news from the very best of authority, one of the cabinet ministers, and urged I should inform my commanding officer, which I declined to do. On entering the building I spoke to the Consul-General of what I had heard. He remarked that the gentleman who informed me was of a rather nervous disposition, and that he placed no credence in his statement, nor did he believe the Queen contemplated any such movement.

At the door of the legislative hall we were met by the Secretary of Foreign Affairs and conducted to seats assigned to us. The legislative hall is a spacious room, about sixty feet long by thirty feet wide, having at one end a raised platform or rostrum and speaker's desk. Just in front of and below the speaker's desk is the clerks' circle, and beyond this was the hall proper, where both nobles and representatives sat together as one body, and behind them was a railing separating the legislators from the section allotted to visitors. Not long after we took our seats, the hall proper began to fill with members of the legislature, foreign officials, and distinguished guests. The space back of the railing was packed with native spectators. Nearly every member of the legislature present was decorated with the various orders of Kamehameha I. and Kalakaua, consisting of great gilded stars, covering the left breast and dangling from the neck by silk bands. I was surprised to notice the entire absence of the white members, and in my cogitations as to the reason of this, began to surmise there was some truth in the information conveyed to me by the gen-

tleman on the outside, in which surmise I became
more convinced when a native nobleman, who sat
to my left and a little to the front, and with whom
I was on quite intimate terms, turned around and
in a boastful tone said to me: "We have them at
last. Wait until we leave the hall and you will see
something. Come over to the palace when you go
out." I asked him what he meant, and he said:
"Never mind, but come over to the palace." I
then inquired: "Do you refer to the new constitution?" and he smiled and nodded his head in assent.
Our conversation was interrupted by the entrance
of the Chamberlain from a side door on the left,
who, with a few assistant attendants, quickly arranged the fixtures upon the rostrum and retired.
Immediately after, a few lackeys entered, followed
by the Governor of Oahu, dressed in a flash uniform, covered with gold lace and embroidery, and
ornamented with orders that would have pleased
the Shah of Persia. He took post on the left side
of the rostrum. From a side door came the royal
procession with all the pomp and paraphernalia this
semi-savage Queen could surround herself with, a
comedy compared with which Pinafore and the
Mikado would be considered Shakesperean.

First came the Chamberlain, supporting in front
of him a large portfolio containing the Queen's
message of prorogation. From it were streaming
the ends of white and blue silk ribbons. Next
came four dusky aides-de-camp in full uniform,
somewhat similar to that worn by a colonel in the

United States army. They were stiff and preten-
tious, varying in personal appearance, size, shape,
and color, and exhibiting the air of fully realizing
the importance of their exalted positions. After
them were the feather kahili bearers, supporting
the emblems of savage royalty. These were followed by her Majesty the Queen, dressed in a light
colored silk which tended to add somewhat to her
dark complexion and negro-like features, and more
plainly exhibiting in the facial outlines a look of
savage determination. The dress was provided
with a very long train, which was supported by four
Kanaka lackeys dressed in blue velvet cut-away
coats, knee breeches, white stockings, and buckled
slippers. They were extremely awkward and
ungainly, and were a source of annoyance to the
Queen, who appeared to be unfamiliar with this
ornamental appendage. Next came four homely
ladies in waiting, dressed in the loud colors so
much admired by all dark-colored races. Then
the two royal princes, modest in demeanor, but extremely spick and span. After them came the newly
appointed cabinet ministers, and then the dignified
justices of the supreme court, whose manly bearing
and intellectual appearance gave a relief to what
had preceded. One of them, Mr. Dole, afterwards
became the President of the Provisional Government and of the Republic.

As the procession entered, the Chamberlain turned
to the right and placed the portfolio on the desk,
opened it, arranged the message for the Queen's con-

venience, and took his stand just to the left. The kahili-bearers formed in line to the rear. The Queen, in turning to face the legislative body, caught her feet in the cumbersome train and partially stumbled. It was due partly to her own awkwardness and turning too quickly, and partly to the slowness and ignorance of the train-bearers. She immediately turned with flashing eyes and angered features and spoke to her lackeys, and then stepped up to the desk and waited. The aides-de-camp formed in a diagonal line on her left, and the maids of honor were similarly disposed on her right, all facing the Queen. The ministers and the justices of the court remained on the right. As soon as all were in position the Chamberlain stepped up, and taking the message from the desk handed it to the Queen, who slowly and deliberately commenced to read it, first in English and then in Hawaiian. While reading she exhibited evidences of both anger and great mental strain. Her eyes flashed, and the facial expressions of a nervous yet determined temperament indicated an excitement in no way associated with what is known as stage fright.

As soon as the Queen had finished reading her proclamation the procession reformed on the rostrum, and in the order of entering passed through to the room then used as an office by the Minister of the Interior, where she held a sort of reception. She took her seat, and, surrounded by the court attendants and cabinet ministers, received the then ex-members of the legislature and other officials.

The Consul-General said he would not go in, and I went into the reception-room alone. As I entered the door the governor of Oahu, who was standing near by, stepped up to me and entered into a short conversation. He was very nervous and his language rather disconnected, conveying to me the impression that he wished to prevent my going further. But as I was there under orders and in an official capacity, and desired to see the remainder of the show, I passed on. Arriving before the Queen I extended my salutations and congratulations, which were coldly received and with evident dissatisfaction that I was there. Her manner and general appearance were such as to convince me that I was right in the opinion I had formed when she was reading her proclamation, namely, that she was under the influence of some intoxicant rather than mere excitement. This opinion was borne out later in the day when a very high and distinguished official, who had been near her person all the afternoon, said to me, " We have at last induced her to postpone her *coup*, and if she had not been full of gin we would have accomplished it long ago." A similar statement was made to me by one of her personal favorites several days later. I paid no attention to her conduct towards me, but entered into a cordial conversation with one of her ministers, of whom I was fond, and from whom I had been the recipient of many acts of friendly hospitality. After a short talk and friendly exchanges of courtesies with some of the attendants, I left the building.

On the outside a large crowd of natives and a
few whites were congregated, while great numbers
were moving towards the palace grounds. I was
again told of the Queen's intention to proclaim a
new constitution, and a half-white by the name of
Wilcox, an ex-member of the legislature and generally mixed up in every revolution that takes
place, in a burst of confidence, said to me that he
would have nothing to do with it; that the
Queen, in anticipation of resistance on the part of
the whites, had sent for him the night before to
take command of four small pieces of cannon
which she had caused to be placed in the upper
halls of the palace, enfilading the approaches to
that building from all sides, and that he had declined. These cannon were still there when the
Provisional Government took possession of the
palace. I also learned that the household guards
to the number of eighty, who were at that time
drawn up in line from the palace to the entrance
gate, were armed with ball cartridges and under
the command of a favorite who had received ex-
plicit instructions. The police-station had been
fortified with two Gatlings and a force of police
under the Marshal, and were in readiness for immediate use. I still had my doubts as to the accuracy
of either the whole or part of the prevailing rumors;
but on entering the palace grounds and noticing
the extraordinary gathering and the position and
armament of the troops, I began to realize the
seriousness of the situation and felt it my duty to

at once go on board ship and report to my commanding officer what was going on, which I did. He was very much surprised, and said he had just before received a message of similar import, but paid little or no attention to it; but from what I reported to him he thought it best to find out all he could. I was then ordered to shift into citizens' clothes and return on shore as soon as possible, and in a quiet way obtain any and all information and keep him posted.

Immediately upon my return on shore, I found at the landing a number of native boatmen loitering about who informed me that the Queen was going to make a new constitution, and that there was much excitement at the palace and uptown. A few minutes later I met an American, who was on his way to the Boston to convey the news to Captain Wiltse. He informed me the Queen had commanded the ministers to countersign the new constitution and they had refused, in consequence of which she had threatened their lives. To avoid personal danger, in great fear and excitement they had hastily made their way down town and appealed to the leading men of the community to protect and sustain them. I was further informed that at the office of W. O. Smith, on Fort street, a large number of prominent men were holding a meeting. I hurried on to that place, only a few hundred yards from the landing, and found the two rooms of the office crowded with the best men of the city, irrespective of political affiliations, busily devising

ways and means to avert serious consequences, and
to prevent, if possible, the Queen from doing such
an unconstitutional act.   Some excitement was exhibited on the part of a few, and much uneasiness
shown by all, yet every one was outspoken in a
determination to do something to prevent the
arbitrary promulgation of a constitution.   Short
speeches were made, voicing this sentiment, but
nothing was said or intimated beyond a condemnation of the Queen's act as unconstitutional, and
threatening the business interests of the kingdom.

I left them still in session and went on to the palace grounds, where the native crowd still remained
waiting for news from the inside of the palace. The
soldiers were still drawn up in line ready for a move.
The natives in the grounds appeared to be unconcerned and quiet.   I made a circuit of the city, and
in the eastern suburbs met a body of natives on
horseback coming in from the country.   I learned
later that they were simply returning from a feast
up the adjoining valley.   I immediately returned
to the center of the town and visited the hotels,
clubs, and public places, and heard the people discussing the situation.   The prevalent talk was a
denunciation of the Queen in no measured terms.
The intelligent people appeared to be alarmed and
exceedingly apprehensive of serious trouble, and
throughout the city the excitement and uneasiness
were growing.   At W. O. Smith's office the crowd
had increased, with many people on the sidewalk,
in front of the door, while those inside were still in

discussion. I then went again to the palace, meeting the Chief Justice coming in a carriage from the palace. He stopped and informed me that, after hours of argument and persuasion, the Queen had been induced to defer her *coup d'état*, but that she had announced her determination to promulgate the new constitution in a few days. The Chief Justice thought she would attempt it again on Monday, and that such was her stubbornness and determination they would have the whole affair to go through with again.

I went on to the palace grounds and there saw the Queen in front of. the palace, standing on the balcony. She had just finished a speech in the throne-room, before a large gathering, stating her desire to promulgate a new constitution, declaring that she had been prevented from doing so by her ministers. She repeated, in substance, this speech from the balcony to the crowd in the grounds. There was no cheering, or any evidence of enthusiasm or regret on the part of the natives. They were simply unconcerned as to what was going on, beyond the novelty of the affair and a morbid curiosity over something that was unusual in their daily life. While the Queen still stood on the balcony, two natives near her began to harangue the crowd, stating that the ministry, under the influence of the whites, had prevented the Queen from giving them a new constitution, and appealed to them to rise and kill those opposing her. A few natives in front, realizing what the effect of such language as this would be, climbed up the balcony and, by force, removed the two incendiary speakers from the scene.   Neither the Queen, nor any one near her, made any effort to stop these speakers, and her actions indicated that she was pleased with their remarks and conduct.   After this the natives began to disperse and leave the palace grounds.   At night quiet crowds gathered about the streets, in the hotels and public places, and the conversations there were universally condemnatory of the Queen's revolutionary act.

From all these sources I learned that the Queen, immediately after leaving the government building, had gone direct to the palace and retired to the blue room, where she summoned the ministers to come to her at once.   She presented to them the draft of the new constitution and demanded their signatures, declaring at the same time her intention to promulgate it at once.   In the meantime a native political association, all dressed in evening dress and tall hats, carrying banners and badges, had marched in columns of two from the government building.   They were headed by their president carrying a large flat package suspended in front of him by ribbons about his shoulders.   This was a draft of the new constitution, a prepared address and petition for the promulgation of the constitution.   All this had been prearranged by direct orders from the Queen.   They marched to the throne-room and took position in regular lines, the president to the front and holding in his hands the

address opened and ready to read at the given
signal when the Queen took her position on the
dais. In the throne-room were also assembled a
few members of the diplomatic corps, two of the
judges of the supreme court, the Governor of Oahu,
the two princes, and a number of the native members of the late legislature, all in position for a state
ceremony, but they were kept waiting by what was
going on in the blue room. Two of the ministers,
Colburn and Peterson, positively refused to sign the
document, and the other two reluctantly followed
their example. The Queen became enraged and,
in most excited and emphatic terms, accented by a
sudden striking of the table with her clenched fist,
informed them if they did not sign the paper laid
before them she would go out on the balcony and
denounce them. To gain time and means of escape, they asked for fifteen minutes to retire and
deliberate. This was at first refused, but finally
granted. They had no sooner left the room than
they hurried over to the government building and
immediately sent word down town calling on the
citizens to support them in their resistance to the
revolutionary acts of the Queen. They sent for
several of their leading opponents of the Reform
party and asked their advice. They were promised
the support of the Reform party, and advised to
resist the Queen ; to issue a proclamation declaring
the Queen in revolution against the constitution and
calling on the people to support them ; also to request the assistance of the American naval forces,

if necessary, to maintain order. The cabinet acquiesced in the plan, if the Queen persisted, and at their request a draft of proclamation and request, in accordance with such advice, was drawn up on the spot. Two of the ministers signed the request to land troops, but it was never delivered. Two of them, Colburn and Peterson, more apprehensive of their safety and impatient of delay, rushed down town and personally addressed the meeting at Smith's office, appealing for their support against the Queen. Leading people hurried together at Smith's office and, after brief consultation, unanimously agreed to support the laws and resist the revolutionary encroachments of the Queen, and sent a message to that effect to the ministers. A document pledging the armed support of the signers, to the Cabinet, for the purpose of resisting the revolutionary acts of the Queen, was drawn up and signed by nearly every one present. The ministers were advised not to resign, and to hold out to the last. Meanwhile the Queen was in the blue room awaiting the return of the ministers. She finally sent a messenger requesting their immediate return. Two of the ministers refused, on the ground that their lives would be endangered. Two went to the palace, and somewhat later, upon receiving assurances of support from the people at Smith's office, the other two reluctantly followed.

In the meantime the Queen's especial favorite, C. B. Wilson, the Marshal, and one who was known to have great influence over her, was sent

into the blue room. He used all his power to induce her to go no further. He even threatened her;
but finding her obdurate, he assured her of his support if she persisted. Just as the ministers returned,
he went to the police-station, called in all the police
that could be spared, appointed and armed a few
white friends as deputies, and made preparations
for armed resistance or aggression, as the occasion
might require. Other efforts were made to induce
the Queen to retrace the revolutionary steps she
had already taken, but without avail, she only con-
senting, with great reluctance, to a temporary post-
ponement of the premeditated *coup*.

The importance of the measures taken by the
Queen, the Marshal, and the Cabinet, above set
forth, consists in the fact that they constitute an
absolute refutation of the reiterated charge made by
Commissioner Blount, Secretary Gresham, and
President Cleveland, that there was profound peace
in Honolulu when the Boston troops landed and
the Provisional Government was formed.

From my personal observation, made at the time,
on the spot, and an intimate personal acquaintance
with all the leading people of all parties, I assert
unhesitatingly that during the three days between
the attempt of the Queen to overturn the constitution and the proclamation of the Provisional Government Honolulu was a slumbering volcano, liable
to break out into bloody conflict at any time on two
minutes' notice. I repeatedly urged Captain Wiltse
to land the troops on Sunday, but he waited until the

evidences of impending conflict became so strong that he would have been wilfully negligent of his duty to have waited longer, and did not land until Monday afternoon.

The assembly in the throne-room, after listening to her announcement, left the building, and the news was sent to the citizens down town of what had transpired. The impromptu meeting at Smith's office, appreciating that the Queen did not intend to give up, and that the trouble had but begun, continued their deliberations. A Committee of Public Safety, composed of thirteen members, was formed, to which the further consideration of the situation was delegated, and the assembly adjourned. The committee remained where they were and continued their deliberations for about an hour, but with little or no plan of operations.

The unanimously expressed opinion was that the Queen, having violated her oath to support the constitution, the people were absolved from further obligations to her; that she was in revolution against the government; that this was only the last act of a series extending over years, all tending in the one direction, viz., the concentration of arbitrary power in the hands of the sovereign, and encroachment upon the just rights of the people; that the limit of endurance had been reached, and the abolition of the monarchy was the sound course to pursue. Before adjourning, the sense of the committee was formally expressed in the following resolution, which was adopted by a vote of 12 to 1, the one explaining that the only reason why he voted "no" was because there was no assurance as to what the United States would do :

"*Resolved*, That it is the sense of this committee that in view of the present unsatisfactory state of affairs, the proper course to pursue is to abolish the monarchy and apply for annexation to the United States."

The committee adjourned about dark, without having come to any decision as to means of carrying the resolution into effect, agreeing to meet on the following morning. Several of the committee and some other leading citizens held an informal meeting that night, at the residence of a prominent citizen, which gathering was reported to the Marshal, who at once informed the Queen and her supporters and requested that she would declare martial law and permit him to arrest the Committee of Safety, but she was afraid to do it. The Marshal deserves great credit for his course throughout this exciting period. Fully realizing and disapproving the Queen's unlawful project, he nevertheless was loyal to his mistress and displayed more judgment and genuine pluck than all of her other followers put together.

The main features of the constitution which the Queen attempted to promulgate had been at her order drafted and submitted to Peterson and Colburn weeks before, meeting at the time with no disapproval by them. Parker and Cornwell, the other two ministers, were in ignorance of its full text.

The knowledge of the extreme character of the instrument, and of the effect which it would have upon the determined characters who had led the fight against both Kalakaua and Liliuokalani accounts for the great fear on the part of the first two and the less anxiety shown by the latter two ministers at the critical moment.

The most objectionable clauses of the proposed constitution provided that the Queen should have the power to appoint and remove at will her ministers; that all members of the upper house of the legislature were to be appointed for life or good beheavior, the choice being absolute with her instead of their being elected by the people for terms of six years as had theretofore been done; that the tenure of office of the Supreme Court judges should be changed to six years only instead of for life, as theretofore; that all whites theretofore possessing the voting right should be disfranchised except those married to native women.

Such was the condition of affairs when I returned to the ship at midnight. I made a detailed statement of the situation, and expressed the opinion that nothing would happen that night, but that, from the state of feeling of the people, serious trouble would come as soon as the counter-revolutionists could organize.

CHAPTER XII.

The following morning, Sunday, January 15, 1893, the Committee of Safety met again, and, after discussing the situation in all its bearings, came to the conclusion that a proclamation should be issued abrogating the monarchy and establishing a provisional government in its place. Word was sent to the Cabinet that, in accordance with their request, the people had organized to support them with armed force against the Queen's revolutionary course; that the Committee of Safety would act in subordination to the Cabinet if they would lead in taking the Queen at her word; but that the committee insisted upon action. The Cabinet were requested to declare that by violating the constitution the Queen had vacated the throne, and were informed that if they failed to take this course the committee would proceed to act without them. The Cabinet asked for time to consider the proposition. They were told that the committee were proceeding with their preparations and would stop for nothing; that it rested entirely with the Cabinet whether they led the movement or not; but in any event the committee would act as soon as it was ready to do so. The committee decided to call a mass-meeting, make a report, and ask this general gathering of citizens to confirm their appointment, and authorize the taking of whatever further steps were necessary to advance the public welfare and secure the rights of the people from future aggression. The mass-meeting, of about 2,000 men, was held on Monday, noon, the report presented, and strong resolutions adopted condemning the Queen, approving the course of the committee and authorizing it to continue to act. The committee continued its meetings and began the work of organization and preparations. Couriers were sent all over town to notify friends of the movement to arm themselves, and be prepared to answer a call when needed. The various old volunteer organizations and the people who had brought Kalakaua to terms in 1887 and put down the revolution instituted by Liliuokalani in 1889 now began to stir themselves, and by night one squad of about 50 men reported with arms at a rendezvous on Emma street. Another squad of 75, mostly Germans, met at a place on Fort street, back of the Chinese church. Posters were displayed calling on the people for a mass-meeting on the following day, to be held in the old armory on Beretania street. The result of the deliberations of the Committee of Safety, the posting of these notices, and the gathering of armed men were known to the Marshal and by him reported to the Queen, but her advisers were afraid to act, and the meetings of the committee and gathering forces were left undisturbed.

The Marshal afterwards told me he had urged the ministers to let him open an attack on the opponents of the Queen before they got too strong, but they would not let him do it. All this time the forces at the palace and station-house were kept under arms. Transpiring events were reported to Captain Wiltse at various times during the day, and he went on shore twice to make personal observations. On his return to the ship he informed me the situation on shore was very critical, and expressed the opinion that he ought to land a force to protect Americans and property, but he did not want to do that unless absolutely necessary. He said he had several interviews with the United States Minister, who informed him that he and the English Minister had used their best influences to stop the Queen, but could do nothing, and that he (Wiltse) and the Minister had agreed upon great caution. In the meantime the aggressive spirit of the Queen had weakened. She began to realize the seriousness of the situation, and exhibited grave fears of being deprived of her throne. She and her followers became frightened at the tone of intense feeling manifested by the people, and began to cast about for means of saving themselves. A peace was patched up between the Queen and her ministers, and for the time being she forgave them for their perfidy. Without a moment's hesitation, and without replying to the proposition of the Committee of Safety, the Cabinet abandoned the citizens whom they had called upon for help, and who had organized in good faith to assist them.

A secret meeting was held on Sunday noon, at the office of the Attorney-General, in the government building, by a few citizens and hangers-on of the palace and the now reconciled cabinet, and they decided to call a counter mass-meeting of natives the next day at Palace Square.   It was decided that the tone of this meeting should be very conservative. A "by authority," to be signed by the Queen and countersigned by the Cabinet, was drawn up, announcing that the Queen had abandoned her intention to force a new constitution, and that in future she would abide by constitutional requirements. Speakers were detailed and posted as to what they should say, in a temperate and peaceful manner. On Monday morning, although outwardly quiet, the city was the recruiting ground for two hostile camps. The Queen, the Marshal, and the Cabinet were increasing their forces and preparing for the demonstration of the people acting through the Committee of Safety, which was preparing swiftly and with little concealment of its objects.   The people were, by this time, organized into armed bodies ready at a moment's call, with squads still forming, of sufficient force to command the entire situation.   The palace guards were kept constantly under arms and ready for active work with a battery of field artillery, while the police-station was barricaded and fortified with two Gatling guns, and nearly the whole police force and a number of special deputies. The city was full of Canadian refugees, beachcombers, and loafers from all over the world, eager

for incendiarism and loot, with two mass-meetings
of opposing factions, to be held in the afternoon at
points only a block apart. The situation was alarming, excitement intense, and a feeling of uncertainty
as to what would take place. The bubble was
likely to break at any moment, and disorder and
riot be precipitated. The Marshal had notified the
leaders of the Committee of Safety that the mass-
meeting should not be held, and receiving no favorable answer, he reported to the Queen's head-
quarters that it would be impossible to stop it without armed interference. A message was sent to the
Committee of Safety by the Cabinet on Sunday, stating the ministers would like to meet and consult
with representatives of their number, which request
was complied with on Monday morning. In that
interview the ministers urged the committee to go
no further, stating that the Queen had agreed to go
no further with the constitution matter. The committee replied they could place no confidence in the
Queen's pledges, that she had gone too far, and
they would proceed with their deliberations without regard to what the Queen said or did.

This alarmed the Queen and her supporters still
more, and impressed upon them the enthusiasm
and determination of the respectable and conservative portion of the community to put and end to the
corrupt monarchy. The ministers made public the
"by authority" referred to, and sent copies to all
the foreign legations in the hope of obtaining their
support, but without avail. Not only was this con-

dition of affairs reported to Captain Wiltse, but, to make sure, he went on shore in the morning to ascertain the facts, and with a personal knowledge of the danger to life and property that existed, there was no other course for him to pursue than to land a force before it was too late, and he made up his mind to do so. Immediately upon his return to the ship, about 10 A. M., he called me to the cabin and with closed doors told me of the condition of affairs as he had learned them, confirming what I had already reported.

The leading citizens of the town were openly and publicly preparing to oust the Queen's government by force of arms. They were making no concealment of their intentions. On the contrary, they informed the Cabinet on Sunday morning, again on Monday morning, and the Marshal on Monday noon, what their intentions were. The Queen and Cabinet were making such preparations as they could to resist.

There were several thousand American citizens and many million dollars' worth of American property at the very focus of this cyclonic condition of affairs.

It was manifest that the government was unable to protect itself, and could not under any circumstances protect life and property.

If ever a situation warranted the landing of troops to protect American interests, this was such an occasion, and Captain Wiltse, after consulting the American Minister and myself, decided that his duty plainly required him to land.

PLOWING A RICE FIELD

A PINEAPPLE RANCH

(From photographs loaned by the San Francisco Wave)

He asked me how long it would take to get ready for landing the two revolving cannon, and two Gatling guns, with ammunition. I replied, half an hour.

Shortly afterwards the executive officer instructed me to get one revolving cannon, and one Gatling gun, with their field carriages, and one caisson ready, and to let him know how many men I needed to fill up the complement, and to get the boats ready for lowering. All of which I did. Other preparations were made and the men of the battalion instructed to get their dinner, and to pack their knapsacks for heavy marching order. Captain Wiltse sent for me again and, in a confidential manner, as was his usual course with me, read his confidential letter of instructions from the Navy Department, and from Admiral Brown, commanding the United States naval forces in the Pacific. In the discussion which followed I fully agreed with him as to the necessity of landing a force. I remarked that the situation was such that great tact and judgment would have to be used to avoid being accused of interfering or taking sides with one or other of the contending parties. His reply was that he intended to maintain a perfectly neutral attitude, but he would prevent any injury to Americans or their property, incendiarism or pilfering, even if he had to fight all hands. As soon as the men had finished their meal, the battalion was gotten ready, ammunition put up, belts filled with ball cartridges, and the men fitted out for heavy marching order, with instructions to be ready to land at 4 o'clock. The time set was supposed to be about the hour the two mass-meetings would finish their deliberations, and should they come together in a hostile manner, we would be on the scene in time to prevent riot and bloodshed within the city proper, or in the vicinity of the innocent women and children. The battalion consisted of one company of artillery, two companies of blue-jackets, and one of marines, with musicians, and hospital corps. The men were provided with knapsacks and double belts, each holding from 60 to 80 cartridges. The caisson and ammunition-boxes were filled with ammunition, taking in all 14,000 rounds of rifle, 1,200 revolver cartridges, and 174 common explosive shells for the revolving cannon.

At 1.30 the citizens began to assemble, and before 2 o'clock the large armory on Beretania street was crowded to its utmost capacity with the largest and most enthusiastic mass-meeting ever held in Honolulu. Every class in the community was fully represented—mechanics, merchants, professional men, and artisans of every kind being present in full force. The report of the Committee of Safety was submitted and unanimously adopted, which was a condemnation of the acts of the Queen and her supporters as being unlawful and unwarranted, endangering the peace of the community and tending to excite riot and cause destruction of life and property. The appointment of the Committee of Safety was confirmed or ratified and they were instructed and empowered to further devise such ways and means as might be necessary to secure the permanent maintenance of law and order and protection to life, liberty, and property in Hawaii.

At the same time that the mass-meeting was in session at the armory, the royalists, under the instruction of the government, were holding a counter demonstration at Palace Square. A resolution, as previously agreed upon by the Queen and her supporters, was adopted, accepting the royal assurance that she would no longer seek to promulgate a new constitution by revolutionary means. Notwithstanding the instructions of the night before for the speakers to be most conservative in their remarks, some of them gave vent to expressions of a desire for bloodshed. During the sessions of the two gatherings the stores in town were closed, business suspended and drinking-saloons stopped from selling liquor, and excitement was intense, while the city was at the mercy of a mob, as most all the policemen had been called into the police-station.

The Committee of Safety met as soon as the mass-meeting adjourned. Numerous citizens, fearing a repetition of the mob of 1874, and probable destruction of the town, outrages upon the persons of women and children, urged the committee to request the American Minister to land a force from the Boston for the protection of life and property. This was prepared but was not delivered until after the Minister's visit to the Boston hereunder referred to, and had nothing to do with the subsequent land-

ing.   While the two mass-meetings were in session
the American Minister came on board the Boston,
several hours after the order had been given for the
battalion to land.   Captain Wiltse immediately
sent for the officers who were to accompany the
men on shore, to come into the cabin, and be present at the interview and consultation with the
Minister.   The Minister spoke of the Queen's
proclamation to abandon her attempt to proclaim
a new constitution, and of the attitude of the leading people of the city in support of the Committee
of Safety; also of the large mass-meeting being
held by order of the committee, and of the counter
meeting, composed mostly of low whites and natives.   He thought they might come into conflict
and that trouble was imminent; that Captain
Wiltse should be prepared to land if necessary.
" Should you land," said he, " you need not ap-
prehend any one firing upon you, as they have
never done such a thing under other and similar
circumstances ; " referring to the landing of American troops in 1874 and 1889.   Captain Wiltse replied
that he realized the necessity and had already given
orders to land the troops at 4 P. M., to protect
American interests.   Then turning to the officers
present he read a short letter of instructions to
them.   These instructions were taken bodily from
his confidential letter from the Navy Department,
and were prepared in the morning when he first
decided to land.   One of the officers present asked
how far he was to go in the event of a change in

the state of affairs, or should he be attacked by either of the contending forces. Captain Wiltse thereupon supplemented his written by oral instructions, to this effect: Under conditions as he then understood them to exist, he would have to largely depend upon the judgment of the officers going on shore; that they had been long enough in Honolulu to be thoroughly acquainted with all Americans and the location of their property; that they should be protected so long as they preserved a neutral attitude.

The Minister, after remarking, " I am glad you are going to land," and that he thought the landing absolutely necessary, left the ship. At 5 P. M. the battalion was landed at the regular landing at Brewer's wharf, and after being formed on shore, marched to the corner of Fort and Merchant streets, where a squad of the marine company was detailed to protect the United States consulate. The rest of the marine company was marched to the United States legation, on Nuuanu avenue. The main body of the force was marched up Merchant street through Palace Square. As it passed the palace entrance, the Queen was seen standing on the front balcony of the palace, whereupon a royal marching salute was given her, arms port, drooping of colors, and ruffles on the drums. As we marched through the city there were no policemen or guardians of the peace at their posts for the protection of the public. A little beyond Palace Square, the battalion halted for the purpose of finding some place to go into camp. An effort was made at first to secure an old armory near the boat-landing, as that was in touch with a base on board ship, but it was refused, as was the opera house, the only two places of suitable dimensions available. These being refused, the forces were marched on out King street, nearly a half mile, to the residence of an American, and in his yard the troops were bivouacked under the trees. About 9.30 P. M. Captain Wiltse drove up, and said he had secured a temporary place in a hall to the rear of the opera house, commonly known as Arion Hall. This building was a small, low, wooden structure with a wide porch front and rear, and was originally erected by the corrupt minister to Kalakaua, Gibson, for the purpose of high carnivals and political gatherings of their ring.

The battalion was immediately formed and marched to the hall and went into camp. I was made officer of the day and posted pickets inside the yard at all the approaches to the camp, and kept watch myself for anything unusual along the front of the opera house. I soon saw that this was the best strategical position in the city for the main body of the troops to encamp, with the two smaller bodies of troops in the narrow business portion of the city, and at the United States Legation. The broad streets diverging from Palace Square afforded an easy means of mobilizing at any point, while the opera house in front constituted a formidable breastwork. From in front of the opera house a good view was obtained of the vicinity of the fortified police-station and center of the business portion of the city, along King and Merchant streets, and of the vicinity of the government barracks across the Palace Square ; the park of the principal hotel ; the approaches to the armory occupied by the citizen forces, and the grounds surrounding the government buildings. The whole section was, with the exception of the government buildings, occupied by American property and residents. I immediately procured several men whom I knew well, and in whom I had implicit confidence, to scour the town and obtain all information possible of the situation, disposition and number of troops on each side, movements of the citizens, and from time to time I received information afterwards corroborated by actual participants. I was informed that the police had all been called in, and a few deputy marshals, newly appointed, in citizen's dress, were the only government officers doing duty in the streets of the city ; that the government forces, consisting of the household guard and policemen, were divided into two detachments, one of 60 men at the barracks and palace grounds, the other of 80 men at the fortified police-station, making in all 140 men. With the exception of a few newly appointed deputy marshals, these were all the forces that the Queen had at her command up to the time of the overturn of the monarchy. At the same time, I learned there were 175 men of the volunteer forces under arms, mostly members of a military organi-

zation known as the " Honolulu Guards," famous
for the aggressive and determined part they had
taken in forcing Kalakaua to terms in 1887, and in
putting down the Liliuokalani-Wilcox revolution
of 1889. They were quartered in three different
sections of the city, within convenient positions for
a quick and easy mobilization of a part or whole
at any desired point within the city.   One of these
squads to the number of 80 men were in a building
on Fort street, in rear of the Chinese church.
Another squad of 50 men were in an old building
on Emma Square, while a third of 45 were
encamped in the armory on Beretania street,
commanding any flank movement from the government barracks.   It was apparent to my mind
that the citizens were the masters of the situation,
as they had much fighting material yet to draw
from, while the Queen's supporters had melted
away. Our forces were so placed as to enforce
upon both sides a proper regard for the safety of
property and the protection of non-combatants, and,
if necessary, to prevent fighting in the streets, as
our forces did when they landed in Panama during
the revolution there in 1885.   Early in the evening
the deputy marshal, dressed in citizen's clothes,
called to see me with an apparent friendly message
from the Marshal, but obviously to find out the
disposition of our forces, and the part we proposed
to take in the event of a fight. I understood his
mission and extended to him a most cordial
reception, took him all through the camp and

emphatically informed him we were there simply
to protect American life and property, and under
no circumstances would we take part with either
side ; but I believed no fighting would be permitted
in the streets or residence portion of the city. He
replied, they knew that, and the next evening the
Marshal told me he knew we would have nothing
to do with either side, and that he wanted to go
out and fight, stating at the same time the cowardly
ministers would not let him. The deputy departed
with a friendly message and with cordial feelings,
and offered to send me something for my comfort
in camp, which he did later that night.

All night long, rumors of an alarming nature prevailed of the intention, by native supporters of the
Queen, to burn the residences of her leading opponents, and the business portion of the city. The
fire-patrol was kept on the alert for immediate use.
Many women were very much frightened, and some
of the people sent their families out of the city to
Waikiki. There were two fires during the night
of an incendiary nature, and on each occasion I
called out the guard ready for a move, and sent couriers to find out where the fires were. Learning
that they were of little importance and that American property was not involved, I returned the guard
to their quarters. This calling out of the guard had
a good effect, and was the means of quieting the
extreme tension of feeling. The fact that we were
ready and on the alert to protect them inspired
confidence among orderly people.

That evening the Committee of Safety continued their deliberations and perfected their plans. They finally decided to abrogate the monarchy and establish a provisional government in its stead, and this accomplished, to submit an appeal for annexation to the United States. Mr. J. H. Soper was appointed to take command of the military forces. A committee of two was appointed to select four persons to constitute an executive council, and others to act as an advisory council. Judge Dole of the supreme court was chosen to act as the head of the government. A messenger from their number was sent to invite Judge Dole's attendance at the meeting. He came, and after hearing their proposition said that he doubted the advisability of abrogating the monarchy yet, and that he did not entirely favor the idea of annexation to the United States. He suggested that it might be better to establish a regency and place Kaiulani on the throne. Kaiulani had been appointed heiress apparent by her aunt, Liliuokalani, and confirmed as such by the legislature. Dole's advice, even at this time, might have been taken and the monarchy preserved, had that young princess been educated in the United States, and not in England under the self-appointed guardianship of T. H. Davies, an Englishman of pronounced bitterness against American interests, and who had repeatedly in the local press of Honolulu, over his own signature, denounced in bitter terms and unfriendly spirit the rights of the United States to establish a naval station at

Pearl Harbor. It was also reported that his son was engaged to marry the princess. Even as it was, there was a long discussion as to the acceptance of Dole's advice, but the feeling prevailed that bitter experience had demonstrated that the Kalakaua blood was not to be trusted, and that if action were not taken now, it would have to be taken at some time in the future, after another struggle, and under, perhaps, more unfavorable circumstances. Finally, upon the earnest persuasion of the committee, Dole consented to take the matter under advisement and further consideration, and give them an answer on the following day. After persistent efforts on the part of the committee, Judge Dole agreed on the following day to accept the responsible position, which acceptance sealed the doom of the monarchy in the Hawaiian Islands.

CHAPTER XIII.

ESTABLISHMENT OF THE PROVISIONAL GOVERNMENT.

Early on the following morning, 17th of January, 1893, the battalion was drawn up in line, mustered and inspected, guards detailed for the day and a routine established. Breakfast was brought off from the ship and served to each company, after which the men were exercised at drill. Every assurance was given to convince both sides that we occupied with our forces a neutral position and were there only for the purpose of protecting American life and property. The men were cautioned not to say or do anything that would cause them to be accused of partisanship, and no one was permitted to leave the limits of the encampment. Whatever rumors either side caused to be circulated to the contrary was due to no word or act of either the officers or men of the Boston's battalion. They were simply there in the performance of duty, as was the case when American forces had been landed in Honolulu on previous occasions of riot or revolution, and this fact was thoroughly understood by both the contending factions in Honolulu. Some of the members of the Committee of Safety made an effort to intimidate the royalists by starting the report that the American forces were on shore for the purpose of supporting them against the Queen and her forces; but Marshal Wilson informed me, the night after the surrender, that he knew better, and that the craven ministers used that canard as an excuse for their own cowardice. The only effect the false rumor had was to induce a few timid whites, who were anxious to join the movement of the citizens but held aloof on account of the fear of reactionary consequences, to become publicly supporters of the committee where they had previously secretly supported it, and it formed a pretext for the protest under which the final surrender of the royalists was made.

The people of the city were astir earlier than usual, yet everything was outwardly quiet. The two hostile forces still occupied the same positions they did the evening before. The royalists kept within their fortified places, well knowing the active progress being made by the Committee of Safety, who were actively at work completing their plans. Several of the prominent members had been to Judge Dole, urging upon him an immediate answer and acceptance of the offer tendered him the day before. Others had waited upon those who had been selected to serve upon the executive and advisory councils of the new government, to obtain their consent to serve. The preliminaries having been attended to, the Committee of Safety met at 10 o'clock A. M. in the office of W. O. Smith and proceeded to organize the Provisional Government. An order was sent out prohibiting the inter-island steamers from leaving for the other islands before the next day. Judge Dole came before the committee and notified them of his decision to accept the presidency, but before doing so he sent in his resignation to the Minister of Foreign Affairs as one of the justices of the supreme court. No better man could have been selected. In fact, there was no one else available gifted with those great qualities which nature lavishes on men born to rule. Quiet and unobtrusive, modest in demeanor and of sterling integrity; possessing a cultivated mind and a benevolent heart; a leader in all the moral, religious, and progressive movements on the islands; careful in thought, fair in judgment, honest in convictions, an excellent lawyer, and a cool, deliberate statesman, Judge Dole was fortified with the universal confidence of the citizens of Hawaii of all nationalities. He was born in Honolulu, of American parentage, in 1844. He was educated in Honolulu, and at William's College in the United States; studied law in Boston and was admitted to the bar in that city before returning to his native country, where he not only became one of the leading lawyers, but a member of the supreme bench.

The Committee of Safety adjourned at noon for lunch, meeting again at 1.30 P. M., when they completed the organization of the Provisional Government upon the plans previously agreed upon. An executive council was appointed consisting of four members, with Dole as chairman and Minister of Foreign Affairs; the other three filled the offices

LOADING SUGAR CANE

(From a Photograph loaned by the San Francisco Wave)

of Ministers of the Interior, Finance, and Attorney-General. An advisory council, to have general legislative duties, was selected, consisting of fourteen members. The proclamation abrogating the monarchy and proclaiming the Provisional Government was signed by the committee, and the executive council confirmed J. H. Soper as Commander-in-Chief of the Military. A guard was sent out to order arms and ammunition, which the committee had in one of the stores in town, to be taken to the armory. A messenger was sent to the government building to ascertain whether there was any armed force there to oppose them. He reported that there were none.

In the meantime the forces from the Boston were being exercised in an afternoon drill within the enclosure, in ignorance of what was going on in town, when a messenger from the police-station came and informed me that the counter revolutionists had completed their organization and were going to make an effort to take the government building at 3 P. M. and from there issue a proclamation formally establishing a Provisional Government, and to prevent this, the Marshal was going to send 50 armed men from the palace and police-station to guard the building. We stopped drilling and the officers went to the front of the yard to see if there was any movement. In a few minutes we saw some men coming up the street headed by Judge Dole, and immediately after heard that a policeman had been shot in town. It looked as though a fight was imminent and the Boston's men were in consequence not dismissed, but kept in the rear of the opera house, with Arion Hall between them and the government building. The shooting of the policeman precipitated matters, and the executive and advisory councils, accompanied by the Committee of Safety, immediately went by different streets to the government building fully half an hour before they intended the *coup* should take place. It appeared that the officer in charge of the squad who were directed to gather the arms and ammunition was seen by one of the special deputies to drive into the back yard of the store where some of these arms were. The special immediately notified the Marshal, who sent out four or five policemen from the station to capture the arms, and in their efforts to do so the officer of the guard shot one of the police. The others permitted the wagon to proceed to the armory and deliver the arms to the men waiting to receive them.

When this shot was fired and the story of its results flew through town, it created a panic in the royal ranks, and all those who could reach the police-station rushed in such numbers to that building for shelter that the Marshal had to close the doors. The Marshal afterwards told me that two of the cabinet ministers, one of whom was the Attorney-General, and the immediate head of the military forces of the kingdom, rushed to the rear of the room and stood there trembling and would not permit the Marshal to either send men to the government building or open a fight, and there they remained, clustered in the closed station-house, afraid to move, while Dole and his party moved on the government building unmolested. Had the plans which the Marshal mapped out been sustained by the ministers, and a guard sent to the government building, supported by the cannon from the palace and the forces at the barracks, with the fortified police-station as a base, it is exceedingly doubtful if the counter-revolutionists could have taken the government building or palace that day, and it would have necessitated the proclaiming of the new government from some other place. In that event they could not have obtained control of the government building and archives, and the treasury, or secured any recognition from the foreign representatives until they had driven the royalists out. They had a sufficient force to eventually capture the place, yet there would have been a fight. The ministers knowing the force and the character of the men opposed to them were afraid to make a stand. However, the leaders of the Provisional Government, while on their way from Smith's office, had grave apprehensions, and the excitement was intense. Several of them told me that they expected at every corner to be fired on.

The armory on Beretania street had been designated as the place of rendezvous for the volunteer forces, and as soon as they heard of the shot on Fort street, they formed their companies and squads and moved towards the government grounds from different approaches. Upon the arrival of Dole and his followers at the entrance to the building, only a few employees were to be found, and the demand upon the chief clerk of the Interior Department for possession of the building was immediately complied with. A crowd began to gather, and from one of the rear gates of the yard a company of about 50 armed volunteers entered and formed in front of the building.

The committee now proceeded to read the proclamation abrogating the monarchy and formally establishing a Provisional Government instead, "to exist until terms of union with the United States can be negotiated and agreed upon." During the reading of the proclamation, armed forces were gathering in the yard, and by the time it was finished fully 175 determined volunteers were in position to guard the building and protect the new government, and the royal forces could never have driven them out. The yard was cleared of all lookers-on, and sentries posted at the gates to prevent outsiders from entering.

After reading the proclamation the councils convened in the office of the Minister of the Interior and issued an order calling upon all persons favorable to the new government to report at the government building and furnish such arms and ammunition as they might have in their possession or subject to their control. Martial law was established, liquor-saloons closed, and letters sent to each of the different members of the foreign diplo-

matic and consular officers announcing the establishment of the Provisional Government, and requesting their recognition.

All this time the American forces were peaceful
spectators from their camp of what was going on.
Captain Wiltse and myself were standing on the
front porch of Arion Hall, where we had a partial
view of the proceedings. Calling me to his side,
he remarked: "This ends it; the royalists are not
going to fight." Just then a messenger from the
Provisional Government came up and reported the
formation of the new government, with a message
from Judge Dole asking if he, Captain Wiltse,
would not recognize them. The reply was that such
recognition could not be made until they were in
possession of the police and military forces, and
fully in condition to protect life and property. A
few minutes later I was ordered to go over to the
building with his compliments to Judge Dole, ask
him what the new government was in possession
of, and to inform him that if he did not have control of the police and military forces Captain Wiltse
could have nothing to do with them. I found
Judge Dole, and the officials of the new government,
and some others, clustered around him, in one of
the large rooms of the government building.
When I delivered my message, with a wave of the
hand Judge Dole said: "You see we have possession of the government building, the archives and
the treasury, which is the government of Hawaii.".
To which I replied, "I see you are here, but how

about the police-station, palace and barracks, and the armed forces at those places?" To this Judge Dole remarked they would soon have them. "Well," said I, "Captain Wiltse directed me to say to you that until you obtain possession of them and are in position to guarantee safety to life and property, he could not recognize you or have anything to do with you." Several persons asked me if we were not going to stand by them. I replied, "Gentlemen, you heard what I said." A few looked at each other in surprise, but the majority and Judge Dole appeared to anticipate my answer.

I reported the conversation and result of my observations to Captain Wiltse on my return, and he repeated in the most emphatic terms that under existing conditions he would have nothing to do with them. Shortly after this another messenger from Mr. Dole came over and requested Captain Wiltse to come and see him, as he desired to speak with him on the situation. The Captain requested me to go with him, expressing a desire to have a witness to his conversation present. The commanding officer of the battalion was standing near and said he would go, and the two went over, resulting in another refusal of Captain Wiltse to recognize them. A summons was sent by Judge Dole to the palace, demanding an immediate and unconditional surrender of the palace, police-station, and barracks. To gain time the ministers who were at the police-station sent a messenger to invite the leaders of the new government to come and

consult with them, which was of course declined, and word sent back that if the ex-ministers
wished to see the Provisional Government they
must come to the government building. Two
of the ex-ministers came in company with two
members of the Provisional Government and after
obtaining an assurance of safety returned for
the other two ex-ministers, when all four appeared
at the government building and entered into negotiations for a surrender.

In the meantime the adherents of the Queen,
realizing that all hopes were gone, appealed to the
American Minister for protection, and being refused,
advised the Queen to take advantage of the presence
of the American forces on shore and to surrender
to them. This proposition was refused by Mr.
Dole on the ground that the United States forces
had nothing to do with the present state of affairs,
and he did not understand why such a proposition
should be made, unless it was a dodge. The
royalists then began to evolve some other means
to escape, and were at a loss for plans, when Paul
Neumann came to their rescue. Neumann was
one of the best lawyers in Honolulu, a thorough
Bohemian, an excellent entertainer, of superior
education. He also had more influence with the
Queen than any other man on the islands. A
German by birth, an American by adoption, and a
Hawaiian by domicile, he was at this time the
Queen's only adviser who possessed more than
ordinary abilities or education, but was not over

scrupulous when a fee was in sight. He drew up terms of surrender by which the Queen was to give up, under the pretext that the armed forces of the United States were the supporters of the new government, and stating that impelled by that force she would, under protest, yield her authority, appealing to the government of the United States to reinstate her upon a presentation of her case. The ex-ministers were no longer trusted by the Queen as advisers, but to give official force to this act they were required to sign the document with the Queen. When the document had been signed, the ex-ministers in company with the agents of the new government, who had been sent to demand the Queen's surrender, returned to the government building and the terms were accepted. The Queen then gave orders to the Marshal to give up the police-station, Oahu prison, and government property under his control, and an officer with a squad of men was sent to take possession. The commander of the forces at the palace and the barracks went over to the government building and offered to surrender, but was instructed to continue in charge until the following day, when those two places were taken possession of.

Late in the evening, and during and following the time of the negotiations between the officials of the new government and the Queen's representatives, I saw a number of the foreign diplomatic corps entering the government building, and was informed at the time that all had verbally recog-

nized the new government as the *de facto* government of Hawaii. Each stated he would confirm
recognition in writing at the earliest opportunity,
and on the following day this was done by all the
representatives of the foreign powers in Honolulu.
With the final surrender the Provisional Government was in full possession of the public buildings,
the archives, the treasury, and in control of the
Hawaiian capital. Armed sentries were posted
about the city and a mounted patrol detailed to
guard the approaches to and the main streets. No
one was permitted to be on the streets after 9 P. M.,
unless provided with a pass from military head-
quarters, and for the first time since Saturday afternoon a feeling of quiet was restored, and the people
were able to retire to rest in full confidence of safety.
The forces from the Boston remained all the
time within the limits of their encampment, and
never lifted a finger in either physical or moral support of either the falling monarchy or the rising
Provisional Government. Their men were amply
protected by the opera house and Arion Hall from
all harm, even if fighting had taken place in the
government grounds.

While at the Hawaiian Hotel that evening, I met
the ex-Marshal, C. B. Wilson, and had a long talk
with him in relation to the past events, before he
became biased by the later false statements made
by the Queen's advisers. The Marshal recounted
to me all his plans and how he had expected to
carry them out, had he not been interfered with

by the ex-ministers. Wilson is a man powerful of
physique, a half white, of strong natural, but un-
cultivated mind ; of good judgment, and possessed
of great confidence in his own prowess. He was
intense in his loyalty to the Queen and bitterly denounced the ex-ministers as cowards and traitors.
He had intended to resist, and said that it was fully
understood that if a fight took place, the government buildings and palace grounds were to be the
scene of battle, as had been the case in all the other
uprisings in Honolulu. Both he and the ministers
well knew that the government building was the
objective point of the counter-revolutionists. The
forces, he informed me, that were under his command consisted of 60 men at the palace and barracks, 85 armed police and a lot of scared and un-
armed refugees, the ex-ministers at the police-station,
and about 20 special deputies in civilian clothes in
the city. With this force so disposed, his plans
were to detail about 30 men early in the forenoon
to guard the government building, and as the volunteers from the armory on Beretania street would
have to approach the government grounds from the
eastern approaches, they would be opened upon by
the cannon in the top of the palace, and the forces
at the barracks and government building. At the
same time he would move up the two Gatling guns
to enfilade the streets from the western approaches
to Palace Square, reserving the station-house for a
base of supplies, and a stronghold to rally on in
case of defeat. Had the Marshal been permitted to

carry out those plans, there would have been loss of life and the Provisional Government would have had difficulty in establishing itself that day. However, the provisional forces had everything their own way from the time of the organization of the military squads on Sunday night, and I am thoroughly convinced, from personal knowledge and careful observations, that the counter-revolutionists, by their superior intellect, greater courage, and superior numbers, would have easily won in any event, and could have sustained themselves when once established.

Without the loss of a single life this remarkable revolution in the Hawaiian Islands came to an end. The Provisional Government immediately received the support of the best citizens, and nine-tenths of the property-owners of the country. It resulted in the complete and final overthrow of the rank hypocrisy and unconcealed paganism of the house that Kalakaua founded and his sister Liliuokalani brought to grief.

CHAPTER XIV.

TEMPORARY AMERICAN PROTECTORATE.

From the preceding it will be seen that for three days, from the 14th to the 16th of January, 1893, inclusive, there were two parties in Honolulu confronting each other in angry hostility, with every indication of an armed conflict at any moment, before the forces from the Boston were landed. When they did land it was purely as a precautionary measure, and in conformity with established precedent and instructions, authorizing and requiring the protection of American lives and property in cases of imminent danger. Their disposition was such as to subserve that particular object, and in their distribution at the Legation, Consulate, and Arion Hall, where they occupied enclosures, they were isolated and inconspicuous, beyond a sentry or two on post. No one was permitted to leave the camp, and no demonstration whatever was made intimidating to the Queen, or in support of the organizers of the Provisional Government. Prior to filing her protest, and twenty-four hours after the troops from the Boston were landed, the Queen and her ministers requested the aid of those troops for her re-establishment and protection, which request was refused and they were again informed that the force would only be employed to protect American property and neutral American citizens. On the other hand, the head of the Provisional Government, late in the evening, and after they were in full possession of the capital of Hawaii, and recognized by the foreign representatives as the *de facto* government, requested the support of the American troops, and further suggested that Captain Wiltse assume command of their forces.

The reply to this request was the same as that given to the ex-Queen and her ministers, and at no time did Captain Wiltse or any officer from the Boston take command of the Hawaiian forces, or permit the troops from that vessel to perform any kind of military duty for the Provisional Government. During the night of the 17th the officers and men from the Boston were kept ready for a moment's call, but everything passed off in a quiet manner. The interior of the government building was transformed into a barrack for the volunteer forces, and the legislative hall and other rooms were assigned as quarters for the different companies.

The household guards completed their surrender on the following day, and they were disbanded, except a small squad that was detailed as a body guard to the ex-Queen, as it was feared some one might attempt to do her bodily injury. The barracks were taken possession of, and all the arms and ammunition of the late government were turned over to the proper officials of the Provisional Government. In view of the unsettled condition of affairs, and the fact that most of the volunteer

forces were men of business, and the police were
in sympathy with the royalists, it was thought to
be to the best interest of the United States for the
Boston's troops to remain on shore. In consequence an unoccupied house on King street,
about 300 yards from the temporary camp at Arion
Hall, was obtained for permanent quarters, and
the Boston's battalion, on the forenoon of the 19th,
was moved into the building, known afterwards as
"Camp Boston," where they remained until finally
recalled on board ship, April 1st. This house was
a square, two-story building of stone, with broad
verandas on three sides, and as it had formerly
been used as a hotel, the accommodations were
excellent for the health and comfort of the men.
Everything was put in order, and the bills for
expenses were paid by the paymaster of the Boston,
although the Provisional Government offered to do
this; but Captain Wiltse refused to accept their
proposition. The lower floor was occupied as barracks for the men, an office for the adjutant, and
officer of the day, and a guard-room. The upper
rooms were assigned to the officers, and an outside
building was set apart for a hospital and armory.
The grounds around the building had a frontage of
about 250 feet separated from the street by a high
stone wall with two broad entrance gates. On the
east side and to the rear was a splendid lawn for
drill, shaded by tropical trees, and enclosed by a
high broad fence having a rear entrance. The
next day after going into the new quarters a com-

"CAMP BOSTON"—HONOLULU

pany was sent through the principal thoroughfares as a grand guard to make observations, and inspire confidence. With the exception of this the men were constantly and rigidily kept within the camp enclosure during their entire stay on shore, except a dress parade every evening in Palace Square, which was attended by most every one in Honolulu.

One of the first acts of the Provisional Government was to appoint a special commission to proceed to Washington, and negotiate a treaty of union of the Hawaiian Islands and the United States. The commission sailed on the 19th of January for San Francisco, in the chartered steamer Claudine, and proceeded thence by rail to Washington, where they presented their credentials at the State Department on the 4th of February. The ex-Queen, to offset the plans of this commission, employed Paul Neumann as her diplomatic agent, to proceed to Washington and present her claim. He was instructed to obtain for her restoration to the throne, or a large indemnity as a price of final abdication, and to try and save her the crown lands. A full power of attorney, signed and acknowledged by Liliuokalani, was given to Neumann, authorizing him in his discretion to release all her claims and make such settlement as he thought best. To inspire Neumann's zeal in this behalf, she paid him $5,000 down, and agreed to pay him $5,000 more should he succeed. This money she had to borrow from one of the local banks, having spent her ready cash on the preparations for change in

the constitution. Neumann sailed on the regular
mail steamer, which left Honolulu a few days after
the Claudine. It leaked out that the ex-Queen in
her instructions had sold out her friends, and they
regarded it as a purely selfish and personal effort on
her part to escape with the spoils of compromise and
leave them in the lurch.

On the 18th the Queen was notified to haul down
the royal standard, which was still flying from
the palace, and to vacate that building. With
her body-guard she accordingly removed to her
private residence on Beretania street, and the palace
was taken for the executive building. Every courtesy and friendly consideration was shown her, even
the salary she had been drawing as Queen was
given her. She was permitted to live quietly in
her own home residence, close by her former palace, and in the fullest enjoyment of all the immunities and privileges of a distinguished citizen. There
she persistently clung to her royal claims, and her
attitude as the rightful ruler of the Hawaiian Islands was not in the least weakened. Her firm confidence in her royal dignity did not show any tremor
in the face of the strong, quiet, and well-ordered
administration of the Provisional Government. She
gathered around her the former ring of political
supporters, and openly threatened and intrigued to
overthrow the new order of governmental affairs.
She was strongly encouraged in this attitude by the
support given by the British residents and officials,
the English Minister being the leader. Prior to her

extreme proceedings just previous to the revolution, he had been an ardent partisan of the Queen. On her retirement he continued a notorious sympathizer, and was a frequent caller at Washington place, the ex-Queen's residence. The rumor was spread broadcast by the royalists that he had requested an English fleet to come to Honolulu and restore her, and that one was coming.

Another source of great uneasiness to the Provisional Government was the fact that there were 20,000 Japanese in the country, over 1,500 of whom were on a plantation only 20 miles from the city. These Japanese had been admitted to the country as contract laborers, under the provisions of a special labor-immigration treaty. The general Japanese treaty gave to Japanese all the immunities of the peoples of the most favored nations. The privilege of the franchise had, however, been denied to them. The royalist leaders made an effort to stir them up to hostility to the government, by making them believe that if the islands became a part of the United States, as proposed by the Provisional Government, they would, under their contracts, become forever slaves, and they promised them full rights of Hawaiian citizenship if the monarchy were restored. There was one Japanese man-of-war in the harbor, and another coming, with every indication of discontent on the part of both the Japanese officers and laborers, and when some 400 of the laborers approached the city one evening, armed with sugar-cane knives, or machetes, and

threatening an attack, the situation became serious.
They were stopped with some difficulty and sent
back by the Japanese officials. There were a
number of renegade whites and of the hoodlum
element of all nationalities ready to nag the Japanese on and for trouble of any kind, and for nights
the town was full of rumors of incendiarism, assas-
sination, and threatened attack on the government
building. The fear entertained by the Provisional
Government, that the captain of the Japanese man-
of-war might take advantage of the discontent of
his people on shore to land an armed force, and
the expected arrival of an English war vessel, by
the aid of which the British Minister would undoubtedly try to embarrass them, decided them to
request the American Minister to assume a temporary protectorate over the Hawaiian Islands for the
purpose of assuring the *status quo* and checkmat-
ing foreign intrigue until the decision of the annexation proposition.

With the flag of the United States over the government building, they felt confident that neither
the Japanese nor English officials would attempt
to insist that their government had a right to interfere. With the sole object, therefore, of holding the existing status unchanged and free from
foreign complications until the United States could
act, the United States Minister acquiesced in the
propriety of this, and on the morning of February 1st the Boston's battalion was paraded and
marched to the government building, where they

THE GOVERNMENT BUILDING—HONOLULU.

were received by the civilian troops in line at a
salute. All the officials of the Provisional Government were present, and the custody of the building was turned over. A proclamation signed by
the United States Minister and approved by Captain
Wiltse was then read by the adjutant, establishing
a protectorate over the Hawaiian Islands in the
name of the United States, pending negotiations
and action in Washington. At the close of reading
the proclamation the United States ensign was
hoisted over the building, the battalion and civilian
forces presenting arms. Then the front of the
battalion was changed to the rear, and the Hawaiian
flag was hoisted to the staff in the grounds in front of
the building, the forces again presenting arms, and
a salute of twenty-one guns was fired from the Boston.
The civilian forces were then withdrawn and the
company of marines of the Boston's battalion took
charge of the building. The rest of the battalion
then returned to their quarters. The assumption
of a United States protectorate, and the hoisting of
the flag, had the effect at once of allaying fears and
restoring confidence, and was approved by all the
leading men of the community. A paper edited by
a Canadian, and one by two adherents of the ex-
Queen, filled their columns with abuse of the
United States officials, and with weird utterances
in the native dialect urged the people to rise
against the government, whereupon the editors
were arrested and brought before the courts, and
their papers suppressed until they gave bond to ab-

stain from such publications. On the 10th of February the U. S. S. Mohican came into port flying the flag of Rear-Admiral Skerrett, the commander-in-chief of the United States naval forces in the Pacific, and he took immediate command of the forces, relieving Captain Wiltse, who was on the 28th of the same month detached and ordered home, his cruise having expired.

The English residents took the American occupation of the islands with bad grace. The English legation was naturally enough the continued center of intrigue, and there the ex-Queen's partisans frequently held consultations. The results of these meetings were promptly reported, and on the 15th of February a ripple of excitement was raised among the ex-Queen's sympathizers by the announcement of the approach of an English man-of-war, the Garnet. As soon as the vessel was sighted off Diamond Head, Englishmen and Hawaiians hurried to the water front and awaited developments. The vessel entered the channel and anchored near the Boston and Mohican, and fired a salute to the Hawaiian flag, which was not returned, for some reason, for nearly three hours after, which was the occasion of a great deal of sensational conjecture. The commanding officer of the Garnet paid an official visit to the Governor of Oahu, the brother-in-law of the ex-Queen, who had not been removed from office upon the change, and neglected to pay his respects to President Dole. The rumor was started, as having come from one of the symposiums at the British legation, that the captain of the English vessel was going to land a detail of his men that night and hoist the English flag over the palace. There appeared to be foundation for this report, and preparations were at once made to land a reinforcement to Camp Boston from the Boston and Mohican to defend the protectorate in case armed men should disembark from the English cruiser. The provisional forces placed the palace in defense and fortified it with a large armed force and six cannon behind sand-bag barricades. The barracks were guarded with Gatling guns and a large force of men, and the water front was patrolled by the police. The news of such precautions was soon carried to the British Minister, and there was no further effort to raise the English flag. It was believed by almost every one in Honolulu that it would have been done had not the United States flag been flying on the government building, as they could not well afford the precipitation of an armed conflict with the American forces.

The result, however, was the generation of ill feeling between the English and American crews, and a few drunken rows between some of their number on shore leave. Several times the English sailors in passing Camp Boston sang tantalizing songs and made use of jeering remarks, making it difficult to control the American troops. Taking advantage of the bitter feeling existing between the two crews, the ex-Queen's native leaders would raise a crowd of hoodlum Hawaiians for the assistance of the English tars whenever a curb-stone encounter took place, in the evident hope that in the excitement something might be done to upset the police power of the Provisional Government, and start a counter insurrection, or cause the English forces to land from the Garnet. To stop this it became necessary to deprive the men of both the American and English ships of their liberty on shore for the time being. After remaining in Honolulu several weeks, the Garnet got under way and left the harbor, leaving the British ship Hyacinth in her place; but no further rumors of English interference were circulated. However, the disaffection among the Japanese spread to the other islands, and upon the arrival of the large protected Japanese cruiser Naniwa, on February 23, they became more bold in their threats, and it soon became necessary to send that vessel to the other islands to check this growing menace towards the government of Hawaii. On one occasion a Japanese convict, sentenced to life imprisonment for murder, made his escape from Oahu prison and took refuge on board the Japanese man-of-war, and upon an application from the Provisional Government for his delivery the Japanese officials refused to give him up. For a time it looked as though there would be a breach in the friendly relations between the two countries, but after a few days' correspondence the Japanese Commissioner delivered the convict to the prison authorities, and from that time peaceable, if not cordial, relations existed.

In the meantime the provisional forces were organized into a company of 100 men under pay, a volunteer artillery company of 60 men, two companies of infantry consisting of 60 men each, and a home guard. The home guard was composed of the leading men of the town, divided into corporal's squads, and each squad had a secret rendezvous at different places in the city. The whole was under the command of one man, and by a system of signals they could be called out at a moment's notice and mobilized at any point, either by squads, companies, or battalion, to the number of over 400. From the time the American flag was hoisted, there was, with the exception of the above, perfect quiet. Political clubs were organized, one of which was called the Annexation Club, which was the largest, and composed of leading whites and natives, having for its object the political union of Hawaii with the United States. A large club of natives was formed for the purpose of supporting the claims of the Queen for restoration. The majority of the English and Canadian residents affiliated with the latter club, and between these two clubs there was intense feeling and race prejudice. President Dole pursued a most conservative policy, retaining the natives in office, which was bitterly opposed by some of the leaders of the Annexation Club, who at times even went so far as to undertake to dictate a policy for the government, and insisted that they should be invested with all power. President Dole, however, continued in his wise policy of tolerance and indulgence, endeavoring to conciliate the native population, and eventually won a very large proportion over to the support of the Provisional Government.

The ex-Queen took advantage of this leniency, and, assisted by a few sympathizing foreigners, continued her plotting and intrigue at her residence, until it became necessary to deprive her of the salary she had been permitted to draw after her retirement from office. Without this salary and the revenues of the crown lands, having spent on the *coup* and in fees to her commissioner all the money she could raise, she was without ready means to do any serious damage.

On Washington's birthday all business houses were closed at noon, the stars and stripes were seen on all sides, the shipping in the harbor was dressed with flags, and the American holiday was celebrated to the fullest extent. The citizens of Honolulu, hearing of Captain Wiltse's detachment, decided upon giving him a farewell reception, and on the evening of February 24th, it was given in the opera house. The parquet was covered over for dancing, and space set apart for the orchestra. The stage, the proscenium arch, and the walls were blazoned with flags, mostly American. President Dole and Captain Wiltse received the more than two thousand guests. The English Minister and officers of the English and Japanese men-of-war in the harbor declined the invitations and were not present. Their absence, however, did not mar the festivities in the least, and the affair was a grand success.

On April 1st the temporary protectorate was removed, and the last of the Boston's troops embarked aboard ship, where they remained until the Boston returned to Mare Island Navy Yard, in September, and was put out of commission.

On the 4th of July, the American Independence Day was celebrated with as much enthusiasm as in any typical town of the United States. Business was suspended and the American flag displayed everywhere, while the people, in holiday attire, gathered in a beautiful grove near the city in such numbers that the place seemed the incarnation of American patriotism. The Declaration of Independence was read, patriotic songs were sung, music was furnished by the band, and appropriate speeches were delivered. Finally, a few days before the Boston left the port for the United States, a grand ball was given to the officers in the executive building, and a great feast to the crew, by the citizens of Honolulu, which was pronounced by all to have been the grandest affair of the kind ever given in Honolulu. The old palace had never presented so fine an appearance as it did that night. The front of the building was hung with hundreds of small and large Japanese lanterns, and all arrangements made to bring out the beauty of the building and add to the festal splendor of the scene. The newel posts and grand stairway were draped with American and Hawaiian flags alternating with each other. The numerous chandeliers of the hallway were trimmed with wreaths and festooned with red, white, and blue ribbons. In the center of the entrance was placed a large ottoman of red silk surmounted by a silver flower-stand filled with red and pink blossoms. The council chamber, where the ball was held, was decorated with festoons of fragrant ferns. The dais, lately occupied by the President's chair, was covered with evergreens, behind which was draped the American flag, over which was placed the single word " Boston" in large gold letters on a blue background. The large mirrors were ornamented by a skilful arrangement and contrasting of colors ranging from the dark green of tropical vines to the brilliant glow of variegated carnations in crystal containers. The gilt window-frames were each surmounted by an alternate gold and silver shield placed at the center. The ceiling was crossed and intercrossed with red, white, and blue ribbons, hung from the crystal chandeliers. In the main hallway above were laid the magnificently provided tables for supper, and the four verandas on the sides of the building were provided with chairs and tables to accommodate the guests. Promptly at the appointed hour the guests began to arrive and it seemed as if the whole population of Honolulu had turned out with the exception of the English officials and a few leading royalists. The guests were received by Mrs. Dole, assisted by several prominent ladies. The music was furnished by the Hawaiian band and that of the United States flagship. At 8 o'clock the grand procession was formed, headed by Admiral Skerrett and staff, who were followed by the other officers of the three American vessels in port, all in full-dress uniform. They were presented to Mrs. Dole and the ladies receiving. The reception of the other guests followed and at 9 o'clock the ball was opened with the Saratoga lancers. Dancing was kept up until a late hour. The entertainment was in every sense a flattering success and the officers of the Boston can forever look back upon it as one of the most agreeable occasions in which they ever participated.

The Boston got under way the following afternoon, and as she left the harbor of Honolulu was followed to sea by the President and government officials on the harbor tug, with the band playing patriotic Hawaiian and American airs. Off Diamond Head they gave farewell cheers and Godspeed to the cruiser that had been in their waters a welcome guest during fourteen months of severe trials and a witness of the triumphal overthrow of the corrupt and semi-savage monarchy which for the past twenty years had been a menace to the Christianity and civilization of the nation. Kalakaua, whose election was secured by American influence, and who was established on his throne by American protection, alienated the support of the foreign residents in his efforts to gain native popularity and revive Hawaiian superstition;

he laid the foundation and commenced the revolution which Liliuokalani carried on with such determination that she thereby lost her crown and relegated herself to private life.

But for the determined retrogression of this family, monarchy would probably have survived for many years in Hawaii, as none of the leading whites thought of such a thing as revolution until they were fairly goaded into it in defense of the elementary principles of freedom and liberty.

The Provisional Government, up to the time of the sailing of the Boston from Honolulu, was moderate in its demands, humane in its actions, uniformly considerate with the whole people, whether native or foreign, and exceedingly patient with the deposed monarch, who was permitted to enjoy every privilege, even when it was well known how sullenly, persistently, and determinedly she was plotting against them, backed by the powerful support of the English Minister and his clique.

CHAPTER XV.

The Provisional Government was administered by men of intelligence, education, and high character, and at the time of departure of the Boston was protected by an efficient military and police force. The officials saw, however, that by reason of the undisguised hostility of the diplomatic representative of the great maritime power of Europe, and his flagrant intimacy with the fallen Queen and her adherents, together with the threat of interference in their internal affairs on the part of other foreign officials, it would not be long before troubles of a serious nature would arise. It was also manifest that the defunct royalist party, under the encouragement thus given by these foreign diplomatic agents, were intriguing in such manner that it was only a question of time when a desperate effort would be made to restore the old régime. This situation necessitated an unusual expense to maintain a force capable of protecting the government against these internal foes. But, to meet the perils from without, it was fully realized that an alliance with some strong nation was necessary. The United States was preferred, and in compliance with the provisions of the proclamation under which the Provisional Government was formed, annexation to that country was attempted, a measure which after many set-backs is now an accomplished fact.

A review of the intrigues in the past on the part of the French and English agents, having for their objects the subversion of the native government and the seizure of the islands, is enough to sustain the grave fears entertained by the supporters of the new government. From the earliest period of discovery of the Hawaiian Islands by the whites, the subject of their control has been one of bitter contention between various foreign governments, and this contention will continue so long as they remain independent. As early as 1794, Vancouver took possession of the islands in the name of Great Britain and hoisted the English flag, but when the news reached London his acts were not ratified. Following upon this, in 1815, the Russian governor of Alaska sent a vessel to Honolulu, and upon her arrival a block-house was built, a few guns mounted and the Russian flag hoisted. A fortified post was also established on Kauai. To resist this encroachment, the King, in the following year and under the advice of John Young, a boatswain of an English ship, who had been detained on shore and raised to the rank of a high chief, built a large fort at Honolulu and mounted upon it about forty guns, as well as a few more on Punch Bowl hill. Upon the completion of these works, Kamehameha gave orders to expel the Russians. In their attempt to depart, their vessel was sunk in the harbor, but the crew was kindly treated by the natives, and the act of the Russian agent was disavowed by the Russian government.

The King, still fearing a repetition of Russian interference, sailed, in 1823, for the United States and England to secure their protection. While in England he and his wife died, but his attendants were sent back with the royal remains, in an English man-of-war, with a promise from George IV to protect them against all foreign aggression. At the same time a coarse and illiterate man, Richard Charlton, was appointed as British Consul, who immediately put himself at the head of a lawless and depraved class of foreigners, and persistently labored to destroy the influence of the American missionaries and attempted to involve the native government in difficulties that would result in hoisting the British flag over the group. This arrogant Consul even went so far as to deny the right of the native chiefs to make laws or treaties without the approval of the British government, and a series of outrages were perpetrated, under his direction, to enforce the repeal of the laws which had been enacted to restrict drunkenness and prostitution. In all his acts he was backed by the crews of the whaling-ships, which on several occasions landed a body of men and committed many acts of a riotous nature, even going so far as to attack the residences of the missionaries, and on one occasion they actually fired upon the town of Lahaina, the then capital of the kingdom. These

lawless acts became so common that an American
man-of-war was finally sent out to suppress them,
and after ridding the islands of a lot of runaway
sailors the captain agreed to the terms of a commercial treaty with the United States, which, however, was not ratified by the home government.
The English Consul bitterly opposed this treaty
and issued a manifesto that the islands were under
the control of Great Britain and that the King,
therefore, could not enter into any treaty with the
United States or any other power.   Following
upon this line of dictation the English Consul, on
the accession of Kamehameha III, made every
effort to lead the King into dissipation and to
estrange him from his political advisers, hoping
thereby to gain his influence.   With the assistance
of a renegade Tahitian he was very successful :
laws were abrogated, distilleries set up, obscene
dances and drunken revels were encouraged, and
heathen practices revived.   The King finally realized the hold these people had upon him, broke
away and asserted himself, which resulted in a
change for the better and the adoption of a constitutional government.

In the meantime a renegade Frenchman by the
name of Rives, a man who had been dismissed as
interpreter to Kamehameha II while on his voyage
to England, went to France, and by false represen-
tations succeeded in getting a few French laborers
and three priests to follow him back to the islands.
The English Consul saw in the landing of these

priests an opportunity to further his designing intrigues with the internal affairs of the government,
and to offset the influences of the American mission, enlisted their support, and together with
Rives plotted to bring about a civil war, which was
only averted by the boldness of the native chiefs.
In 1831 the council of high chiefs, in opposition to
the advice of the American missionaries, passed a
formal order for the departure of the priests, and
they sailed for California. This banishment, however, was of short duration, for the exiled priests
soon returned to the islands in an English vessel,
but in an attempt to land they were sent back to the
vessel. The captain refused to receive them, whereupon they were put on board by force. The captain in consequence sent the crew ashore and hauled
down his flag, and made a protest to the English
Consul, who was always on the alert for some pretext to force the native government into a quarrel.
The Consul declared that the vessel had been seized
by the Hawaiian government, for which he made
claim for $50,000 damages. An English and a
French man-of-war shortly after came into harbor,
and their commanding officers, upon exaggerated
reports by the Consuls of their respective countries,
made a vigorous protest against the detention of
the priests on board ship. The native government
was forced to permit the landing of the priests, but
under a solemn promise that they should depart as
soon as an opportunity would permit. The port
was declared under blockade, and the French cap-

tain in a brief conference with the King forced him
to sign an agreement to accord to the French equal
advantages with those of the most favored nations.
The two men-of-war then sailed away.

For the next five years the French and English
became very active in their efforts to occupy the
islands of the Pacific, and the Hawaiian government more than ever became a bone of contention.
The French made another effort to land Catholic
priests on the islands as a pretext to opening hostilities with the native government, but after a vigorous protest, the King, in June, 1839, met the demands of the French by issuing an edict of toleration
for all religions on the islands.   This was not what
the French wanted, and the captain of the man-of-
war, in the following month, drew up a series of
articles by which the King was to grant not only
the freedom of the Catholic religion and the erection of a Catholic church in Honolulu, but the flag
of France must be saluted with twenty-one guns.
The sum of $20,000 was exacted from the govern-
ment.   A battalion of one hundred and fifty men,
with fixed bayonets and a band of music, were
landed and took possession of the King's residence,
and after the priests had celebrated mass, the King
was made to sign the convention without amend-
ments.   Under duress the series of articles were
agreed to, and, in addition, French merchants were
granted extraordinary commercial privileges, and
in future all Frenchmen who should commit any
crime in the islands were to be tried by a foreign

jury, selected by the French Consul. Following upon this the Catholic mission became a settled institution. Shortly after, a bishop and many priests arrived in the islands, and a considerable number of natives were enrolled as converts. Petty disputes arose between the Catholics and Protestants, and the French Consul endeavored to support the former by constantly interfering in the internal affairs of the government.

This state of affairs continued until 1842, when another French man-of-war arrived in Honolulu, and from the very first exhibited an unfriendly disposition by failing to exchange a national salute. The captain made a number of demands, which were answered by the King in a dignified manner, stating an embassy had been sent to France to negotiate a new treaty. The English Consul, stimulated by the French action, and jealous of the advantages that might be obtained by a rival country, thereupon manufactured a lot of grievances intending to involve the native government in difficulties that would result in hoisting the English flag over the islands. The King, after vainly trying to satisfy the Consul, petitioned the British government to remove him. The Consul, failing to produce an open rupture, engaged in another move by taking advantage of the schemes of a private firm who, by a secret contract, had obtained a lease of a large tract of land at a low rental.

The Hawaiian government, realizing the danger that would follow the designs of the English Consul, made an effort to avoid a crisis by appointing a commission to visit the United States, Great Britain, and France, with power to negotiate new treaties, and, if possible, to obtain guarantees of the independence of the kingdom. This embassy quietly embarked in a small schooner for Mazatland, and crossed to Vera Cruz. As soon as it was known that they had left the islands on such a mission, the wily English Consul secretly embarked for London, leaving an English adventurer as his deputy to carry out the designs in which both were interested. The hostility of this deputy to the native government was so well known that the King refused to recognize him, whereupon he sent dispatches requesting that a man-of-war be sent to protect him, and representing that the property and persons of his countrymen were in danger. The complaints of the Consul induced the British Admiral to send an English man-of-war, under the command of Lord George Paulet, to Honolulu to investigate. The Consul had met Paulet on the Mexican coast, and made a convert of him to his schemes. Hence, upon arrival, Paulet, without ceremony, demanded the recognition of the English Vice-Consul and immediate submission to the English government. The peaceful submission of the King was not what the hot-headed Paulet wanted, and he followed these demands up with one for the absolute cession of the islands to the Kingdom of Great Britain. The King, amid perplexity and the indignation of the American residents, was forced to sign a provisional cession and the Hawaiian flag was hauled down and the British colors hoisted instead. The officers of the American man-of-war in the harbor, after doing all in their power short of open hostilities, showed their displeasure at this outrageous seizure of the islands at the cannon's mouth, gave a ball and declined to invite the officers of the English vessel. Paulet appointed a commission, including himself, to govern the islands, which arrogated to itself executive, legislative, and judicial powers. It seized all the lands claimed by the English Consul, and expelled all natives living on the same. It abrogated all laws against vice, released all prisoners, and enlisted a small army of natives, who were made to swear allegiance to Great Britain, and were drilled by English officers. Heavy drafts were made on the Hawaiian treasury, and the seizure of the national archives was threatened. The impetuous anxiety of Paulet to inform the home government of his acts caused him to send his dispatches by the Vice-Consul direct to England instead of through his Admiral, as he should have done. This offended the Admiral, and upon his arrival, when informed of what had taken place, he became so indignant over the presumption of his subordinate that he not only disapproved of Paulet's acts, but restored the King to authority after obtaining his signature to a convention which fully guarded English interests. The 31st of July, the day of this restoration, has ever since been a national holiday, and the place where the ceremonies were held was made into a public square, and called Thomas Square, after the Admiral.

These interferences in Hawaiian affairs by the French and English officials, and their encroachments upon the commercial rights of other nations in these islands, were encouraged by the absence of any pronounced policy on the part of the United States. When the Hawaiian Commission represented to the Washington government the true condition of affairs, the United States immediately declared that no power ought to take possession of the islands, either as a conquest or for the purpose of colonization. Daniel Webster, then Secretary of State, while declining at that time to recognize their full independence, announced definitely that as between Hawaii and all other governments Hawaii must be considered absolutely independent. This declaration on the part of the United States operated, without doubt, to prevent England or France from taking possession of the islands. The Hawaiian Commission at first met with indifferent reception in England. The British officials refused to receive them, claiming that the influence of the United States was detrimental to British interests. But when the French government treated the Commissioners with every. consideration, and promised to recognize the independence of Hawaii, the English officials thought better of their former course, and not only recognized the independence of the native government, but promised to remove Charlton, the objectionable

English Consul. They also assured the United States and France that the English government had no intention of retaining possession of the Hawaiian Islands. Finally, on the 28th of November, 1843, France and England entered into a joint declaration not only recognizing the independence of the island kingdom, but agreeing never to take possession, either directly or under the title of a protectorate, of the whole or any part of the islands. The United States followed up their friendly act by immediately sending a Commissioner, and the English replaced the troublesome Charlton as Consul-General for Great Britain. The French, a few years later, attested their friendly relations by restoring the $20,000 extorted by the French captain in 1839.

Notwithstanding these treaties and avowed relations of an amicable nature, the foreign consular and diplomatic representatives continued to intrigue and harass the native government by asserting the rights of ready access to the King, diplomatic interference with internal affairs, and efforts to discredit the native government abroad and break it down at home. Old claims were revived, and for several years the government was involved in disputes with the English Consul-General over the illegal Charlton claims, which had already been settled by the courts and confirmed by Great Britain in favor of the Hawaiian government. The French Consul attempted to reopen the old disputes and manufactured new grievances, for which the Hawaiian government was compelled to request his recall. Instead of complying with this request, a French frigate arrived in 1849, and the Admiral in command supported the Consul in ten most unjust demands. An armed force was landed, and, against the urgent protests of the American and English Consuls, the custom-house and public buildings were seized, the fort dismantled, and much property destroyed, the King's yacht confiscated, and communication with the other islands cut off. Although the French government disavowed the acts of the Admiral, the King was, nevertheless, apprehensive, and for his better guidance installed some of the leading foreigners as his advisers.

A second commission was dispatched to the United States, England, and France, and a new treaty negotiated with the two former countries, but they met with opposition in France. This opposition was indicative that the acts of the Admiral were in accord with instructions from Paris, and as further evidence that such was the case, the French sent out a counter commission, who, to the surprise of every one, renewed the demands of the Consul and assumed a policy of interfering with the internal affairs of the kingdom. The King and Privy Council became alarmed at the new aggression of the French, and issued a proclamation on March 10th, 1850, placing the islands under the protection of the United States. This document was duly signed and deposited with the government archives. When it became known, the

French Commissioner modified his demands, and although arbitrary and unjust they were submitted to by the native government. The officials of the United States from this time on assumed a more active policy, and in 1851 Secretary Marcy apprised both France and England of the determination of the United States not to allow the Hawaiian Islands to be owned by, or fall under the protection of, either of those two powers, or any other European government. In 1854 the Secretary directed the American Minister at Honolulu to negotiate a treaty of annexation. Sailor riots and threatened filibuster raids from California kept the native government in a constant state of alarm, which, together with internal political agitation and party strife induced an active agitation in favor of annexation to the United States. A committee was appointed to carry out these objects, which was vigorously protested against by the British and French Consuls. Petitions were presented to the King based upon strong commercial interests, and he favored such a course as a refuge from the annoying demands made upon him by the foreign powers and the intrigues of their agents.

The prospect of annexation to the United States stimulated speculation and led to new enterprises. The King in February, 1854, agreed to an annexation treaty, which was duly drawn up, but before it was signed he died, and his successor, Kamehameha IV, declined to carry the negotiations further. A treaty of reciprocity was concluded instead with the United States, but it failed of ratification at Washington.

In 1867 a minister was sent to the United States to negotiate a treaty of reciprocity, and though it was approved by the Hawaiian legislature and the President of the United States, it failed of ratification by the United States Senate. Secretary Seward instructed the United States Minister at Honolulu that the peaceful annexation of the Hawaiian Islands was more desirable. In 1868 President Johnson, in his message to Congress, recognized the precarious condition of the Hawaiian people, caused by the unfriendly proceedings of the foreign powers, and favored a treaty of reciprocity until the people applied for admission to the Union. Again, in 1881, Secretary Blaine, in his dispatches to the American Minister, spoke of the advantage to be derived from the annexation of the Hawaiian Islands and the settlement of their future upon an American basis, and not upon an Asiatic or British solution. Secretary Bayard and other American officials have since reiterated the same sentiments.

Finally, in 1876, a treaty of commercial reciprocity with the United States, together with the enactment of laws to carry it into effect, was entered into in spite of strenuous opposition on the part of a large party in the islands led by the English residents. Under the provisions of this treaty, the United States became the controlling influence in the commercial affairs of the island kingdom, and an era of unexampled prosperity followed for the people of Hawaii. So great was the influence thus obtained by the United States that the French officials have stopped their interference in Hawaiian internal affairs. The immense and growing importance of American interests in the Pacific led to an amendment to the original treaty of reciprocity, in 1887, whereby the United States obtained the exclusive right to use Pearl Harbor as a coaling depot and naval station, thus completing her commercial control of the islands so long as the treaty continues. The effect of the treaty was, for the time being, to silence the discussion of annexation, and it was not renewed again until the continuous aggressions of Kalakaua and Liliuokalani upon the rights of the people forced it to the front.

In the meantime the English Minister, supported by British resident subjects and naval officers, made an effort to offset American influences, and by his support of the fallen Queen and her adherents was the means of giving intense alarm. Aside from this hostile British influence, there was a new factor of trouble in the Japanese, who even now threaten future interference of a most serious nature.

There are about 25,000 Japanese in Hawaii, of whom over 19,000 are adult males. Nearly all have had a military training, many having served in the war with China. The adult male natives number only about 10,000, and the adult male whites of all nationalities only 7,500. Japanese immigration increased to an alarming extent, and threatened by sheer force of numbers to possess the country and make it practically, if not formally, Japanese. By a clause in the treaty between the two countries, the privileges of the most favored nations were accorded Japanese residents in Hawaii, and the government of Japan was continually demanding for its subjects the right to vote,—which the Hawaiian government persistently refused. Acting upon this refusal, and with a determination of ultimately seizing the islands, the Japanese government, in 1897, sent as many as 2,000 emigrants a month to Hawaii, and amongst these emigrants were a number of trained soldiers disguised as laborers. An attempt by Hawaii to limit this invasion resulted in a demand by Japan for damages, for an apology, and a promise not to further interfere with Japanese immigration. All that prevented the enforcement of these demands was the pendency of the annexation treaty with the United States, and the result was, for the time being, the creation of most bitter feelings between the Japanese and the people of the United States. On several occasions our sailors were attacked by a mob in Kobé and American tourists in Japan were insulted. The difficulty was finally settled by the political changes in the Orient, and the Hawaiian government agreeing to pay an indemnity of $75,000, which was accepted by Japan with reluctance ; and were it not for the fact she has to watch the political agitation in the Orient, early and certain aggression by Japan against the claim of the United States to Hawaii might be looked for.

CHAPTER XVI.

The great strategical value and commercial importance of the Hawaiian Islands, and the frequent interferences by foreign nations in the internal affairs of the island kingdom, have warned the Hawaiian people of their inability to permanently maintain an independent government. For more than seventy years Americans and American influence have been dominant in Hawaii, and annexation to the United States has during all these years been the subject of careful study and contemplation. This has always been regarded by them as the ultimate destiny of the country, whenever the exigencies of fate should compel them to make choice between independence and foreign domination. In this they have been encouraged by the public declarations of American statesmen, and the diplomatic correspondence of the United States with its Ministers to Hawaii, which has from time to time been made public or communicated to the Hawaiian officials. In this correspondence frequent and favorable allusion is made to " closer relations " between the two countries, the term " annexation " being sometimes used, and at others, more general language. Many times the subject of annexation has been dealt with in a spirit

of friendly consideration for the advantage of the
country and the people. Daniel Webster, John
M. Clayton, W. L. Marcy, William H. Seward,
Hamilton Fish, Thomas F. Bayard, and James
G. Blaine as Secretaries of State, and Presidents
Pierce, Lincoln, Johnson, and Grant, all equally
maintained a settled policy that all other foreign
nations must be excluded from Hawaii, and that
if it should turn out that Hawaii could not maintain an independent stable government it should
be encouraged to gravitate towards political union
with the United States. It became a conceded
axiom on the part of Great Britain, Germany, and
France that the islands would in the course of time
drift to the United States. The result has been
that the progress, education, development, laws,
commerce, and government of Hawaii have become
so closely identified with those of the United
States that there has developed an ever-increasing
mutuality of interests and gravitation of Hawaii
toward political union with the United States.
This peculiar relationship has repeatedly been
evidenced by official declarations that no intervention would be permitted in the affairs of Hawaii
by any foreign power which might tend to diminish
American control, or to gain any advantage over
the Americans who may have settled in that
country. Finally a treaty of reciprocity was
agreed upon between the two countries, by which
the Hawaiian trade, both export and import, is
practically confined to the United States, while at

the same time its terms are highly advantageous to Hawaii. It, moreover, prevents the disposal of Hawaiian bays, harbors, and territory, either by lease or otherwise, to other countries so long as the treaty lasts, and gives to the United States the exclusive right to Pearl Harbor as a coaling depot and naval station. Hence when the Provisional Government assumed the sovereign power, their avowed purpose to secure the annexation of the Hawaiian Islands to the United States was but an event in the natural order of development; an event which had been predicted, looked forward to, and hoped for by two generations of American statesmen. The proclamation inaugurating the new government explicitly stated that it would exist " until terms of union with the United States of America have been negotiated and agreed upon." Therefore, the Executive and Advisory councils proceeded to immediately carry out the provisions of the proclamation under which they assumed office, by appointing a commission to go to Washington, where they negotiated and signed a treaty in conjunction with Secretary Foster for the annexation of the Hawaiian Islands to the United States, which was approved by the President and sent to the Senate for ratification.

When the news reached Honolulu that the treaty had been signed by the President and sent to the Senate the majority of the people went into a fever of enthusiam and blossomed out with handkerchiefs and head-coverings made of the stars and stripes; the American flag was displayed from almost every house-top and flag-staff, and the Hawaiian band played the " Star-Spangled Banner." The Senate of the United States delayed action until after the 4th of March, when another administration came into power and Mr. Cleveland, the new President, disapproving of the acts of his predecessor, withdrew the treaty from the Senate and appointed Mr. Blount, of Georgia, a special Commissioner to Hawaii to make an investigation and report upon the causes that led to the overthrow of the Hawaiian monarchy. When the news reached Honolulu of the withdrawal of the treaty from the Senate it caused serious misgivings in the minds of the government officials, and the royalist faction exhibited their feelings in a series of jollification-meetings, and drinking-bouts in the bar-room of the Hawaiian Hotel, and at night the old court circles gathered at the ex-Queen's residence, and between poi, gin and music the party had a royal time. On the other hand, while disappointment was felt on the part of the leading citizens, they nevertheless took a philosophical view of the situation and fully appreciated the fact that the President was new to the subject, and was entitled to know the facts. They therefore welcomed the news of a Commissioner from the United States to inquire into the state of affairs, and without fear of the result, awaited and courted a fair, complete, and impartial investigation and report to the President of the United States. But they were sadly disappointed.

Commissioner Blount, with " paramount authority," and accompanied by a stenographic clerk,
arrived in the harbor of Honolulu on the United
States Revenue Cutter Rush, about noon of the
29th of March, 1893. By the time the Rush came
to anchor an immense crowd of men, women, and
children had gathered on the wharves in expectation
of seeing the Commissioner. The United States
Minister and a delegation of leading gentlemen of
Honolulu immediately went on board to receive the
high official and extend to him offers of assistance and friendly courtesies. They informed him
that the manager of the Hawaiian Hotel was intensely partisan in his royalist sympathies, that
the hotel was the rendezvous of the royal supporters,
and for him to go there would simply be to place
himself within the circle of their influence. They
further informed him of a comfortable residence
then vacant, but furnished, removed from annoyances and interferences, which he could have on
his own terms. These courteous salutations and
friendly offers were met with a bluff refusal, and
in the midst of the conversation Mr. Blount ab-
ruptly turned on his heel and returned to the cabin,
leaving his visitors standing in amazement on deck.
Shortly after this incident the Commissioner left the
vessel and went on shore, where he was met by the
Chamberlain of the ex-Queen, who offered him the
use of her coach, which he politely declined, his
manner being in marked contrast with the treatment accorded the diplomatic representative of the

United States.   Entering a cab, he drove to the
Hawaiian Hotel, where he took up his residence in
one of the cottages in the hotel grounds, and from
the very first, free access was given to the ex-
Queen's ministers and the royal supporters, while
the members of the government and the leading
whites of the community were either denied that
privilege or put off with the remark that when they
were wanted they would be sent for.

Grave anxiety on the part of the government
officials began to assume shape, notwithstanding
Mr. Blount's letter of credence was to that government and of a most friendly and cordial nature.
They feared a partiality to the ex-Queen, and as
the methods of interrogation of a class of irresponsible persons became known in the progress of the
investigation, these fears increased.   Friendly over-
tures and disinterested offers of ordinary courtesies
and civilities by the leading whites were met by
cool and deliberate snubs, which caused them to
refrain from calling or volunteering information.
The first two days were occupied by Mr. Blount in
presenting his letters of credence to the Provisional
Government and notifying the United States
officials, both diplomatic and naval, of his " paramount authority."   On the afternoon of March 31st
he notified the President of the Provisional Government of his intention to haul down the American
ensign and issued a written positive and direct order
to Admiral Skerrett, commanding the United States
naval forces in the Pacific, to haul down the United

States flag from the government building at 11
o'clock on the 1st of April and embark the troops
on shore to the ship. This unusual and unprece-
dented order was obeyed by Admiral Skerrett,
although he exhibited unmistakable signs of irri-
tation and humiliation, and afterwards wrote a complaint to the Navy Department.

Coming into town early in the morning of April
1st, in company with a friend at whose country
cottage I had spent the night, we passed the residence of the ex-Queen, where we met a couple of
native women coming out, who informed us they
had spent the night with the ex-Queen; that she
and her ex-ministers had been informed the evening before that the United States flag was going to
be hauled down that day at 11 o'clock; that the
Commissioner was going to restore her, and that
she was very nervous and excited. On arrival on
board ship I found that no one there had as yet
been informed of the fact, the orders from the Admiral coming later. At the appointed time the flag
was hauled down and the troops embarked, a humiliation which was keenly felt by both men and
officers. No demonstration was made by the people present, and no exhibition of disturbance, yet
the immediate effect of this movement was to increase the membership of the Annexation Club in
the city. No notice was given by Mr. Blount to
the government of what he was doing, nor was any
request made of them to present evidence or argument. He simply commenced and carried through

a secret and ex-parte investigation, examining only those witnesses whom he selected, nearly all of whom were avowed royalists. His method of examination was to put leading questions upon a few points, either shutting off altogether or manifesting by his manner that he did not wish to listen to evidence on other points. It soon became manifest that it was his purpose to obtain evidence in support of a restoration of the ex-Queen, and in support of the theory that the American Minister and the officers of the Boston were parties to the overthrow of the monarchy. The causes of the revolution, the grievances of the people, the justness of their action, the rottenness, immorality, and irresponsible character of the late King, the ex-Queen, and the entire court influence—all this was ignored, and the investigation conducted as though he were an attorney working up one side of a case. The royalists were kept well informed of what was going on, and freely predicted what the report would show. Mr. Blount's stenographic clerk was a frequent visitor and most intimate associate at the house of a leading royalist, one of the most notorious native gamblers and smugglers in Honolulu, and from this house frequent reports came of what Blount's doings and intentions were, that were afterwards corroborated in the published report of the Commissioner. So-called patriotic societies, headed by some of the worst characters on the islands, including the drunken Bush of Samoan fame, were the first to present a series of resolutions. The

statements of these men were given careful attention, and serious consideration without inquiry as to
their standing in the community. The ex-Queen's
ministers were examined at length, and encouraged
to state all they were supposed to know in support
of their cause; while, on the other hand, the few
officers from the Boston, and all the sympathizers
with the Provisional Government, were asked leading questions, skilfully framed, to bring out any
facts tending to support " the theory," while further
explanatory evidence, which would have absolutely
refuted such conclusion, was suppressed. Any information or suggestions from the naval officers or
the United States Minister were met with the reply
that he simply wanted answers to the questions put.
I am not speaking from hearsay, but of my own
knowledge, when I say that Mr. Blount did not attempt to make either a fair investigation or a truth-
ful report.

I was called before the Commissioner and made
several suggestions in relation to the revolution.
When I came to the statement that Captain Wiltse
would not have allowed any fighting in the streets
in the vicinity of the residences of Americans, Mr.
Blount eagerly asked me to write that down, saying
he did not care for the rest. On several occasions
I suggested the names of old white residents, of
high standing, who were familiar with the entire
history and progress of the islands and the events
leading up to the revolution, and in each case he said
he did want anything to do with them ; whereas those

who were in accord with the fallen Queen were
either sent for or permitted to make all manner of
statements, many in the form of written affidavits,
drawn up by themselves, without the slightest regard to their character or standing.   In no case was
there anything in the nature of cross-examination
to test the credibility of the royalist witnesses or
the correctness of their statements.   One noticeable
instance was that of the manager of the Hawaiian
Hotel, who was repeatedly sent for, and at all times
had ready access to the Commissioner's cottage.   I
called Mr. Blount's attention to the fact that this
man was an intense royalist, and misrepresenting
facts to him.   From what he had told me in relation
to the examination and his answers, I knew he was
not telling the truth ; yet in the published report
of the Commissioner this man is represented as a
person of the greatest integrity and high social
standing.

One day I was passing through the corridor of
the hotel and met the ex-Marshal, Wilson, who requested me to look over and comment upon a type-
written manuscript which he held in his hand, and
which he informed me was prepared at the request
of the Commissioner.   Upon looking over the document I observed the first few pages were devoted
to vilification and abuse of the American Minister,
and advised him to expunge it.   I remarked that
the whole paper bore the earmarks of Peterson,
the ex Attorney-General to the Queen, as I recognized some of the phrases that I had heard Peter-

son use, to which Wilson replied that Peterson did write it from his notes, and that the part about Minister Stevens was known to Mr. Blount, who told him to put it in, as he, the Commissioner, wanted full information about Stevens. The document, among other things, purported to give a statement of the military forces at the disposal of the Queen at the time of her overthrow and the plans for a fight, had such an affair taken place, and the number of men under arms as eight hundred. I remarked that the number given was false; that I was cognizant of the exact number, which was only one hundred and forty-five. Wilson acknowledged that I was correct; but said that in a conversation with the Commissioner, the day before, he, Wilson, had said to the Commissioner that he could have gotten that many if he had been given time, and that the Commissioner directed him to put as many men down as he could have obtained. Therefore the paper would go in as it was, and if the Commissioner wanted more he would give them to him. Whether the Commissioner " wanted more," or whether Wilson's imagination fed upon itself, I cannot say, but the identical report shown me by Wilson appears in Mr. Blount's report to Secretary Gresham, with the available force changed from 800, the number stated when I saw it, to 700, " and a reserve of about 500 men, mostly foreigners," or 1,200 altogether. The utter unreliability of the statement is demonstrated by the fact that another statement sworn to by Wilson and also printed in

Blount's report says that the police-station force was 224, and an affidavit by Nowlein, commander of the palace troops, gives the number at the palace as 272, or a total of 496.

A summary of these statements, which are about as near the truth as most of the evidence on which Mr. Blount based his report, is as follows:

The real number of armed men supporting
  the Queen was........................ 145
The number sworn to by Wilson and Nowlein was............................ 496
The number enumerated in Wilson's statement when he showed it to me was...... 800
The number enumerated in Wilson's statement when printed in Blount's report is.. 1,200

I called on the Commissioner the following morning, informed him of this conversation, told him that of my own knowledge the paper was full of misstatements, and that if he desired the facts I could recommend a few actual participants, men of standing, both Provisional Government men and royalits, who would give them to him. He appeared much embarrassed, but made no reply except to ask: "Did he show you that paper?" In the published report the paper appears in its entirety, with the remark that the ex-Marshal was a man who could be relied upon, and that he believed his statements to be substantially correct.

On another occasion I met several native politicians, ex-members of the legislature, coming out of the cottage. They told me they had just been examined by the Commissioner, and that from his manner and the character of his questions they were sure he was making an effort to secure information in favor of the royalists.

Rumors began to be circulated that the Commissioner was strongly in favor of the monarchy and had made secret visits to the residence of the ex-Queen, which rumors came from the ex-ministers, who were constant at and around the cottage. These rumors appeared to irritate the Commissioner, and when he accepted an invitation to visit one of the other islands in company with a party of the ex-Queen's adherents, who made the most of the opportunity to augment the foundation for these rumors, the Commissioner issued an explanation and denial. Another annoying episode to the Commissioner was the arrival in Honolulu of two persons on the 7th of April, one a New York correspondent and the other an ex-U. S. Consul to Samoa. It was given out that they were special officers of the United States and were fully informed as to the intent of the President to annex the islands. They were said to have stated that the ex-Queen and the President of the Provisional Government had agreed upon terms of settlement for a monetary consideration to the ex-Queen, who was to abdicate, and that her attorney was going to Washington to close the deal. This was in accord with the known instructions to her attorney when he went to Washington before, and credence was therefore given to the rumor. This was

decidedly distasteful to the Commissioner, as it was
directly opposed to his too apparent efforts to
secure evidence in support of the royalists and
against the annexation of the islands and he warned
the Queen against having anything to do with
them or with such a settlement. The American
Minister was accused of trying to support these two
supposed agents. The Commissioner intimated
that he was trying to mould native opinion in favor
of annexation of the islands to the United States,
which accusation brought about pronounced friction between the two. Mr. Blount's treatment
of Mr. Stevens was discourteous in the extreme.
Although the latter was instructed to assist the
Commissioner in his investigation, and possessed
the fullest knowledge of every detail, he was ignored
by the Commissioner, and virtually told to remain
silent in all matters connected with the Commissioner's investigation. The Minister was from
that time on such in name only. Shortly after, he
was recalled and Mr. Blount appointed in his
stead.

The active measures taken by a club, favorable
to annexation, to increase their rolls, and their
suggestions that the ex-Queen should be deported
in the interest of peace, together with a few edito-
rials to that effect in a paper controlled by the club,
brought forth a letter of complaint from the Commissioner to the President of the Provisional Government, although the paper was controlled by a
private corporation and not under governmental

control. The native clubs and patriotic leagues
were differently treated ; their memorials, reflecting
upon the existing government and condemnatory of
American officials, were not only received and
encouragement given, but the Commissioner, ignoring not only the amenities of civilized international
intercourse, but the first principle of international
law, caused to be published in the royalist paper a
proclamation, over his own official signature, entitled
" An address to the Hawaiian people," ignoring
the government to which he was accredited, setting
forth what his instructions were, what he proposed
to do, and wound up by stating that in the event of
any conflict, he would protect those Americans
who took no part therein. As practically all the
white men in the country had taken an active part
in the recent troubles, in common defense of their
elementary rights, this proclamation was looked
upon as a direct threat that the Americans of Honolulu were to be abandoned to their fate, so far as Mr.
Blount could accomplish it. It was interpreted by
the natives as a censure for the landing of the
Boston's troops and a hint for them to rise and by
force restore the Queen, and an assurance that
all domiciled Americans would have to keep off.

In the meantime two persons arrived in Honolulu who undoubtedly influenced greatly the results of the investigation. These two gentlemen
were Charles Nordhoff, a newspaper correspondent, and Claus Spreckles, the sugar king. Nordhoff, while on the steamer on his way to Honolulu,

and before he had any opportunity to investigate the situation, wrote an article for his paper denouncing the action of the Provisional Government and reflecting upon the troops from the Boston, giving the keynote of the course he intended to pursue. This article was so full of misstatements and of such a libelous nature that when it was republished in the local papers he was threatened with prosecution before the courts of law. The Commissioner immediately came to his rescue, and notified the officials of the Provisional Government that Mr. Nordhoff should not be molested, nor should he be deported, and the two became almost inseparable companions. This encouraged the wily correspondent, and he continued to send out false and inflammatory articles to the press of the United States, which were republished in the papers of Honolulu hostile to the existing government. The tenor of these dispatches followed closely the outlines of the leading questions and the desired answers thereto that leaked out through those examined by the Commissioner, leaving no doubt in the minds of the people that Nordhoff possessed the confidence of the Commissioner, and that his press dispatches outlined the tone of the final report of that official in censuring the American Minister and the officers of the Boston, and in favor of the restoration of the Queen. This impression became so fixed in the minds of the royalists that one day the leader of the ex-Queen's Cabinet told me that he had learned from a reliable source that such would be the report, and offered to bet a large sum of money the Queen would be restored. That Nordhoff had intimate connection with Blount is demonstrated by the fact that considerable portions of his letters, published months before Blount's report was made public, are verbatim copies of evidence appearing in Blount's report. Who paid Nordhoff for his services is a question which I cannot undertake to answer. Mr. Spreckles claimed that he did, as appears hereinafter. Whether he did or not is a question for those gentlemen to settle. Claus Spreckles, upon his arrival in Honolulu, called a meeting of the sugar stockholders on the islands, and at the meeting attempted to obtain the support of the planters to oppose annexation and continue the government as an oligarchy, so that cheap Chinese labor could be continued, which could not be done if annexation took place. The planters almost unanimously rejected his proposition. This defeat not only irritated him, but broke his prestige with the sugar-growers who were in favor of securing stable government, which they believed could be obtained only through annexation to the United States. Spreckles thereupon became an open and violent opponent of the Provisional Government, denouncing it and " the missionaries " in the most abusive language in the most public manner, and became an enthusiastic supporter of the ex-Queen, advocating her restoration and predicting the early downfall of the existing government. One morning a sign of a skull and crossbones was found pinned to his gate. It was

generally believed that he had it placed there himself. In any event, he immediately raised a hue
and cry, claimed that the Annexation Club were
trying to assassinate him, and called upon Mr.
Blount to protect his life. Mr. Blount had no
more jurisdiction over the matter than the King of
Dahomey, but the desired protection was promptly
promised. Referring to the matter one evening at
the residence of his neighbor, a well-known royalist leader, Spreckles boastingly remarked, in my
presence, that Blount would protect him, and that
he knew the Commissioner had no use for the set
who were running the government nor for the
"annexation missionaries." His neighbor asked
on what he based that opinion, and what he
thought would be the character of the report of
the Commissioner? Spreckles' reply was to the
effect that he had Blount in the palm of his hand,
that he would do just what Nordhoff said, and
that he, Spreckles, was "paying Nordhoff to work
Blount."

The intimacy between the British Minister and
the Commissioner was also a matter of amazement
to the community. The Minister took up his residence in a cottage in the hotel grounds, just across
the street from the ex-Queen's residence. From
this cottage he became a frequent caller and adviser to the Queen, and was often the companion
to the Commissioner, over whom he appeared to
have much influence. He constantly sent out
word through his adherents that he knew the
Queen was to be restored by the Commissioner.

After the Commissioner had completed his reports and forwarded them to Washington, he became very restless to return home. Finally, the
permission came, and Admiral Skerrett, commanding the United States naval forces in the
Pacific, was placed in charge of the legation, without any diplomatic authority. When the Commissioner left, the entire royalist faction followed him
to the steamer and loaded him down with flowers,
while the notorious Bush mounted a pile and in
fervid language thanked the Commissioner for his
services to the Hawaiian people and violently
abused the officials of the Provisional Government,
the former United States Minister, and officers of
the Boston. The royalists had been given direct
information of what his report would be, which
preliminary information was borne out when the
report was made public. They freely discussed
the Queen's restoration as a foregone conclusion.
The Queen herself firmly believed such would be
the case, and in consequence, the night following
the departure of the Commissioner, she gave a big
reception and luau to her especial favorites. On
the other hand, the officials of the Provisional Government were kept in the dark, being able to draw
inferences only from the one-sided partial method
of the examination, the Commissioner's friendly
intimacy with every royalist leader and opponent
of the Provisional Government, and his persistent
avoidance of examination of those who were in a
position to give him reliable information.

CHAPTER XVII.

EFFORTS TO RESTORE THE EX-QUEEN; AND ESTABLISHMENT OF THE HAWAIIAN REPUBLIC.

The uncertainty respecting the outcome of Mr. Blount's report caused serious depression in business circles on the islands. Both public and private enterprises were hampered, for capital is wary in the face of possible political overturn. The royalists, believing firmly that the Commissioner had recommended restoration of the Queen and that the United States would act favorably upon the recommendation, renewed their secret intrigues, and, assisted as they were by the English Minister, they became a constant menace to the peace of the community. There were constant rumors of an uprising, and reports of filibuster expeditions from the coast to assist the royalists, keeping the community in a condition of excitement and disquietude. In addition to the interference with business, created by this condition of affairs, it necessitated the government keeping up a comparatively large force of armed men to prevent sudden uprising, at an expense which the depleted treasury inherited from the monarchy could ill afford.

The Hawaiian Minister in Washington made every effort to find out the intentions of the government in regard to Hawaii, but without avail. This failure was still further depressing to the cause of the Provisional Government.

The report of the Commissioner was received at Washington in July, but no action was taken until in October, 1893, when Mr. Willis was sent to Honolulu as Minister of the United States and publicly accredited to the Provisional Government but actually and covertly for the purpose of destroying that government and restoring the ex-Queen before Congress should meet. Mr. Willis had received both oral and written instructions to do this. Upon his arrival in Honolulu he was received by the Provisional Government with great cordiality, and an interchange of the usual courtesies was had between them. Little did the Hawaiian officials think that under the guise of this amicable representation Mr. Willis had secret instructions to take the earliest opportunity to inform the ex-Queen that the treaty withdrawn from the Senate would not be returned, and that if she would promise amnesty to all persons who had been engaged in overturning the monarchy, she would be restored to the throne by the United States. Suspecting nothing of this kind, the officials of the Provisional Government were greatly encouraged by the friendly attitude of the United States as manifested by accrediting a Minister to the new government after full investigation by a manifestly hostile Commissioner. Simultaneously with the arrival of Mr. Willis, Admiral Skerrett was relieved and ordered to command the naval forces in China, and Admiral Irwin took his place. The American Minister lost no time in carrying out his instructions relating to the ex-Queen. Without a word to the government to which he was accredited, he sent for Liliuokalani, and early in the forenoon of November 13th she called, accompanied by her former Chamberlain. She was informed that through the unauthorized intervention of United States officials and the troops from the Boston she had been obliged to surrender her sovereignty, and that if she would bind herself to grant amnesty to all persons who had been engaged against her authority, it was the intention of the United States to restore her to the throne. To this proposition the ex-Queen would not assent, replying that she would cause those people who had been instrumental in her overthrow to be beheaded and their property confiscated to the government. This startling statement amazed the Minister, and put a stop to further negotiations for the time being. The Minister faithfully reported the facts to Washington, and notified the ex-Queen that he had no further communication to make until he heard from his government, which would be in three or four weeks.

Every precaution was taken to keep this interview and the ex-Queen's declaration a secret from the Provisional Government. The Minister frankly informed the American Secretary of State that, from actual information received in a conversation with the ex-Queen's best friends, it was plainly evident that in the event of restoration there would be a concerted movement to overthrow the constitution and limited government, and establish the absolute dominion of the Queen, as was attempted in the *coup d'état* which caused her downfall. Notwithstanding the great secrecy maintained in regard to this interview, the officials of the Provisional Government got some inkling of it, for that very evening the tension of feeling became so great as to threaten disastrous consequences, and the town was filled with rumors of an outbreak. The greatest excitement prevailed at the executive building, in consequence of which the military forces were increased and the volunteer companies were ordered on duty at night. This condition of affairs continued for nearly two months; business was practically suspended; the people subjected to a severe strain of excitement, and the military was again increased to meet apprehended contingencies.

On November 24th and December. 2d, respectively, a British and a Japanese man-of-war arrived in the harbor, and, on the same day that the English vessel came in, a letter of the Secretary of State recommending the restoration of the monarchy was published in the Honolulu papers. Although this was simply a newspaper publication, it was given credence and created a great sensation. Crowds gathered and the excitement became intense. A public meeting was called for the following night of all friends of the Provisional Government, at which over 1,200 men were present, and at which the Vice-President presided, and vigorous protests voiced in several speeches by leading men of the community. The Provisional Government withdrew its permission, formerly given to Admiral Irwin, to land troops for drill, and a protest against the use of force by the United States against their persons or property was presented to the Minister by a large number of American residents. Not until the Hawaiian Minister in Washington notified his government that the publication of Secretary Gresham's letter in the American press was official, and that it was not only unfriendly towards the Provisional Government, but actually recommended hostile action, did the Hawaiian officials become satisfied that the intentions of the American Minister were other than favorable, as indicated by his letter of credence to their government. This absolute proof of a contemplated overthrow of their existence as a sovereign power through the secret agency of the Minister accredited to them forced the Provisional Government to decide upon a course of action, either to submit or fight. President Dole, accompanied by his Attorney-General, called upon the Minister and requested to know what the United States intended to do, receiving the reply that he was unable at that time to comply with their request. To obtain some authentic utterance in reference thereto, President Dole that afternoon addressed a formal letter of inquiry, dated November 29, 1893, to the United States Minister, as to the authenticity of the published letter. The Minister did not answer this communication until December 2d, and then he evaded the question by referring to it as a domestic transaction and intimating that something of a serious nature would occur, but it was not in his power to indicate what it would be until he had received further instructions in answer to letters recently forwarded by him to his government.

No possible information could be obtained from the Minister as to his course, but on the 29th of November a local paper published the remarks of the Minister made to one of the native leagues, in which he stated the policy of the United States regarding the islands was already formulated, and as an executive officer he would act when the proper time came. This implied threat, and the inability to obtain information whether the Minister intended to use force, or not, in support of his policy, emboldened the royalists and made it necessary for the Provisional Government to make further preparations for defence. After full deliberation and consultation with nearly all the leading men of the city, the decision was reached, practically unanimously, to resist to the last the attempt to restore the Queen, even though it involved a conflict with the United States troops. The executive building was fortified with bags of sand, both in front and around the various balconies. The volunteer forces were again increased and the citizens armed as if in a state of war. Following upon this the American Minister became more active, sent for the ex-Marshal to the Queen, and on December 5th had an interview with him in regard to the restoration, well knowing that person would have command of the royal forces if such an event should occur.˙ The ex-Marshal submitted a paper containing a method of procedure upon the restoration of the Queen which had been approved by her attorney and by all the members of her former Cabinet. This paper had been drawn up months before and contained a list of special advisers, all of whom were English or natives who had distinguished themselves by their ultra hostility to American interests. They were almost, without exception, men of low character and without responsibility or property interests. A provision was made for the support of autocratic authority by the Queen, and the trial of all those who had taken part against the monarchy, by a special court martial to be appointed for that purpose. This extraordinary document shows the confidence these people had in the information they had received prior to Mr. Blount's departure that the Queen was to be restored, and it should have convinced the Minister that the Queen had made up her mind to do what she originally proposed to him—assassinate all enemies and confiscate their property. He was informed that this program had. been agreed upon after a consultation with the leading royalists, who would constitute that court, and that she had decided upon the course she intended to pursue long before his interview. Any one acquainted with her stubborn disposition well knows that she would have carried it out to the letter. Yet, on December 14th, the Revenue Cutter Corwin arrived in Honolulu from San Francisco, bringing further instructions in answer to the Minister's letter reporting the ex-Queen's refusal to accept the amnesty proposition directing him to proceed with the restoration program. Minister Willis thereupon renewed his efforts to restore the dusky, bloodthirsty Queen.

The unexpected arrival of the Corwin created intense excitement, which was increased when it became known that immediately after the arrival of that vessel the liberty of the men on the United States man-of-war in the harbor had been stopped; that the battalion was made ready to land at a moment's notice, and that the wives of the naval officers in Honolulu had been instructed by their husbands to make preparations for an immediate removal, indicative of possible hostilities. The Minister was instructed to carry out his original instructions, was urged to prompt action, but to insist upon amnesty and recognition of obligations of the Provisional Government as essential conditions to restoration. Accordingly he made arrangements for another interview with the ex-Queen, which was held on Saturday, December 16th, in the presence of Mr. J. O. Carter, her immediate friend. In this interview the ex-Queen was informed of what had previously been said and reported to Washington. In a long interview, assisted by Carter, the ex-Queen remained firm in her determination to kill or banish all those who took part against her, and their children, and to confiscate

their property.   Shortly after, the ex-Queen and
Carter left the legation, the latter becoming uneasy
as to the outcome, and in the hope of getting the
ex-Queen to change her mind, returned and
requested another interview for Monday, which
was granted.   In the meantime the ex-Queen had
seen some of her adherents, who, together with
Carter, urged her to abandon her savage purpose.
As though to assist these supporters in their efforts
to induce her to give up this purpose, the Minister
followed them up by calling at her residence, and
further notified her that should she refuse assent to
the written conditions, he would cease interference
in her behalf.   These extraordinary efforts at last
brought this bloodthirsty barbarian to terms, and
she drew up a letter promising to permit no
proscription or punishment of any one, and virtually
accepting the written obligations submitted by the
Minister.   For fear she might change her mind,
J. O. Carter immediately obtained an agreement
signed by herself to that effect, and delivered it to
the American Minister at the legation.

It will be seen that four days had elapsed since
the arrival of the Corwin before the ex-Queen could,
under all this pressure, be induced to accept the
terms proposed.   Carter, who had full information
of what had been said and done, understanding
that force was to be used by the sailors and marines
of the U. S. S. Philadelphia, and well knowing
that the ex-Queen would be liable to violate any
agreement she had entered into as soon as restored,

became apprehensive for the safety of his nephew, one of the officials of the Provisional Government, and after informing him of the purpose to restore the ex-Queen, advised him to join the royalist forces. The nephew, instead, informed President Dole of what had been told him. The frequent and secret interviews of the Minister with the ex-Queen and her partisans, together with the preparation on board the Philadelphia, produced an almost universal belief in the city that the naval forces of the United States would land to restore the Queen. In anticipation of such a move the wharves were for days lined with crowds of people, waiting to see the troops land. At no time did the American Minister attempt to deny this rumor, notwithstanding the German Consul called and begged him to speak, and relieve the public from the state of extreme tension they were in, which was becoming unbearable. The British and Japanese Ministers shared likewise in a failure to obtain an answer, and they became alarmed. They requested permission from the government to land a force from their men-of-war in the harbor to protect their respective legations, and it was granted. The Japanese Minister, realizing the status of those Americans supporting the Provisional Government, through the published notice that only those not engaged in conflict would be protected by the American Minister, and knowing that the entire American population were supporting that government, sent word to a number of Americans offering them the use of the Japanese Legation as a refuge for their families in case of attack by the American troops upon the government. Was there ever a more humiliating situation since the Declaration of Independence, that, in the interests of humanity, a Japanese official, in a foreign country, should feel called upon to offer asylum to American women and children, to protect them from American troops, who were being used to force back into power a bloodthirsty and dissolute Queen, against the armed protest of an intelligent people, largely of American birth, who had been forced into revolution against her by her attempt to overthrow the constitution and establish an absolute monarchy?

The President of the Provisional Government that same day addressed a letter to the American Minister calling his attention to the fact that he was informed of what was going on, and that he, the Minister, was acting in a way hostile to the Hawaiian government, to which he was accredited, and asking for immediate confirmation or denial. In answer to this the Minister on the following day called upon the President of the Provisional Government by appointment, and in the presence of his ministers notified him of the Queen's acceptance of the proposals submitted, and demanded " in the name and by the authority of the President of the United States" that President Dole forthwith relinquish to her the sovereign power. He concluded by asking if President Dole was willing to abide by this decision of the President of the United

States. Nothing was said in regard to whether the decision would be enforced in case of rejection.

The Corwin was placed under sailing orders to leave for San Francisco to carry the answer of President Dole to Washington. To prevent the news getting out in the press, the captain was instructed to enter the harbor of San Francisco at night. No mails were permitted to be sent on the vessel, not even the official mail of President Dole to the Hawaiian Minister in Washington, although he requested permission from Mr. Willis to forward such mail. On December 23d, after a conference at a special session of the Advisory Council, President Dole wrote a lengthy document in answer to the United States Minister's demands, giving a full résumé of the situation and the events leading up to the establishment of the Republic. He claimed to have been no party to the Blount investigation; never to have seen the Blount report upon which the action of the American official was based, and, as no court of arbitration existed, he denied the right of the United States to interfere in the affairs of the sovereign state of Hawaii. He therefore declined to entertain the proposition to surrender the authority of the government to the ex-Queen.

The Corwin sailed on the following day, December 24th, and on the 26th the Minister acknowledged the receipt of Dole's reply, and notified the ex-Queen of the result.

If the excitement of the last few days had been great, it now bordered upon terrorism. Threats to assassinate the Provisional officials were made; royalist conspiracies were formed, and the passions of all parties were aroused, which made it probable that a disturbance might occur at any time. To relieve the tension and restore confidence, President Dole again addressed the United States Minister a letter on December 27th, calling his attention to the apprehension existing, and urgently requesting that some assurance be given as to whether or not he intended to use force in regard to his policy, but Mr. Willis still withheld all information. At last, President Cleveland's special message to Congress, transmitting copies of Blount's report, and submitting the Hawaiian problem for Congressional solution, as published in the American papers, was received, giving the desired information for the first time. A rather spicy and unpleasant correspondence between President Dole and the United States Minister followed, closing the attempt, by direct act of the American executive, to restore the ex-Queen. In the meantime the Senate of the United States, by a formal resolution, directed its Committee on Foreign Affairs to investigate the Hawaiian situation. The Committee, under a Democratic chairman, made an exhaustive and careful investigation, examinations being under oath, and the witnesses subjected to rigid cross-examination, in place of Mr. Blount's method of affidavits and simple interrogation of an *ex parte* nature. Leading men of all parties, and others having no interest in the matter, were placed on the witness stand, and the

result was a lengthy report unqualifiedly exonerating
the officers of the Boston and Minister Stevens, and
reflecting upon the methods of Mr. Blount.

January 17, 1894, the first anniversary of the
Provisional Government, was celebrated with great
enthusiasm, in public receptions, a military parade,
and a mass-meeting at night. The American Minister declined an invitation to be present, and the
other foreign representatives in Honolulu followed
his example by failing to participate in the observance
of the day. No salutes were fired from any of the
men-of-war in the harbor, a tacit recognition of the
monarchical government and an apparent discourtesy
to the Provisional Government for refusing to step
down and out. The English Minister made good
use of the situation by actively influencing opinion
inimical to the interests of the United States and in
support of the ex-Queen and her party. The
officials of the Provisional Government now fully
realized that their case was in the hands of Congress, the proceedings of which were reported by
their Minister at Washington, who, after filing a
protest with the Secretary of State against the
unwarranted demands of the United States, returned
to Honolulu to post his superiors on the situation
in the United States. In consequence the hope of
early annexation was abandoned by the Provisional
Government, and steps were immediately taken to
establish a republican form of government. The
office of Minister of Foreign Affairs was separated
from the person of the President, and the Executive

Council was increased to five members. A constitutional convention was called to assemble May 30, 1894, for a revision of the constitution by which the Provisional Government was to transfer its authority to the Republic of Hawaii. The convention finished its labors on the afternoon of July 3d, and on the same day the Advisory Council passed the act to provide for the proclamation of the Republic. On the following day the general public were invited to participate in the ceremony. At 8 A. M. July 4th, 1894, President Dole, accompanied by his Cabinet and staff and other officials, delivered the proclamation ushering into existence another republic, and that, too, on the anniversary of American Independence. Official notification was sent to all foreign powers of the changed form of government, and it was promptly recognized by them. The constitution adopted by the convention went immediately into force as the supreme law of the Republic, and Sanford B. Dole by virtue thereof assumed the office of President. The new constitution was fashioned after the general form of that of the United States and of the individual States. An educational qualification was required of voters for both houses, and a property qualification for electors of Senators, by which the ignorant and irresponsible of all nationalities are eliminated from control of the political life of the community. The legislature was divided into two branches, consisting of fifteen members each, a Senate and a House of Representatives. A Council of State was also provided for, consisting of fifteen members, five of whom are appointed by the President and five elected by each branch of the legislature, and these together with the President and Executive Council act in times of emergencies when the legislature is not in session. Provision was made for the bestowal of special letters of denization on those who assisted in establishing the Provisional Government, entitling them to all privileges of Hawaiian citizenship without having to renounce allegiance to their own government. The President is elected for a term of six years by a joint vote of the two houses, and cannot be elected to a second consecutive term. The Senators are elected for six years and the Representatives for two. A small property qualification is required for a Representative and a larger one for Senators. The authority of each house is similar to that of other legislative bodies. There is a special provision by which the President is empowered, with the approval of his Cabinet, to make a treaty of political union with the United States.

In opposition to this excellent form of government the royalists were warmly supported by the British residents and officials to continue their intrigues under the stimulus of a supposed American unfriendliness. The English Minister and his wife were not only notorious sympathizers with the ex-Queen, but were in constant communication with her, and the officers of the British man-of-war in the harbor took part in secret meetings of the leading royalists to consider what action should be taken to reinstate the monarchy. This British sympathy and support constituted not only a serious element of peril, but stimulated the naturally peacefully inclined natives and half-whites to look forward to, and work for, the return of the monarchy, and they largely failed to qualify as voters for the first election called by the Republic for the election of Senators and Representatives. About 5,000 voters qualified, and all the members of both houses were elected on a platform in favor of annexation of the islands to the United States, both houses subsequently passing resolutions unanimously approving such proposition. This is worthy of note, as the majority of the lower house, including the Speaker, were full-blooded native Hawaiians.

Secret plotting and serious disaffection were reported, and some arrests were made, but this did not put a stop to the continued intrigues. In the meantime, Rear-Admiral J. G. Walker, whose professional abilities, tact, and judgment are unexcelled by those of any other officer in the United States Navy, by orders of the Navy Department, was placed in command of the naval forces in the Pacific. He relieved Rear-Admiral Irwin on April 14, 1894, and at once proceeded to obtain all the information possible on the political situation, and in several communications to the Department made exhaustive reports. The accurate and reliable information transmitted to the Department by the Admiral was not of an *ex parte* nature, but based upon knowledge obtained in conversations with men of all parties, and clearly defined the condition of affairs. He plainly demonstrated how the English were interfering in the political affairs of the islands ; reported their efforts to seize Necker Island for a cable landing, and pointed out the necessity of strengthening the United States naval forces in Hawaii, urging that another vessel be sent to Honolulu, which recommendation was not complied with.

The establishment of a permanent form of government and a settled policy was discouraging to the royalists ; nevertheless their leaders held a series of conferences, and as a result sent a committee of three, headed by one of the ex-Queen's Cabinet, to the Coast to purchase arms and munitions of war, and make other arrangements to assist in a secret uprising. The committee visited Washington, called upon the Secretary of State, and made an effort to obtain the support of the United States in case of such a move. They were informed that the United States would not interfere in the domestic affairs of Hawaii. They informed Secretary Gresham that if the American men-of-war were recalled from Hawaii, they would have no difficulty in overthrowing the Republic and re-establishing the monarch. There is no record of his reply. The committee reported back that the United States ships were going to be withdrawn. They returned to California, purchased arms and munitions, and caused them to be shipped to the islands. Admiral Walker was, by telegram of July 9th, instructed to proceed with the Philadelphia to Mare Island, California, but as soon as it was known that the Philadelphia was to leave, the British Minister ordered the Champion, a British war ship, to remain in port. The Admiral had full confidence in the Republic's ability to preserve order, but he well knew that in the event of an uprising of the royalists, with only an English man-of-war in the harbor, the forces from that vessel would, in all probability, land to assist them in the restoration of the Queen, and he very wisely postponed the departure of the Philadelphia. The English and royalists were greatly elated at the intended departure of the Philadelphia, leaving the Champion in port, while the supporters of the government regarded the situation with anxiety. A petition was sent to the Admiral, signed by prominent merchants and business men, representing large American moneyed interests, requesting him to remain. The Admiral not leaving, he was again ordered by telegram, via San Francisco, to leave at once with the Philadelphia, and this time, having no discretion in the matter, he obeyed his instructions and sailed on the 12th of August, leaving the islands virtually under British protection.

This withdrawal of the Philadelphia left Honolulu, for the first time in twenty years, without United States naval supervision. The royalists believed and announced that it was done to afford them an opportunity to revolt against the Republic. The timidity of the royalist leaders, however, caused the contemplated move to be put off until January 6, 1895, when a lot of natives and low whites, instigated by agitators of foreign birth, and acting with the full knowledge and consent of Liliuokalani, met at a secluded spot about four miles from the city for the purpose of commencing hostilities. Arms and ammunition, having been previously purchased in San Francisco by the royalists, were landed from a small coasting vessel, and placed in the hands of these men, from the house of one of the conspirators, at the foot of Diamond Head. Preparations were made for a night attack on the city, which, had it been successful, would have resulted in the killing of many innocent men, women, and children, the looting of buildings and the destruction of much property. The armed forces were led by the mutinous Wilcox and others of unsavory record, while the instigators remained in the city to assist when the attack was made if the appearances were favorable to success. The telephone wires were cut and a number of foreigners out for a stroll were taken prisoners by the rebels, as a precautionary measure. The news of a suspicious gathering at the place of rendezvous reached the authorities, and the deputy marshal, with a few police, was sent with warrants to arrest the conspirators. Upon their arrival at the place they were fired upon, resulting in the killing of young C. L. Carter, who had been one of the annexation commissioners who went to Washington in 1893, and the wounding of two police. The regular troops and volunteer forces were immediately called out, and for several days there was desultory fighting, resulting in the complete overthrow of the revolution and the capture of the rebel forces. The leaders as soon as captured became anxious to reveal the inner history of the movement, and the names of the parties connected with them. A search was made of the ex-Queen's residence, and a lot of bombs, rifles, and ammunition found there. She was arrested, together with several prominent foreigners, mostly English and Canadians. The town was placed under martial law, and a military commission appointed to try those implicated. Nowlein, one of the leaders, turned state's evidence. Those found guilty were either deported or sentenced to imprisonment for a stated period and fined. Some were fined only, and four were sentenced to be shot, all of whom in the course of time were pardoned. The ex-Queen, hoping to avoid trial and consequent punishment, voluntarily executed a document renouncing and abdicating all pretensions or claims whatsoever to the throne of Hawaii, and took the oath of allegiance to the Republic; but she was tried, nevertheless, for "misprision of treason" and sentenced to imprisonment and to pay a fine, but was afterwards released and placed on indefinite parole.

Following upon this revolution frequent reports of filibuster expeditions from Puget Sound and British Columbia came to disturb the peace and quiet.

To make matters worse, there was sprung upon the government an unexpected claim of a serious nature. It was a demand from the American Minister, by order of Secretary Gresham, claiming a large indemnity for the imprisonment of an American subject who had been found guilty of engaging in the late revolution and sentenced to a short term of imprisonment. This man's affidavit was taken by the American Consul and the Minister without any inquiry being made of the government officials. Upon that affidavit alone the demand was made, and that, too, after an official publication stating that no American engaged in a conflict would be protected. Hence when the demand came it was regarded as another act of hostility by the Washington government and caused grave apprehension, as the British government at the same time presented several claims of a similar character. It was feared that the United States was going to combine with England in crushing exactions and ruinous demands for the treatment of those who had been in active revolution against the Republic.

The Hawaiian Minister in Washington, who, by his exertions against restoration of the Queen, had lost favor with the Secretary of State, was, in the early part of April, recalled by his government upon request of Secretary Gresham, but the position was filled later on and did not interfere with the formal diplomatic relations between the two countries.

Major Wodehouse, the English Minister, continued his hostility to the Republic so openly that the government finally, in self-defense, demanded to know his intentions and meaning. He became so offensive that his government finally recalled him. Upon his retirement from office he declined to notify the President of the change, and failed to exercise the invariable courtesy of a formal farewell to that official, but, instead, upon his departure, he requested permission for himself and wife to bid adieu to the ex-Queen, who was then in prison. This request was denied. Both Major Wode-house and his wife had stimulated to the utmost the ex-Queen's hopes of restoration, and prior to and during the revolution of 1895 they gave active encouragement to the royalists. This official had been at Honolulu nearly thirty years, in a constant struggle to promote English influence at the expense of American interests, and his policy was to maintain the monarchy as a means of maintaining English influence.

The successful establishment of the Republic upon the eve of his retirement made him bitter and hostile, and though holding the position of British Minister and transacting diplomatic business with the *de facto* government, he continued to be a pronounced royalist. He was succeeded by an official who was not involved in local politics, but who possessed the English proclivity for British supremacy, and was, consequently, a sympathizer with the royalists. But the change was welcomed by the republican officials.

The first legislature of the Republic met on June 12, 1895, and adjourned August 15th, after passing an elaborate act providing for dividing the government and crown lands into homesteads, which are now being rapidly taken up by actual settlers on very favorable terms. As though the political turmoil on the islands had not caused sufficient suffering, the overtaxed patience of the people was further burdened by an infliction of the cholera. A passenger steamer from China brought the disease to the islands in August, 1895, and though a strict quarantine, thorough sanitary treatment, medical and police inspection were maintained, the disease was not stamped out before the end of September, resulting in the death of 85 persons, mostly natives.

The government of the new Republic was at last firmly established, with ample strength to maintain itself against any and all phases of hostile domestic sentiment; an organic law had been put in force and faithfully and judiciously administered, distinctly closing the chapter in Hawaiian political history which relates to the transition from a monarchy to a republic. The entire community accepted the situation and settled down to comparative peace and contentment. The regular legislature was chosen and passed many acts of a beneficial nature, with every indication of a most favorable outlook for political stability and commercial prosperity.

CHAPTER XVIII.

THE STRATEGIC VALUE OF HAWAII.

It is interesting to note that upon the strength of Balboa's discovery of the Pacific Ocean, in 1513, Spain continued, until not much over a hundred years ago, to claim that entire ocean and all the countries bordering thereon as her property. When Sir Francis Drake circumnavigated the globe, the claim was advanced that the Pacific was a *mare clausum*, and his sailing across that sea was resented as a trespass upon Spanish property. As late as 1789 Spanish war vessels seized several English fur-trading vessels on the northwest coast, and the Commandant at San Francisco was ordered to seize the Columbia, the first vessel that carried the American flag around the world, for having invaded those waters. Spain's greatness was already on the wane, however, and she was unable to maintain her preposterous claims.

Early in the present century the nations of the world began to realize, in a faint way, that the Pacific and its adjacent shores were eventually to become valuable, and in ever accelerating degree began an international scramble for dominion therein until, with the exception of the territory owned by the United States or protected by the Monroe doctrine, China, Japan, and Hawaii, every island in the Pacific, and the shores bordering thereon, have become the property of some European country. Japan is one of the wonders of the modern world. It is the one country not of the Aryan race which has evinced ability to withstand the aggressions of that race. It has taken its position as one of the forces, not only of the Pacific, but of the world, which must be calculated upon by international statesmen, not only in a negative way, but as one of the active and aggressive forces, not only of the future but of the present. Japan already has a navy nearly as strong as that of the United States, and has more naval vessels in course of construction than any other country, except Great Britain. Moreover, her people are of an active, mercurial, and belligerent disposition, with unbounded faith in their own prowess and ability. In possession of the magnificent navy which they are building, they are liable to be in the position of a boy with a new toy, with which he wishes to experiment. While the traditional relations of Japan and the United States are friendly, the rapid prospective commercial development of both countries is liable to bring them into conflict of interest. A conflict of commercial interest is growing more and more to be the basis of international hostility. No American statesman can in the future leave Japan out of sight as one of the dominating powers in the Pacific.

Although the great powers began to absorb Pacific territory in the early part of the century, it
was not until some ten or twelve years ago that the
available territory began to become exhausted. At
that time a final division of the Pacific into "spheres
of influence" was made among Germany, France,
England, and Spain, which partitioned and divided
off among these four powers all the territory not
theretofore absorbed, except Samoa, which the sudden and unexpected intervention of the United
States finally left in the anomalous control of united
England, Germany, and the United States; and
Hawaii, which has remained in a semi-independ-
ent position simply because the United States has
for forty years reiterated at frequent intervals that
it would consider interference in that group as an
attack upon the United States. It is idle to claim
that other countries have not desired, and do not
desire, the control of Hawaii. At various times
Russia, England, and France have each seized the
country, and Japan has had serious intentions looking in that direction. To England, especially, the
control of Hawaii would be of inestimable value. It
has become fashionable of late to rhapsodize over the
unity of the English-speaking race and their community of interest; and now that England is facing
a hostile Europe it is manifestly wise policy on
her part to cultivate every possible appearance of
friendly feeling toward the United States. American statesmen, however, cannot and do not lose
sight of the fact that sentiment has little effect upon

international relations when material interests are involved. It is to England's material interest to-day to cultivate friendship with the United States. The fact cannot be lost sight of, however, that the United States, more than any other country, is the rival of Great Britain in almost every great material interest. Producing, as the United States does, all the necessary raw materials, this country, in an ever-accelerating degree, is destructively competing with Great Britain in the markets of the world. To a still greater degree is this competition on the part of the United States going to be injurious to the other European countries. While present conditions have produced a temporary estrangement between Europe and Great Britain, driving the latter to a seeming friendship toward the United States, it is a moral certainty that the near future will draw Great Britain and the countries of Europe, by mutuality of interest, into an antagonism to the United States. The map of the Western Hemisphere demonstrates that Great Britain recognizes that America is her greatest rival, and that she is preparing to treat her as her greatest foe. Beginning with Halifax and including Bermuda and the Bahamas, Jamaica and St. Lucia on the east and south, and ending with Esquimalt and British Columbia on the west, she has established a series of impregnable fortresses, each equipped with dry-docks and fortifications second in strength and capacity to none in the world, and connected them all with expensive cable systems for which there is no commercial call.   All this has been done with no logical purpose except to prepare for eventual hostilities with the United States.   The one link omitted in this chain of hostile forts surrounding the United States is Hawaii. Not only is Hawaii a missing link in an otherwise continuous chain, but it directly divides England's greatest Anglo-Saxon colonies, Canada and Australia, the distance between which is so great that it is impossible for even merchant steamers to traverse it without recoaling at Hawaii, as there is no other supply station available.

The importance of Hawaii as a strategical position is no more a matter of opinion than is a geometrical axiom.   It is a primal, incontrovertible fact.   It is second in importance to no other single point on the earth's surface.   England seized, and with bull-dog tenacity has held, Gibraltar for its strategical value alone ; but there is no country the route to which lies past Gibraltar which cannot be reached by several other different ways.   The distinctive feature of Hawaii, wherein it is unique among the strategical points of the world, is that it lies at the center of an area so great that commercial and military operations across it are practically impossible, except by using Hawaii as a coal and supply station.   Eliminate Hawaii from the map, and there are scarcely any battle-ships in existence which can operate across the Pacific, by reason of the fact that they cannot carry coal enough, and the problem of coaling at sea has not yet been solved.

It has been repeatedly and officially pointed out by the naval authorities, not only of the United States but of the world, that the trans-Pacific countries and islands, with the exception of Hawaii, are so far distant from the American continent that, unless the ships of such nations can recoal at Hawaii, it is practically impossible for them to get to the Pacific Coast for the purpose of conducting military operations there. The most efficient ships could not get there at all, and those which do carry sufficient coal to cross would have no coal with which to operate, much less to return to their base of operations. In other words, it is impossible to maintain naval or military operations at a distance of from 3,500 to 5,500 miles from a base of operations. This fact was definitely established in the late war with Spain, as every United States man-of-war and transport for troops, in their efforts to reinforce Admiral Dewey's fleet in the Philippine Islands, had to stop at Honolulu for coal, repairs, and supplies.

As long ago as 1851, Congress by formal resolution requested the Navy and War Departments to report upon the conditions and requirements of the coast defenses of the United States. By instructions of the Navy Department, Admiral Dupont drew up a report in reply to this resolution, in which he said, in connection with the defense of the Pacific Coast:

"*It is impossible to estimate too highly the value and importance* of the Sandwich Islands, whether in a commercial or military point of view. Should circumstances ever place them in our hands, they would prove the most important acquisition we could make in the whole Pacific Ocean—an acquisition intimately connected with our commercial and naval supremacy in those seas."

This opinion has been fully approved by United States naval officers from that day to this. That United States control of Hawaii can be made both effective and economical is demonstrated by a brief examination of the facts.

Although the Hawaiian Islands are eight in number and extend over a distance of about 400 miles, with the exceptions of Honolulu and Pearl harbors the ports are all open roadsteads, in which vessels are compelled to lie at distances of approximately half a mile from shore, obliged at all times to land and ship all freight in small boats, hampered by the restless swell of the ocean and exposed to constant interruptions by storms. The port of Hilo could be partially protected by building a breakwater several miles long, at an expense of an unestimated number of millions of dollars, but even then it would not be protected from northerly storms. With the exception, therefore, of Honolulu and Pearl Harbor, all points in the island may be eliminated from consideration as possible naval stations.

Pearl Harbor and Honolulu harbor are both located upon the south side of the Island of Oahu, and are only seven miles apart. Any effective military control of the one must necessarily include the control of the other, for they are so close together that heavy artillery located at either point would be within easy range and have full control of the other.

Fortifications for the defense of the two need be of the most inexpensive kind. Both Honolulu and Pearl Harbor are protected by natural fortifications which need nothing but the placing of guns in position to become impregnable. Three miles east of Honolulu, projecting out into the deep water, its summit only about a quarter of a mile from the water's edge, rises Diamond Head, a hill of solid rock, with an almost perpèndicular face, reaching an elevation of 750 feet.

In the very heart of Honolulu, within three-quarters of a mile of deep water, lies a second hill of solid rock, with almost perpendicular face, rising to an elevation of 500 feet. Four miles west of Honolulu, just half way to Pearl Harbor, lies a third hill, of the same rocky perpendicular character, reaching an elevation of 400 feet. A battery of modern guns can be mounted on each of these three hills at so little expense as to practically eliminate the amount as a factor for consideration in an estimate of cost. To the rear of Honolulu the only pass through the mountain is a narrow cut, twenty feet wide, to approach which an invading army would have to climb an almost perpendicular bluff, nearly a thousand feet high, that would preclude any attack from that direction.

Honolulu is an absolutely safe land-locked harbor, but is unsuitable for a naval station, for two reasons : first, because it is so small that it will not accommodate more than a hundred vessels at the outside, and the rapidly growing commercial use of the port will very soon tax its limit to the utmost.   In the second place, the shores of the harbor are distant only from a half to three-quarters of a mile from deep water.   The dry-docks, machine shops, and magazines of a naval station should be located at such a distance from deep water as to practically put them beyond the reach of an ordinary bombardment.   While Honolulu can be so fortified as to absolutely prevent an effective landing being made, it lies so close to deep water that a heavy battle-ship might easily, before being driven off, annihilate the effectiveness of the station by a few well-directed shots.

Pearl Harbor is an arm of the sea, a lagoon, connected with the ocean by a long, narrow, river-like entrance, some three miles in length ; the inner end expanding and dividing into three locks, having together an interior frontage of some 30 miles, with an average depth of from 30 to 60 feet.   Its banks are formed of coral and sandstone with a top layer of soil.   In many places the banks are so perpendicular that a full-rigged ship could lie alongside without excavation or dock-building.   The entire harbor is surrounded by abundant springs of pure, fresh water, and artesian wells reach fresh water at any point at a depth of approximately 400 to 425 feet, which rises to an elevation of about 30 feet above sea-level. The shores are well wooded with Algeroba forests, and the country on the land side is a rich, fertile district covered with rice, banana, and sugar plantations, capable of furnishing an unlimited amount of fresh supplies for the use of the station. A barrier reef extends parallel with, and distant about a mile from, the shore, and the water beyond does not reach a depth of over 100 feet for a distance of about another mile, being well suited, therefore, for marine mining. These, with the assistance of the fortifications already spoken of and inexpensive fortifications at the mouth of the harbor, would be absolutely prohibitive of any successful attack on the station from the sea. The Navy and War Departments have already executed most minute surveys of the harbor and its entrance, and caused expert reports to be made thereon. As early as 1872, Generals Schofield and Alexander, of the United States Army, reported unequivocally in favor of the military value of this harbor to the United States. The surveys of the Navy Department have been made under the direction of Admirals Irwin, Walker, and Miller. They disclose that there is a sand-bar across the extreme outer entrance of the harbor, consisting almost exclusively of soft disintegrated coral sand, which can be disposed of by a suction dredge at an estimated expense of not more than $150,000. The rise and fall of the tide is less than three feet, and there are no currents which need be feared to re-form the bar. A bar similar in character, somewhat smaller in extent, was pumped out from the entrance to Honolulu harbor in 1891, a depth of over 30 feet being secured, which has not since changed a particle. The expense of clearing the Honolulu harbor bar, exclusive of the cost of the dredge, was only about $40,000. This dredge was the property of the Hawaiian government, and is now available at any time for use by the United States Government at Pearl Harbor, if desired.

The United States had for a long time, by means of treaty rights, the exclusive use of this harbor as a coaling and naval station, but nothing was ever done to avail itself of this privilege other than making the few surveys mentioned. It was fully realized that a mere sheet of water carried with it few advantages, and to be effective for the purpose intended, to protect a fortified port of call, must necessarily be able to control the territory for a sufficient distance therefrom to prevent its occupation by a hostile power. As there was no grant of territory by that treaty, the United States consequently had no claim to the jurisdiction over the lands adjacent to Pearl Harbor, and the Hawaiian government used this fact as a lever to either perpetuate the treaty of reciprocity or force the acceptance of the islands as a whole by the United States. It argued, and that forcibly, that by the terms of the treaty the claim of the United States to Pearl Harbor was coterminous with the treaty itself, and that if the treaty terminated, the American rights to the harbor terminated also. Finally, when the war commenced between the United States and Spain, and Admiral Dewey made his celebrated attack upon Manila, the importance of this harbor became more than ever apparent, and the Hawaiians, on the alert for such an opportunity, immediately declined to pass any act of neutrality. Consequently the men-of-war and transports with soldiers on their way to the Philippine Islands made Honolulu a port of call, as was necessary. They were welcomed by the people of the city and given a most hearty reception. American flags were displayed, American airs were played, and the inhabitants regarded the temporary occupation as a propitious omen. The result was that the United States saw no alternative but to accept the islands as a whole, and the Senate failing to take up the treaty of annexation, Congress passed the Newlands act, and the Hawaiian Islands at last became an American possession. Now, with the control of this stronghold of the Western world the United States becomes the dominant power over the entire North Pacific, both from a naval and a commercial standpoint, and our Pacific Coast is afforded a military protection, as well as command over the trans-Pacific commerce, which could never have been obtained as long as these islands were subject to seizure by the commercial powers of Europe. The American merchant marine is now greater in the Pacific than in any other ocean, and will in the near future increase with giant strides under the new régime. With a little addition to the present force, occupation and a strengthening of the fortifications of Pearl Harbor and Honolulu, the United States can never be evicted from the islands except by an expenditure of blood and treasure that will make the effort one of the greatest naval and military feats of history.

CHAPTER XIX.

THE HAWAIIAN ISLANDS BECOME AN AMERICAN POSSESSION.

The withdrawal of the treaty of annexation of Hawaii to the United States by President Cleveland, and the subsequent efforts to restore Liliuokalani to the throne, was a severe blow to the advocates of American absorption. They were, however, encouraged by the result of the investigation and report upon the situation by the Committee on Foreign Affairs in the United States Senate, and they patiently waited for the proper time to renew their efforts. Finally, when a change in the administration took place, and President McKinley assumed office as the Chief Executive of the United States, the Hawaiian statesmen renewed their efforts to carry out the provisions of the proclamation inaugurating the Republic of the islands, which explicitly state that such form of government would exist " until terms of union with the United States of America have been negotiated and agreed upon." A new treaty of annexation was drawn up and, through diplomatic agents in Washington, it was submitted to President McKinley for his inspection and comment. Meeting with his approval it was in a short while ratified by the Hawaiian legislature. In the meantime, President McKinley submitted the treaty to the Senate of the United States for its action, but it met with such opposition in that body that those having it in charge hesitated to report it from the committee. Sporadic efforts of a few of the advocates of the treaty were made to get it before the Senate, but each time it was met with such pronounced opposition that Senator Davis, the Chairman of the Committee on Foreign Affairs, would not report it to the Senate. This strong and unexpected attack on the part of the Senate aroused the enthusiasm of the advocates of the treaty in the House of Representatives. The result was that after the introduction of a number of bills favorable to annexation and some heated political discussion, the Newlands resolution was adopted by both houses of Congress, and approved by the President on July 7th, 1898. The following is the full text of the resolution that made Hawaii a portion of the United States :

" Whereas the government of the Republic of Hawaii having in due form signified its consent in a manner provided by its constitution to cede absolutely and without reserve to the United States of America all rights of sovereignty of whatsoever kind in and over the Hawaiian Islands and their dependencies, and also to cede and transfer to the United States absolutely free the ownership of all government or crown lands, public buildings, edifices, ports, harbors, military equipment, and all other public property of every kind and description belonging to the government of the Hawaiian Islands, together with every right and appurtenance thereunto appertaining ; therefore

"*Resolved,* By the Senate and the House of Representatives of the United States of America in Congress assembled, That said cession is accepted, ratified, and confirmed, and that the said Hawaiian Islands and their dependencies be, and they are hereby, annexed as part of the territory of the United States, and are subject to the sovereign dominion thereof, and that all and singular property and rights thereinbefore mentioned are vested in the United States of America.

" Existing laws of the United States relative to public lands shall not apply to such lands in the Hawaiian Islands, but the Congress of the United States shall enact special laws for their management and disposition, provided that all revenue from or proceeds of the same, except as regards such a part thereof as may be used or occupied by civil, military, or naval purposes of the United States, or may be assigned for use of the local government, shall be solely for the benefit of the inhabitants of the Hawaiian Islands for educational and other public purposes.

" Until Congress shall provide for the government of such islands, all civil, judicial, and military authority exercised by the officers of the existing government of said islands shall be exercised in such a manner as the President of the United States shall direct, and the President shall have power to remove said officers and fill the vacancies so occasioned. -

" Existing treaties of the Hawaiian Islands with

foreign nations shall forthwith cease and determine, being replaced by such treaties as may exist and may be hereafter concluded between the United States and such foreign nations. Municipal legislation of the Hawaiian Islands, not enacted for the fulfillment of treaties so extinguished, and not inconsistent with this joint resolution, nor contrary to the Constitution of the United States, nor to any existing treaty of the United States, shall remain in force until the Congress of the United States shall otherwise determine.

" Until legislation shall be enacted extending the United States customs laws and regulations to the Hawaiian Islands, existing customs regulations of the Hawaiian Islands with the United States and other countries shall remain unchanged.

" The public debt of the Republic of Hawaii lawfully existing at the date of the passage of this joint resolution, including the amounts due to depositors in the Hawaiian Postal Savings Bank, is hereby assumed by the Government of the United States, but the liabilities of the United States in this regard shall in no case exceed $4,000,000.

" So long, however, as the existing government and the present commercial relations of the Hawaiian Islands are continued as hereinbefore provided, said government shall continue to pay the interest on said debt.

" There shall be no further immigration of Chinese into the Hawaiian Islands, except upon such conditions as are now or may hereafter be allowed to enter the United States from the Hawaiian Islands.

" The President shall appoint five commissioners, at least two of whom shall be residents of the Hawaiian Islands, who shall, as soon as reasonably practicable, recommend to Congress such legislation concerning the Hawaiian Islands as they shall deem necessary or proper.

" Section 2. That the commissioners hereinbefore provided for shall be appointed by the President by and with the advice and consent of the Senate.

" Section 3. That the sum of $100,000, or so much thereof as may be necessary, is hereby appropriated out of any money in the Treasury not otherwise appropriated, and to be immediately available, to be expended at the discretion of the President of the United States for the purpose of carying this joint resolution into effect."

Admiral Miller, of the United States Navy, was instructed to carry the message of acceptance to the President of the Hawaiian Government. He arrived in Honolulu in his flag-ship, the Philadelphia, and at noon of August 12th, 1898, the imposing ceremony of transferring the Hawaiian Islands to the United States took place. The ceremonies began by the appearance of the Hawaiian National Guards, headed by a detachment of police, at the boat landing, where they met the sailors and marines from the two United States men-of-war in the harbor, the Philadelphia and the Mohican. From

the landing the Hawaiian Guards escorted the
American troops to the gate of the Executive Building and there deployed to positions near the platform, with the Hawaiian band on one side and the
American band on the other.   In the grounds and
all around the approaches were crowds of onlookers.
The platform for the exercises and the verandas
of the Executive Building were crowded with the
élite of Honolulu.   Exactly at fifteen minutes to
noon President Dole and his Cabinet came from the
Executive Building to the platform.   The Justices
of the Supreme Court followed, and after them
Admiral Miller, United States Minister Sewell,
Consul General Hayward, and the Commanding
Officers of the American men-of-war.   The ceremonies opened with prayer, after which Minister
Sewell rose and presented a certified copy of the
joint resolution to President Dole, who, in the interest of the Hawaiian body politic, yielded up to
the representatives of the United States the sovereignty and public property of the Hawaiian Islands.
Minister Sewell accepted the same, when Admiral
Miller directed the transfer of flags.   As the Hawaiian flag came down the band played Hawaii-
Ponoi, and a salute of 21 guns was fired from the
National Guard battery on shore, which was answered by a similar number of guns from the Philadelphia.   A few minutes later the United States flag
was hoisted, the American band played the Star
Spangled Banner, and a salute of 21 guns was fired
from the Philadelphia, answered by the National
Guard on shore.

One of the most gratifying spectacles of the occasion, especially to those Americans who witnessed our flag being hauled down by Blount, was the re-hoisting of the same flag on the same flag-pole, over the same building, simultaneously with the lowering of the Hawaiian flag on the Executive Building. I was enabled to obtain this flag immediately after it was hauled down five years previously and carefully preserved it, fully believing that sooner or later there would be a call for it to go up again. When I was ordered to Cuban waters last May, in command of the U. S. S. Hist, to take part in the war with Spain, I gave this flag to L. A. Thurston, with the request that it be re-hoisted on the same flag-staff from which it had been lowered. Mr. Thurston communicated with President McKinley, and he approved of the proposition, as did President Dole ; so the result was, the flag that Blount hauled down rose proudly to its old position.

The flag-raising being over, a proclamation was read by Mr. Sewell in which the civil, judicial, and military officials of the Republic of Hawaii in office prior to the transfer of sovereignty should continue to exercise authority until Congress should provide for the government of Hawaii, and they took the oath of allegiance to the United States. All treaties entered into between the Hawaiian Government and foreign powers, except those inconsistent with the provisions of the joint resolution, or contrary to the Constitution of the United States, or to any existing treaty of the United States, were to remain in force until Congress should otherwise determine.

The ceremonies concluded at night with a popular ball and public reception at which Admiral Miller, President Dole and Mrs. Dole, Mr. and Mrs. Sewell received the people. The grounds of the Executive Building were the scene of the most elaborate fire-works ever displayed in Honolulu.

The cession of the Hawaiian Islands to the Great Republic of North America having been accomplished, the President of the United States, in compliance with the joint resolution of Congress, appointed a commission, headed by Senator Cullom, to visit Honolulu, and upon careful investigation devise a system of government for the islands. They carried out their instructions, and after careful and mature deliberation reported favorably upon placing Hawaii on the plane of an organized Territory of the United States, to enjoy the same degree of self-government that is accorded to New Mexico, Arizona, and Oklahoma. They based their opinion upon the fact that the people of Hawaii had already demonstrated their capability of self-government by the establishment and maintenance of the Republic of Hawaii, and that they were already more or less familiar with the institutions and laws of the United States, from which most of the Hawaiian laws were drawn. President Dole made a minority report recommending a Board of Advisers to the Governor of the Territory in all matters of public policy, stating as his reason for so doing that he feared the

Governor would arrogate to himself greater power than was contemplated. The commissioners also recommended the construction of a cable to the Hawaiian Islands, to be under the control of the United States, as required by the military conditions existing or liable to exist at any time.

In accordance with the recommendations of this Board, three bills were sent to Congress by President McKinley, and were introduced in the Senate by Senator Cullom, and in the House by Representative Hitt. By the provisions of these bills, safeguards, such as educational and limited property qualifications, are thrown around the suffrage so as to insure the domination of Americans and persons of American descent in the government of the islands. All white persons, as well as Portuguese and persons of African descent, and all persons descended from the Hawaiian race on either paternal or maternal side, who were citizens of Hawaii immediately preceding the annexation, were made citizens of the United States. It will be seen from this that all Japanese and Chinese laborers on the islands are barred from citizenship, and the importation of coolie labor into Hawaii forever prevented. The labor laws of the United States are extended over the islands so as to prevent all kinds of foreign contract labor from entering the Territory.

This closes the long chapter in Hawaiian history through which American influence has wonderfully developed the islands until now the government in Hawaii is the same as the Government of the United

States. There can no more be any overthrow of
this or that monarchy or little republic. It is at
last planted, as it were, upon a rock where capital
will soon recognize its solidity, and with the introduction of capital will come power to develop varied
industries. Agricultural resources will be improved,
manufactures will be established, and a further increase of population and accumulation of national
wealth will naturally result. Hawaii is now in
truth the Paradise of the Pacific and the jewel in
the diadem of our western possessions, as the Pearl
of the Antilles is the gem of our eastern acquisi-
tions.

APPENDIX.

[The following appendices set forth in abbreviated form nearly all the latest and most reliable information relative to the Hawaiian Islands that has been gathered within the last ten years. They have been compiled from pamphlets issued by the Secretaries of State and of Agriculture of the United States, reports of commissions, consular reports, official correspondence and the like, and are in every sense authoritative.]

A.

LAND.

SETTLEMENT ASSOCIATIONS IN THE HAWAIIAN ISLANDS.

Six or more qualified persons may form a " Settlement Association " and apply for holdings in one block.

The provisions for cash freehold apply to the settlement of such blocks, but first auction sale is confined to members of such Settlement Association.

Any lot in such block which may be forfeited or surrendered, or which is not taken up by any member of the Settlement Association within three months, shall be open to any qualified applicants.

Disputes, disagreements, or misunderstandings between the parties to certificate of occupation, homestead lease, right of purchase lease, or cash freehold, and relating thereto, which cannot be amicably settled, shall be submitted to the Circuit

Judge in whose jurisdiction the premises are situated, and his decision shall be final, subject only to appeal to Supreme Court.

CASH SALES AND SPECIAL AGREEMENTS.

With consent of Executive Council, public lands not under lease may be sold in parcels of not over 1,000 acres, at public auction, for cash, and upon such sale and payment of full consideration a land patent will issue.

Parcels of land of not over 600 acres may, with consent of Executive Council, be sold at public auction upon part credit and part cash, and upon such terms and conditions of improvement, residence, etc., as may be imposed.

Upon fulfilment of all conditions a land patent will issue.

GENERAL LEASES.

General leases of public lands may be made for a term not exceeding twenty-one years.

Such leases are sold at public auction, and require rent in advance quarterly, semiannually, or annually.

The conditions of general leases are made at discretion of the Commissioners, and may be made for any class of public lands.

METHODS OF ACQUIRING LAND.

Land can be obtained from the Government by two methods, viz., the cash freehold system and the right of purchase leases. Under the first system the land is sold at auction. The purchaser pays one-quarter in cash and the rest in equal instalments of one, two, and three years, interest being charged at the rate of six per cent. upon the unpaid balance. Under this system the purchaser is bound to maintain a home on the land from the commencement of the second year to the end of the third. The right of purchase leases are drawn for twenty-one years at a rental of eight per cent. on the appraised value of the land. The lessee has the privilege of purchasing the land after the third year at the original appraised value, provided twenty-five per cent. of the land is reduced to cultivation and other conditions of the lease filled. In this case a home must be maintained from the end of the first year to the end of the fifth year. The limit of first-class agricultural land obtainable is 100 acres. This amount is increased on lands of inferior quality. Under the above conditions the applicant must be eighteen years of age and obtain special letters of denization. Land can also be obtained from the various land and investment companies and from private parties.

GOVERNMENT LANDS.

The total area of Government lands is fixed at 1,782,500 acres, classified as follows:

Class of land.	Acres.
Valuable building lots	145
Coffee	76,270
Cane	25,626
Rice	977
Homesteads, Government interest in	20,000
Grazing	451,200
Forest lands, high	681,282
Rugged mountain tracts	227,000
Barren lands	300,000

The above classification is somewhat arbitrary because of the lack of positive knowledge of quality and adaptability of soil in untried sections. The area of coffee lands on the island of Maui will probably be increased by further investigations on the windward side of the island.

These Government lands are located on the several islands as follows :

Islands.	Coffee.	Cane.	Rice.	Grazing.	Forests, etc.	Estimated value.
	Acres.	*Acres.*	*Acres.*	*Acres.*	*Acres.*	
Hawaii..............	62,800	18,156	140	368,849	749,302	$1,874,900
Maui................	8,180	520	110	112,570	58,550	453,800
Oahu................	800	2,050	327	71,414	13,778	983,500
Kauai	4,400	4,900	400	80,050	86,650	648,000
Molokai.............				40,625		77,500
Lanai and Kahoolawe				77,669		70,000
Laysan, etc..........						40,000
Total..........	76,270	25,626	977	751,177	908,280	4,147,700

AGRICULTURAL INDUSTRIES.

The mainstay of the Hawaiian Islands has, for the last thirty-five years, been the sugar industry. From this source a large amount of wealth has been accumulated. But the sugar industry requires large capital for expensive machinery, and has never proved remunerative to small investors. An attempt has been made at profit-sharing and has met with some success, the small farmer cultivating and the capitalist grinding at a central mill. Of late years, moreover, the small farmer has been steadily developing in the Hawaiian Islands and attention has been given to other products than sugar.

Rice neither the European nor the American can cultivate as laborers. It requires working in marshy land, and though on the islands it yields two crops a year, none but the Chinaman can raise it successfully. A dry-land or mountain rice has been introduced, which will be treated under the head of agricultural possibilities.

The main staple after sugar and rice is coffee. Of this hundreds of thousands of trees have been planted out within the last five years. This is essentially the crop of the future and bids fair to become as important a staple as sugar. Coffee does not require the amount of capital that sugar does, and it can be worked remuneratively upon a small area. It is estimated that at the end of the fourth year the return from a 75-acre coffee plantation will much more than pay the running expenses, while from that time on a return of from eight to ten thousand dollars per annum may be realized.*

Fruits can also be cultivated to advantage. At present the banana trade of the islands amounts to over 100,000 bunches per annum, valued at over $100,000, and the quantity might be very easily quadrupled. The banana industry may be regarded as in its infancy. The export of the fruit is only from the island of Oahu, but there are thousands of acres on the other islands of the group which could be profitably used for this cultivation and for nothing else. The whole question of the banana industry hinges on the market. At present the market is limited.

Limes and oranges can be cultivated and the fruit can be easily packed for export; at present the production does not meet the local market. The fruits can be raised to perfection. The Hawaiian orange has a fine flavor, and the Hawaiian lime has an aroma and flavor far superior to that cultivated in Mexico and Central America. In the uplands of Hawaii and Maui potatoes can be and are raised. Their quality is good. Corn is also raised. In these industries many Portuguese, Norwegians, and others have embarked. Both these products find an ample local market. The corn is used largely for feed on the plantations. The corn is ground with the cob and makes an excellent feed for working cattle, horses, and mules.

In the uplands, where the climate is temperate, as at Waimea, Hawaii, vegetables of all kinds can be raised; excellent cauliflower, cabbages, and every product of the temperate zone can be grown to perfection.

* See page 315 of this appendix.

Cattle-raising in so small a place as the Hawaiian Islands does not present great opportunities except for local consumption. Pigs are profitable to the small farmer. In the Kula district of Maui pigs are fattened upon the corn and potatoes raised in the district. The price of pork, dressed, is twenty-five cents per pound in Honolulu and about fifteen cents per pound in the outside districts. The Chinese, of whom there are some fifteen thousand resident on the various islands, are extremely fond of pork, so that there is a large local market, which has to be supplemented by importations from California.

Attention has lately been given to fibre plants, for which there are many suitable locations. Ramie grows luxuriantly, but the lack of proper decorticating and cleaning machinery has prevented any advance in this cultivation.

Sisal hemp and sanseveira have been experimented with, but without any distinct influence upon the trade output.

The cultivation of pineapples is a very growing industry. In 1895 pines were exported from the islands to San Francisco to the value of nearly $9,000. This has grown up in the last half-dozen years. There is every reason to think that canning pineapples for the coast and other markets can be made profitable.

The guava, which grows wild, can also be put up to profit for the manufacture of guava jelly. It has never been entered upon on a large scale, but to the thrifty farmer it would add a convenient slice to his income, just as the juice of the maple adds an increase to the farmer of the Eastern States. Well-made guava jelly will find a market anywhere. In England it is regarded as a great delicacy, being imported from the West India Islands. Besides the guava there are other fruits which can be put up to commercial profit, notably the poha or Cape gooseberry (Physalis edulis). This has been successfully made into jams and jelly, which command an extensive local sale and should find their way into larger markets.

In the Hawaiian Islands a simple life can be lived, and, entering gradually upon the coffee industry, a good competence can be obtained long before such could be realized by the agriculturalist elsewhere. However, it is useless to immigrate to the islands without the necessary capital to develop the land that can be obtained.

Between arriving and the time that the crops begin to give returns there is a period when the living must be close, and cash must be paid out for the necessary improvements. The land is cheap, the climate equable; it only requires brains, a small capital, and energy to realize such comfort and independence as cannot be realized in old countries in one-fourth of the time.

B.

COFFEE.

Estimate of cost of establishing and maintaining a coffee plantation of 75 acres from the first to the seventh year.

FIRST YEAR.

Purchase of 100 acres of Government land at $10 per acre.......	$1,000
Manager's house and water-tank...	600
Laborers' quarters and water-tank.	350
Clearing 50 acres of land at $20 per acre...........................	1,000
Fencing	300
Purchase of 65,000 one-year-old coffee plants at $5 per thousand....	325
Lining, holing, and planting 50 acres...........................	600
Manager's salary, one year........	1,200
Labor of six Japanese, one year, at $15 per month.................	1,080
Purchase of tools and starting nursery............................	500
	$6,955

SECOND YEAR.

Manager's salary.................	1,200
Labor, six Japanese..............	1,080
Extra labor, lining, holing, and planting 25 acres...............	300
Sundries........................	500
	3,080
	10,035

THIRD YEAR.

Manager's salary..................	$1,200
Labor, nine Japanese	1,620
Pulping-shed and drying-house....	500
Pulper, with engine and boiler....	500
Extra help for picking, pulping, and drying 20,000 pounds of coffee from 50 acres at 4 cents per pound	800
Hulling, polishing, and grading 20,000 pounds of coffee at 1 cent.	200
Sundries (bags, freight, etc.)......	250

$5,070

15,105

CREDIT.

By sale of 20,000 pounds of coffee at 18 cents ....

3,600

11,505

FOURTH YEAR.

Manager's salary.................	1,200
Labor, nine Japanese............	1,620
Extra labor picking, pulping, and drying:	
50,000 pounds of coffee from 50 acres at 4 cents per pound ..	2,000
10,000 pounds from 25 acres (three-year-old trees).......	400
Hulling, polishing, and grading 60,000 pounds at 1 cent	600
Sundries (bags, freight, etc.)......	400

6,220

17,725

CREDIT.

By sale of 60,000 pounds of coffee at 18
  cents................................ ..... $10,800

6,925

FIFTH YEAR.

Manager's salary................. $1,200
Labor, nine Japanese............   1,620
Picking, pulping, and drying 60,000
  pounds of coffee from 50 acres
  and 25,000 pounds from 25 acres
  at 4 cents.   3,400
Hulling, polishing, and grading
  85,000 pounds at 1 cent per pound.   850
Sundries (bags, freight, etc.)......   500

7,570

14,495

CREDIT.

By sale of 85,000 pounds of coffee at 18
  cents.............................   15,300

      Balance on hand.   905

SIXTH YEAR.

Manager's salary.................   1,200
Labor, nine Japanese............   1,620
Picking, pulping, and drying 75,000
  pounds of coffee from 50 acres
  and 25,000 pounds from 25 acres
  —100,000 pounds at 4 cents......   4,000
Hulling, polishing, and grading
  100,000 pounds at 1 cent..   1,000
Sundries (bags, freight, etc.)...,. ..   1,000

8,820

CREDIT.

By sale of 100,000 pounds of coffee at 18
cents.......................... $18,000

Balance on hand. 10,085

SEVENTH YEAR.

Manager's salary. $1,200
Labor, twelve Japanese.......... 2,160
Picking, pulping, and drying 125,000
pounds of coffee at 4 cents...... 5,000
Hulling, polishing, and grading
125,000 pounds at 1 cent........ 1,250
Sundries (bags, freight, etc.)...... 1,200
————— 10,810

CREDIT.

By sale of 125,000 pounds of coffee at 18
cents.......................... 22,500

Balance to credit of plantation at
end of seventh year............. 21,775

INTERVIEWS WITH PLANTERS.

Plantation No. 1.—This place is situated in Hamakua, and is owned by a Portuguese, Narcizzo
de Mello. It shows what can be done by a man
without means. It must be borne in mind, however, that this man was on the ground making a
living, and had every opportunity to select his land.
In all probability a stranger would spend nearly
as much as this man owns before he got fairly
started. This place consists of 17 acres, 13 of
which are in coffee. The land cost $10 per acre,

and he estimates that the clearing did not cost him more than $3 per acre, as he did most of the work himself.　His plants cost $5 per thousand, the trees now being from six months to four and one-half years old.　They are planted 7 by 6 feet at an elevation of 1,750 feet.　He employs no labor, with the exception of one Portuguese woman at 50 cents per day at picking time, who, together with his own wife and two children, is sufficient.　His land is not paid for, he paying interest at five per cent.　He has a small house of two stories, 20 by 20 feet, with a 7-foot veranda, which cost $650, with a detached kitchen costing $55.　He estimates that it costs him $20 per month to support his family, outside of what he raises in the way of vegetables.　His tools cost $5, and his stock, consisting of a horse and cow, $70.　The crop of last year amounted to 2,560 pounds; this year he expects to get 4,800 pounds.　The coffee was sold in the parchment, to a local shopkeeper, for 10 cents per pound, which was 2 cents under the price paid in Honolulu.　Mr. de Mello has owned his place for six years and estimates that it has cost him, exclusive of land, $1,000.　He owes $700.　His trees look very well, and show careful planting and intelligent cultivation.　The older trees were laden with berries, and the estimate made that there would be an average yield of 1½ pounds of clean coffee per tree is conservative.　Some trees must have had 4 pounds of clean coffee on them.　De Mello never had any previous experience in raising coffee, but raised fruit in Portugal.　He frequently works for others, earning about $150 per year.　He will work at planting by the day for new settlers, and would be a good man to employ to show strangers around the Hamakua district.

Plantation No. 2.—The owner of this place is also a Portuguese.　He owns 15 acres of land which cost $10 per acre.　He had 4½ acres in coffee, the trees being three and one-half to six years old. Last year he received $150 for his crop. The man probably works at times for others. It costs him in money from $20 to $25 per month to support a family of twelve. He raises hogs, chickens, and vegetables. He estimates that his place has cost him, all told, $700.

Plantation No. 3.—This place is owned by a gentleman who is engaged in other business besides coffee. He has 40 acres planted. The cost of clearing his land was $100 per acre. The trees are from six months to seven years old. They are planted 7 by 8 feet at an elevation of 1,800 feet. Five Japanese are required to take care of the place, who are paid $15 per month. Last year 4,225 pounds of coffee were marketed. It was sent in parchment to the coast, and brought at the rate of 19½ cents for clean coffee. On this place are a number of trees which have been badly planted. Upon pulling the tree up it is usually found that the tap-root was bent or that the lateral roots were growing in a bunch around the main stem.

Plantation No. 4.—This is a new place of 90 acres which cost $12.50 per acre. The clearing cost $25 per acre. Ten acres have just been planted, the plants costing $5 per thousand. The trees are planted 8 by 8 feet at an elevation of 1,800 feet. Four Japanese are employed at $15 per month. About $800 has already been spent, in addition to the cost of the land. This gentleman is a firm believer in plants raised from Guatemalan seed.

Plantation No. 5.—This place belongs to two young men. They have spent rather more than usual for a place of its size and age. They have 147 acres, the cost of which averaged them $12.50 per acre. This is one of the new homestead lots in Hamakua opened up by the Government the first part of the year. The land is covered with heavy timber and a thick tropical undergrowth. It cost to clear $25 per acre. Eight acres have just been put in coffee. The plants were bought at $5 per thousand. The trees are planted 8 by 8 feet and 7 by 7 feet. The land has an elevation of from 1,600 to 2,300 feet. Four Japanese are employed at $15 per month. They estimate their living expenses to be $40 per month. They have spent so far $5,000. Their buildings have cost $2,000, the dwelling costing alone $1,750. This place is a good illustration of what it costs to build on a new place before roads are made. The material for the house had to be packed on mules over a miserable trail, and then carried by Japanese over a deep gulch. The freight cost as much as the material and labor.

Plantation No. 6.—This place is owned by Mr. J. M. Horner, and is the show place of Hamakua. He is also a large sugar-planter. He has 125 acres in coffee. The land cost to clear $40 per acre. He sells plants raised from Guatemalan seed at $10 per thousand. He has also sold considerable seed at $1 per pound. His land has an elevation of from 1,400 to 2,000 feet. He considers 2,000 feet the best. His trees are from one to five years old. They are planted 7½ by 7 feet. He employs twenty-five Japanese, four being women, paying $15 to the men and $10 to the women. In 1894 he picked 2,000 pounds of coffee; in 1895, 12,000 pounds; in 1896, 68,000 pounds, and this year expects 80,000 pounds. He has received 15 cents per pound for his coffee. Mr. Horner has paid great attention to his nurseries, his plants being in great demand. After planting the seed, all of which is Guatemalan, he covers the ground with fern leaves and does not remove them until the plants are well out of the ground. The ground is watered every day. Mr. Horner claims that a tree raised from Guatemalan seed is as far advanced at four years as a native one would be at six years. Cutworms appear on the ridges and not in the valleys. This year he has been experimenting with fertilizing. He hopes by expending 5 cents per tree to double the crop. His coffee looks very fine.

As the case now stands for the investor, land can be obtained for coffee-growing in:

ISLAND OF HAWAII.
    North and South Kona,
    Hilo,
    Puna, including Olaa,
    Hamakua.

ISLAND OF MAUI.
    Keanae,
    Nahiku,
    Lahaina,
    Kaupo.

ISLAND OF MOLOKAI.

ISLAND OF OAHU.

ISLAND OF KAUAI.

C.

SUGAR.

Sugar is the great staple of these islands, and the whole production goes to the United States.

The total amount shipped during the first six months of 1897 was 186,517 tons, valued at $11,093,-516.82. Of this amount, 70,503 tons, valued at $4,235,613.85, went to New York, consigned to the American Sugar Refining Company, and 116,014 tons, valued at $6,857,902.97, went to San Francisco.

One hundred and forty-six vessels were employed, of which 123, or 84 per cent., were American, carrying 143,270 tons.

Hawaii can never produce enough sugar to supplant the beet or any other sugar in the United States. The sugar consumption of the United States was approximately two million tons during 1896, which consumption is rapidly increasing year by year. During 1896 Hawaii produced a little over two hundred thousand tons, or approximately one-tenth of the consumption of the United States. This is the highest output ever made by Hawaii, and is the best it has been able to do after twenty years of encouragement under the reciprocity treaty with the United States.

All of the natural cane lands of Hawaii are already under cultivation.

The only remaining lands which can possibly be cultivated with sugar-cane are those now dry and barren, which can only be cultivated by artificial irrigation, by pumping water to an elevation of from one hundred and fifty to six hundred feet.

It goes without saying that such irrigation must be limited in area and problematical in profits.

SUGAR-PLANTATION STATISTICS

From 1875 to 1897 inclusive.

YEAR.	SUGAR.		MOLASSES.		TOTAL EX-PORT VALUE.
	Pounds.	Value.	Gallons.	Value.	
1875	25,080,182	$1,216,388.82	93,722	$12,183.86	$1,228,572.68
1876	26,072,429	1,272,334.53	130,073	19,510.95	1,291,845.48
1877	25,575,965	1,777,529.57	151,462	22,719.30	1,800,248.87
1878	38,431,458	2,701,731.50	93,136	12,107.68	2,713,839.18
1879	49,020,972	3,109,563.66	87,475	9,622.52	3,119,185.91
1880	63,584,871	4,322,711.48	108,355	29,753.52	4,352,464.73
1881	93,789,483	5,395,399.54	263,587	31,630.44	5,427,020.98
1882	114,177,938	6,320,890.65	221,293	33,193.95	6,354,084.60
1883	114,107,155	7,112,981.12	193,997	34,819.46	7,147,800.58
1884	142,654,923	7,328,896.67	110,530	16,579.50	7,345,476.17
1885	171,350,314	8,356,061.94	57,941	7,050.00	8,363,111.94
1886	216,223,615	9,775,132.12	113,137	14,501.76	9,789,633.88
1887	212,763,647	8,694,964.07	71,222	10,522.76	8,705,486.83
1888	235,888,346	10,818,883.09	47,965	5,900.40	10,824,783.49
1889	242,165,835	13,089,302.10	54,612	6,185.10	13,095,487.20
1890	259,789,462	12,159,585.01	74,926	7,603.29	12,167,188.30
1891	274,983,580	9,550,537.80	55,845	4,721.40	6,555,258.20
1892	263,636,715	7,276,549.24	47,988	5,061.07	7,281,610.34
1893	330,822,879	10,200,958.37	67,282	5,928.96	10,206,887.33
1894	306,684,993	8,473,009.10	72,979	6,050.11	8,479,059.21
1895	294,784,819	7,975,590.41	44,970	3,037.83	7,978,628.24
1896	443,569,282	14,932,172.82	15,885	1,209.72	14,933,382.54
1897	520,158,232	15,390,422.13	33,770	2,892.72	15,393,314.85

AMOUNT OF SUGAR SHIPPED FROM THE HAWAIIAN ISLANDS FROM JANUARY 1st TO JUNE 30th, 1897.

From whence shipped.	To New York.	To San Francisco.	Total.
	Pounds.	*Pounds.*	*Pounds.*
Kahului....................	14,671,387	28,967,601	43,638,988
Mahukona.................	....	22,976,550	22,976,550
Hilo	15,897,831	39,482,113	55,379,914
Honolulu.....	110,437,950	140,602,431	251,040,381
Total.................	141,007,168	232,028,695	373,035,863
Total tons.	70,503	116,014	186,517

VALUE OF ABOVE.

From whence shipped.	Value to New York.	Value to San Francisco.	Total.
Kahului.....................	$439,673.89	$906,748.06	$1,346,421.95
Mahukona........	....	658,843.43	658,843.43
Hilo.	472,050.71	1,137,683.28	1,609,733.99
Honolulu.	3,323,889.25	4,154,628.20	7,478,517.45
Total..................	4,235,613.85	6,857,902.97	11,093,516.82

NUMBER AND NATIONALITY OF VESSELS.

```
American............................................................. 123
Hawaiian..... ........... ....... ........... .................... 13
British................................................... ... .......... 5
German...... ...................................................... 5
```

LIST OF SUGAR PLANTATIONS, MILLS, AND CANE GROWERS THROUGHOUT THE ISLANDS.

Those marked with an asterisk (*) are planters only; those marked with a dagger (†) are mills only; all others are plantations complete, owning their own mills.

NAME.	LOCATION.	MANAGER.	AGENTS.
American Sugar Co.	Molokai.	P. McLane.	C. Brewer & Co.
Beecroft Plantation*.	Kohalo, Hawaii.	H. R. Bryant.	Davies & Co.
Eleele Plantation.	Eleele, Kauai.	A. Dreier.	Schaefer & Co.
Ewa Plantation.	Ewa, Oahu.	G. F. Renton.	Castle & Cooke
Gay & Robinson*	Makaweli, Kauai.	Gay & Robinson.	H. Waterhouse.
Grove Farm*	Nawiliwili, Kauai.	G. N. Wilcox.	Hackfeld & Co.
Haiku Sugar Co.	Haiku, Maui.	H. A. Baldwin.	Alexander & Baldwin.
Hakalau Plantation Co.	Hilo, Hawaii.	Geo. Ross.	Irwin & Co.
Halawa Sugar Co.	Kohala, Hawaii.	T. S. Kay.	H. Waterhouse.
Hamakua Mill Co.†	Hamakua, Hawaii.	J. R. Renton.	Davies & Co.
Hamakua Plantation Co.*	Hamakua, Hawaii.	A. Lidgate.	Davies & Co.
Hamoa Plantation.	Hana, Maui.	W. H. C. Campbell.	C. Brewer & Co.
Hana Plantation Co.	Hana, Maui.	K. S. Gjerdrum.	Grinbaum & Co.
Hanamaulu Sugar Plantation*	Hanamaulu, Kauai.	A. S. Wilcox.	Hackfeld & Co.
Hanamaulu Mill†.	Lihue, Kauai.	C. Wolters.	Hackfeld & Co.
Hawi Mill & Plantation.	Kohala, Hawaii.	J. Hind.	Davies & Co.
Hawaiian Agricultural Co	Kau, Hawaii.	C. M. Walton.	Brewer & Co.
Hawaiian Com'l & Sugar Co.	Spreckelsville, Maui	W. J. Lowrie.	Alexander & Baldwin.
Hawaiian Sugar Co.	Makaweli, Kauai.	H. Morrison.	Alexander & Baldwin.
Heeia Agricultural Co., Ltd	Heeia, Oahu.	E. K. Bull.	Grinbaum & Co.
Hilo Sugar Co.	Hilo, Hawaii.	John A. Scott.	Irwin & Co.
Hilo Port. Sugar Mill Co.	Hilo, Hawaii.	W. von Gravemeyer.	Hackfeld & Co.
Kona Sugar Co.	Kona, Hawaii.	J. Coerper.	M'Chesn'y & Sons.
Honolulu Sugar Co.	Halawa, Oahu.	Jas. A. Low.	......
Honokaa Sugar Co.	Hamakua, Hawaii.	John Watt.	Schaefer & Co.
Honomu Sugar Co.	Hilo, Hawaii.	Wm. Pullar.	Brewer & Co.
Hutchinson Sugar Co.	Kau, Hawaii.	G. C. Hewett.	Irwin & Co.
Kahuku Plantation	Kahuku, Oahu.	George Weight.	Grinbaum & Co.
Kaiwilahilahi Mill	Laupahoehoe, Hawaii.	C. McLennan.	Davies & Co.

LIST OF SUGAR PLANTATIONS, ETC.—Continued.

Name.	Location.	Manager.	Agents.
Kekaha Sugar Co.	Kekaha, Kauai.	Otto Isenberg	Hackfeld & Co.
Kilauea Sugar Co.	Kilauea, Kauai	G. R. Ewart	Irwin & Co.
Kipahulu Sugar Co.	Kipahulu, Maui	Oscar Unna	Hackfeld & Co.
Kihei Plantation.	Kihei, Maui	W. F. Pogue	Alexander & Baldwin.
Kohala Plantation.	Kohala, Hawaii	E. E. Olding	Castle & Cooke.
Koloa Agricultural Co.	Koloa, Kauai.	J. K. Farley.	Castle & Cooke.
Koloa Sugar Co.	Koloa, Kauai	A. Cropp.	Hackfeld & Co.
Kukaiau Mill Co.	Hamakua, Hawaii	Jas. K. Renton	Davies & Co.
Kukaiau Plantation Co.*	Hamakua, Hawaii	J. M. Horner	Hackfeld & Co.
Laie Plantation.	Laie, Oahu.	S. E. Wooley.	H. Waterhouse.
Laupahoehoe Sugar Co	Laupahoehoe, Hawaii.	C. McLennan.	Davies & Co.
Lihue Plantation.	Lihue, Kauai.	C. Walters.	Hackfeld & Co.
Makee Sugar Co.	Kealia, Kauai.	G. H. Fairchild.	Brewer & Co.
Nahiku Sugar Co.	Koolau, Maui.		Davies & Co.
Niulii Mill & Plantation.	Kohala, Hawaii	Robert Hall.	Hackfeld & Co.
Oahu Sugar Co.	Waipahu, Oahu.	A. Ahrens.	Irwin & Co.
Olowalu Sugar Co.	Olowalu, Hawaii.	A. Hanneberg.	Castle & Cooke.
Onomea Sugar Co.	Hilo, Hawaii.	John T. Moir.	Irwin & Co.
Ookala Sugar Co.	Ookala, Hawaii.	W. G. Walker.	Irwin & Co.
Paauhau Plantation Co.	Hamakua, Hawaii.	A. Moore.	Irwin & Co.
Pacific Sugar Mill†	Hamakua, Hawaii	D. Forbes.	Schaefer & Co.
Paia Plantation.	Paia, Maui.	D. C. Lindsay	Alexander & Baldwin.
Pioneer Mill Co.	Lahaina, Maui.	L. Ahlborn.	Hackfeld & Co.
Pepeekeo Sugar Co.	Hilo, Hawaii.	H. Deacon.	Davies & Co.
Union Mill Co.	Kohala, Hawaii.	J. Renton.	Davies & Co.
Waiakea Mill Co.	Hilo, Hawaii.	C. C. Kennedy.	Davies & Co.
Waialua Agricultural Co.	Waialua, Oahu.	W. W. Goodale.	Castle & Cooke.
Waianae Plantation.	Waianae, Oahu.	D. Center	J. M. Dowsett.
Wailuku Sugar Co	Wailuku, Maui.	C. B. Wells.	Brewer & Co.
Waimanalo Sugar Co.	Waimanalo, Oahu.	G. C. Chalmers.	Irwin & Co.
Waimea Sugar Mill Co	Waimea, Kauai.	E. E. Conant.	Castle & Cooke.

D.

POPULATION AND AREA.

	Square Miles.
Niihau	97
Kauai	590
Oahu	600
Molokai	270
Maui	760
Lanai	150
Kahoolawe	63
Hawaii	4,210
Total	6,740

The islands that interest an intending immigrant are Hawaii, Maui, Oahu, and Kauai. It is on these islands that coffee, fruits, potatoes, corn, and vegetables can be raised by the small investor, and where land can be obtained on reasonable terms.

The different nationalities represented among the population of the islands are distributed as follows:

POPULATION BY NATIONALITIES.

Hawaiians	35,000
Part Hawaiians	10,000
Chinese	15,000
Japanese	24,000
Portuguese	9,000
American and European	14,000
Total	107,000

In the matter of the general population of the islands the subjoined table has been compiled from the last census returns.

	Male.	Female.	Total.	DWELLINGS.			
				Inhab-ited.	Unin-habited.	Build-ing.	Total.
Oahu.........	26,164	14,041	40,205	6,685	1,065	60	7,010
Hawaii	22,632	10,653	33,285	5,033	955	35	6,027
Molokai.....	1,335	972	2,307	651	92	3	746
Lanai........	51	54	105	23	13	....	36
Maui........	11,435	6,291	17,726	3,156	650	18	3,824
Niihau	76	88	164	31	3	....	34
Kauai.	10,824	4,404	15,228	2,320	299	8	2,627
Totals....	72,517	36,503	109,020	17,099	3,081	124	21,104

SCHOOLS.

SCHOOL STATISTICS, HAWAIIAN ISLANDS.

(From Reports of the Department of Education.)

COMPARATIVE TABLE OF SCHOOL POPULATION, 1897–98.

ISLANDS.	NO. SCHOOLS 1898.	IN SCHOOL, JAN. 1898.			NO. SCHOOLS 1897.	IN SCHOOL, JAN. 1897.		
		Boys.	Girls.	Total.		Boys.	Girls.	Total.
Hawaii	60	2,055	1,773	3,828	64	2,008	1,703	3,711
Maui and La-nai	36	1,321	1,167	2,488	37	1,319	1,151	2,470
Molokai	5	90	67	157	6	114	64	178
Oahu	73	3,638	2,790	6,428	71	3,429	2,670	6,099
Kauai & Nii-hau........	18	913	708	1,621	17	878	687	1,565
Totals.	192	8,017	6,505	14,522	195	7,748	6,275	14,023

The main plan of the school system is modelled upon the public-school system of the United States, modified to meet the wants of a heterogeneous population. The children are instructed in writing, reading, composition, arithmetic, geography, both local and general. The books are uniform and obtainable at the same price as in the United States. The schools are strictly non-sectarian. There is no district, however remote, in which there is no school. The only people who cannot read and write are those who come from abroad. Those born on the islands are compelled by law to take advantage of the education offered. Besides the common-school education, opportunities are given at various centres for a higher education equivalent to the grammar grade of the United States, and in Honolulu a high school and collegiate course can be obtained at a small cost.

CLIMATIC CONDITIONS.
RAINFALL THROUGHOUT THE HAWAIIAN ISLANDS,
1897–98.

Locality.	Feet Ele-vation	1898.						
		Jan.	Feb.	Mar	Apr.	May.	June.	Total.
HAWAII.								
Waiakea	50	41.51	6.94	49.75	6.95	7.25	4.30	173.47
Hilo	100	38.64	3.95	45.41	7.12	8.19	4.23	361.39
Kaumana	1,250	49.61	7.76	55.58	12.70	15.58	6.54	230.99
Pepeekeo	100	33.14	8.66	42.37	5.94	8.87	4.17	152.62
Honomu	300	35.44	7.28	49.49	....			
Hakalau	200	31.90	6.53	38.72	6.32	8.48	3.85	147.92
Laupahoehoe	600	41.60	8.28	31.70	7.50	11.56	4.80	169.86
Ookala	400	32.85	6.52	28.43	6.33			
Kukaiau	260	28.20	4.72	20.59	4.96	3.96	3.88	91.01
Paauhau	300	18.31	2.90	12.23	4.46	3.32	2.73	62.41
Honokaa	425	16.24	3.56	12.79	5.39	2.93	3.19	66.54
Waimea	2,720	3.62	2.62	6.39	3.60	2.54	4.66	34.64
Kohala	350	6.61	.....	16.54	3.15	4.84		....
Kailua	650	1.33	4.10	8.67	2.48	7.28	7.26	67.62
Kealakekua	1,580	1.61	4.53	6.99	2.03	7.81	7.36	69.39
Kalahiki	800	1.27	3.88	6.80	2.19	4.74	3.59	51.27
Naalehu	650	4.34	3.77	20.62	0.71	3.47	0.62	55.39
Pahala	1,100	5.82	5.34	.....	0.54	1.21	0.34	.....
Olaa	1,650	51.46	10.16	52.44	13.86	13.66	8.18	227.00
Kapoho	110	15.64	11.41	24.86	3.26	4.17	4.19	108.86
Pohoiki	10	18.04	15.26	19.87	3.05	3.48	6.50	....
MAUI, ETC.								
Haleakala Ranch	2,000	3.97	3.83	9.46	1.17	1.55	1.18	38.49
Puuomalei	1,400	9.93	5.91	13.38	3.21	5.32	2.78	.....
Paia	180	3.08	4.35	5.03	1.80	.....		
Kahului	10	0.88	5.16	1.74	0.75	.....	..	
Kaanapali	15	3.64	8.71	4.80	..	.....		
Olowalu	15	0.00	4.15	0.70	0.00	0.00	0.00	....
Kaupo	300	14.21	6.84	20.96	2.17	2.94	1.96	.....
Mapulehu, Molokai	70	3.68	8.66	8.69	1.02	2.23	1.43	45.49
Koele, Lanai	1,600	0.23	7.92	9.22	0.39	0.32	5.02	.....
OAHU.								
Punahou	50	6.26	8.49	12.70	2.42	1.35	2.90	.....
Kulaokahua	50	3.99	7.62	10.66	1.20	0.68	2.07	34.26
Kapiolani Park	10	1.39	6.63	7.95	0.23	0.21	0.37	19.94
School Street	50	5.56	9.15	12.03	2.22	1.84	3.05	49.59
Nuuanu Avenue	50	.	9.04	11.79	1.67	1.47	2.63	....
" Valley	405	18.89	10.82	26.17	4.32	4.31	7.10	108.70
Luahaka	850	22.00	20.44	40.13	7.45	0.30	10.25	166.16
Waimanalo	25	1.87	11.20	12.35	1.68	1.26	2.74	46.27
Maunawili	300	4.93	10.72	15.69	2.42	2.92	4.51	80.46
Kaneohe	100	2.02	.....	16.34	1.77	1.58		....
Ahuimanu	350	4.54	12.75	28.87	4.05	3.51	6.95	103.22
Kahuku	25	2.57	6.58	16.15	1.72	1.24	1.91	45.49
Waianae	1,700	2.96	13.93	11.20	4.40	2.45	3.01	64.73
Honouliuli	60	0.42	11.01	7.02	0.38	0.22	1.53	30.43
KAUAI.								
Lihue	200	4.03	6.65	11.60	2.00	1.89	2.51	40.46
Hanamaulu	200	2.68	5.06	19.39	1.54	1.73	2.83	35.46
Kilauea	325	8.79	7.44	18.01	5.27	4.46	4.09	73.39
Hanalei	10	13.20	4.71	27.67	7.03	6.10	3.49	98.72

SUMMARY OF METEOROLOGICAL OBSERVATIONS AT HONOLULU, 1897-98.

(Compiled from Records of Weather Bureau by C. J. Lyons.)

Month	Barometer		Rainfall	Rel. Humid.		Temperature						Absolute Humidity Gr. to Cu. Ft.	Cloud Amount.	Wind Force.
	9 A.M.	3 P.M.		9 A.M.	9 P.M.	Min.	Max.	6 A.M.	2 P.M.	9 P.M.	Aver.			
July	30.009	30.03	1.31	68.0	73.8	72.5	83.9	74.2	80.8	73.5	76.8	6.9	5.0	4.0
August	30.079	30.024	1.23	67.9	71.3	72.6	85.4	73.9	81.6	75.8	77.4	7.1	5.0	3.0
September	30.58	29.990	3.41	70.0	76.6	71.3	84.4	74.2	80.8	75.4	76.8	7.1	4.0	3.0
October	30.075	29.990	1.81	72.7	79.1	72.5	83.1	73.1	80.1	75.1	76.1	7.5	5.0	3.0
November	30.032	29.956	0.07	67.9	70.6	66.6	80.5	69.6	77.3	77.8	73.0	6.6	6.0	3.0
December	30.100	30.020	0.84	69.8	77.0	65.8	78.8	68.0	75.0	75.0	73.2	6.3	6.0	3.0
January	30.116	30.043	6.20	74.7	76.4	67.0	77.0	68.0	74.0	71.0	71.2	6.3	5.2	3.0
February	29.996	29.912	8.99	78.2	79.8	62.9	76.1	64.2	73.0	67.9	68.8	6.4	7.2	1.4
March	30.086	30.000	13.70	75.3	77.5	65.2	74.6	67.1	73.0	69.5	69.9	6.4	3.9	3.3
April	30.133	30.048	2.47	66.5	73.6	65.3	77.4	67.3	75.7	70.4	71.2	6.8	5.2	2.6
May	30.120	30.072	1.35	66.3	73.6	63.8	79.2	70.0	77.3	72.5	73.5	6.8	4.2	3.4
June	30.088	30.031	2.90	67.3	75.2	69.9	81.5	71.5	79.5	74.0	75.0		5.1	2.5
Year	30.088	30.011	43.79	70.4	76.1	68.4	80.2	70.3	77.5	72.6	73.4	6.7	5.1	2.9

G.

EXPORTS AND IMPORTS.

EXTENT OF HAWAIIAN TRADE WITH UNITED STATES.

In the fiscal year ending June 30, 1897, the aggregate trade between the Hawaiian Islands and the United States reached $18,385,000.

This is greater than our total trade with Argentina, which amounted to $17,157,000 in the same year.

It was greater than our total trade with Central America, which amounted to $16,464,000 last year.

It was greater than our total trade with Spain, which amounted only to $14,600,000.

It was greater than our total trade with Switzerland, which amounted only to $13,950,000.

It was greater than our total trade with Venezuela, which amounted only to $12,960,000.

It was greater than our total trade with Austria, which amounted only to $12,200,000.

It was greater than our total trade with Russia, which amounted only to $10,700,000.

It was greater than our total trade with Denmark, which amounted only to $10,500,000.

It was greater than our total trade with Colombia, which amounted only to $8,540,000.

It was greater than our total trade with Norway and Sweden, which amounted only to $7,963,000.

It was greater than our total trade with the Guianas, which only amounted to $6,770,000.

It was greater than our total trade with Chili, which only amounted to $6,370,000.

It was greater than our total trade with Uruguay, which only amounted to $4,729,000.

It was nearly four times greater than our total trade with Portugal, which amounted only to $4,750,000.

It was nearly seven times greater than our total trade with Turkey, which only amounted to $2,821,000.

It was ten times greater than our total trade with Peru, which only amounted to $1,830,000.

It was more than twenty times greater than our total trade with Greece, which only amounted to $850,000 in the last fiscal year.

COMPARATIVE TABLE OF IMPORT VALUES FROM VARIOUS COUNTRIES SINCE 1891.

Countries.		1892.	1893.	1894.	1895.	1896.	1897.
United States	Dutiable	$533,800.94	$568,345.31	$544,275.79	$619,150.78	$665,834.67	$725,862.90
	Bonded	87,456.31	87,106.45	86,257.65	73,015.22	40,187.48	38,761.12
	Free by Treaty	2,340,717.24	2,413,369.35	2,738,213.68	3,018,755.42	3,235,659.80	4,318,944.30
	Free by Civ. Code	870,524.61	1,257,079.08	986,043.30	805,912.86	1,532,526.25	1,716,460.02
Great Britain	Dutiable	333,767.75	362,093.45	397,054.77	413,223.64	636,238.19	774,476.22
	Bonded	18,730.44	22,694.06	16,643.63	12,091.67	12,690.45	14,223.09
	Free by Civ. Code	28,581.70	36,230.82	51,781.32	45,807.67	106,782.75	77,081.94
Germany	Dutiable	89,057.34	64,821.43	98,020.41	64,318.76	103,058.59	149,526.30
	Bonded	6,795.40	5,309.18	7,377.23	6,970.10	8,406.76	8,799.44
	Free by Civ. Code	3,260.13	3,825.70	33,935.43	39,482.75	36,561.13	34,606.45
Brit. Col. and Canada	Dutiable	25,159.00	18,102.28	41,312.05	8,846.02	9,493.12	12,606.75
	Free by Civ. Code	33,874.10	483.88	3,088.72	4,560.17	2,086.83	2,684.11
Australia and New Zealand	Dutiable	2,463.20	46,766.35	73,797.80	17,335.02	41,402.05	43,484.07
	Bonded	68,866.12	42,871.07	94,697.78	66,460.36	24,175.54	19,001.99
	Free by Civ. Code	125,853.59	16,096.33	1,110.62	2,865.05	1,534.30	209.26
China	Dutiable	27,621.52	67,077.03	90,440.35	53,469.19	87,934.81	103,241.94
	Bonded	1,221.87	141,666.56	181,997.24	164,239.17	236,148.73	242,477.69
	Free by Civ. Code	58,481.55	29,248.92	46,551.40	59,452.39	62,306.00	17,293.04
Japan	Dutiable	1,218.46	1,218.46	1,751.77	10.00	616.25	646.67
	Bonded	731.29	120,263.33	170,044.37	183,487.51	264,849.34	267,819.84
	Free by Civ. Code	791.03	1,437.97	3,391.40	18,124.46	3,330.83	4,513.64
France	Dutiable	3,267.38	18,057.54	10,431.75	5,213.62	8,303.63	19,982.86
	Bonded	1,297.17	5,215.63	8,215.53	7,849.90	8,322.98	13,050.74
	Free by Civ. Code	77.76	476.98	476.98	......	5,794.08	5,122.48
All other countries	Dutiable	291.11	93.80	93.80	......	3,603.96	12,824.10
	Bonded	......	85.35	1,555.83	597.87	6,239.60	28,513.06
	Free by Civ. Code	4,517.75	400.59	21,260.83	22,377.84	2,908.10	47,668.80
			16,965.60			27,865.12	137,419.38

COMPARATIVE TABLE OF PRINCIPAL ARTICLES OF EXPORTS, 1867 TO 1897.

Yr.	Sugar Lbs.	Molas. Galls.	Rice Lbs.	Paddy Lbs.	Coffee Lbs.	Hides Pcs.	Tal'w. Lbs.	Goat skins	Wool Lbs.	Pulu Lbs.	Fungus Lbs.	Salt Tons.	Bunches Bananas	Total Val. All Dom'stic Exp.
1867	17,127,187	544,994	441,750	572,099	127,546	11,207	60,936	51,889	409,471	203,058	167,666	107	2,913	$1,324,123.02
1868	18,312,926	492,839	40,450	862,954	78,373	11,144	104,504	57,670	258,914	342,882	76,781	540	3,566	1,450,269.26
1869	18,302,110	338,311	48,800	1,586,059	340,841	12,803	85,937	62,736	318,753	622,498	85,215	1,152	6,936	1,743,891.59
1870	18,783,639	216,662	152,669	535,453	415,111	13,695	90,238	67,413	234,699	233,803	41,960	2,513	4,007	1,514,425.06
1871	21,760,773	271,291	417,011	867,452	46,926	19,384	185,240	58,920	471,706	202,740	37,475	711	3,896	1,731,094.46
1872	16,995,402	192,105	455,121	894,562	39,276	27,006	493,078	51,592	203,546	421,227	33,161	572	4,520	1,462,645.18
1873	23,129,101	146,459	941,438	597,045	262,025	20,677	604,655	66,702	364,507	412,123	57,536	445	6,452	1,721,507.78
1874	24,566,611	90,660	1,187,956	439,157	75,492	22,620	125,596	71,935	199,936	418,330	50,955	730¼	6,494	1,622,455.37
1875	25,080,182	93,721	1,573,739	550,495	105,077	27,777	51,920	50,531	505,489	379,003	45,093	98	10,518	1,835,302.91
1876	26,072,429	739,673	1,289,134	1,542,603	153,607	11,105	327,291	45,205	405,544	314,432	35,891	5	14,982	2,955,133.55
1877	25,575,965	151,402	2,761,370	2,571,917	101,345	22,164	509,129	51,551	375,703	150,560	11,029	322	15,995	2,461,416.66
1878	35,431,45	93,136	2,707,766	2,754,861	127,993	25,309	339,941	84,525	522,757	212,740	22,364	120¼	15,431	3,333,679.49
1879	49,020,972	87,475	4,792,613	33,515	74,275	24,385	......	24,940	464,390	137,001	2,571	50	12,399	3,665,593.76
1880	63,584,871	192,355	6,495,840	......	99,593	22,945	19,169	51,013	331,316	44,846	14,601	14¼	19,164	4,889,194.40
1881	93,789,447	203,587	7,082,700	102,370	18,912	21,972	118,931	31,307	525,489	53,415	4,262	302	20,276	6,784,976.38
1882	114,177,493	221,293	12,160,473	459,613	8,131	26,007	77,869	23,401	528,913	......	2,111	......	25,846	8,165,931.34
1883	114,107,155	193,497	11,519,000	1,306,703	16,957	38,055	32,257	24,795	318,271	......	3,78,	......	44,992	8,036,227.11
1884	142,654,923	11,330	9,403,000	46,224	4,231	21,026	2,364	30,125	407,623	465	2,247	......	58,040	8,067,648.82
1885	171,350,314	57,911	7,307,743	......	1,575	19,043	......	19,782	474,121	......	1,137	......	60,246	8,958,663.88
1886	216,223,615	113,137	7,338,615	......	5,931	31,207	21,305	21,173	418,784	......	......	......	45,862	10,540,375.17
1887	212,763,647	71,223	13,884,200	400	5,360	28,039	56,713	65,233	75,911	......	......	......	58,930	9,435,204.12
1888	235,888,346	47,905	12,898,600	......	7,130	24,404	204,743	17,589	562,528	Pine-	......	......	71,335	11,631,434.88
1889	242,163,835	54,012	9,606,896	......	43,673	27,158	97,125	11,715	241,925	apples	......	......	105,630	13,810,070.54
1890	259,798,462	74,926	10,579,000	......	88,593	28,106	33,876	8,661	371,724	Pcs.	......	Guano Tons.	97,204	13,023,104.16
1891	274,983,580	55,845	4,900,450	......	3,051	20,427	27,225	7,316	47,119	5,368	......	1,217	116,660	10,107,315.67
1892	263,636,715	47,958	11,516,328	......	13,368	21,622	702	3,449	585,999	46,171	......	61	105,375	7,959,938.05
1893	330,632,579	67,382	7,421,024	......	49,311	19,859	13,250	5,911	391,952	19,042	......	......	108,239	10,742,958.50
1894	306,614,993	73,979	7,803,972	......	14,150	21,603	......	......	264,337	44,993	......	......	123,204	9,253,359.87
1895	204,734,819	44,970	3,768,762	......	116,755	10,185	......	6,466	227,987	65,213	......	......	105,085	8,358,106.79
1896	443,569,281	15,885	5,025,491	......	255,655	25,079	......	12,647	462,819	147,451	......	......	126,413	15,436,037.23
1897	520,158,231	53,770	5,499,499	......	337,156	25,140	9,000	6,085	249,860	151,715	......	......	75,835	16,021,775.19

DUTIES ON IMPORTS.

Articles.	From United States.	From other Countries.
Ale, beer, cider, and porter............	20 cts. per dozen.	20 cts. per dozen.
Animals and birds....................	Free............	10 per cent.
Building materials...................	....do.........	Do.
Asphaltum, fire clay, window glass, plaster of Paris, stone, and tiles..........	10 per cent......	Do.
Clothing, boots and shoes.............	Free............	Do.
Linen collars, collars and cuffs, hats, jackets, ladies' cloaks, oil clothing, rubber clothing, linen shirts, underclothing..........................	10 per cent......	Do.
Skirts, suits..........................	....do.........	Do.
Coal and coke	Free............	Free.
Crockery and glassware...............	10 per cent......	10 per cent.
Lamp fixtures.....	Free............	Do.
Drugs and medicines..................	10 per cent......	Do.
Artificial limbs and sponges...........	Free............	Do.
Dry goods............................	....do.........	Do.
Linens...............................	10 per cent....	Do.
Silks.....	25 per cent.....	25 per cent.
Woollens............................	Free............	10 per cent.
Fancy goods..........................	....do.........	Do.
Beads, bonnets, buttons, binding, collars............................	10 per cent......	Do.
Feather dusters	....do.........	Do.
Embroidery and feathers..............	25 per cent.....	25 per cent.
Kid gloves...........................	$3 per dozen....	$3 per dozen.
Silk gloves...........................	25 per cent.. ...	25 per cent.
Gold-leaf.............................	10 per cent.....	10 per cent.
Hook and eyes, hoods.................	....do...... ..	Do.
Parasols, pins, veils, suspenders, linen thread, trimmings, umbrellas, assorted	....do.........	Do.
Lace, mitts, sewing silk, silk umbrellas.	25 per cent.....	25 per cent.
Fish, dry and salt...	Free............	10 per cent.
Flour................................	....do.........	Do.
Fruit, fresh...........................	....do.........	Do.
Furniture............................	....do.........	Do.
Oilcloth...........	10 per cent......	Do.
Looking-glasses......................	... do.........	Do.
Grain and feed.......................	Free	Do.
Groceries and provisions..............	....do.........	Do.
Chocolate, cocoa, condensed milk, glucose, honey, indigo blue, lye, sago, tapioca.............................	10 per cent......	Do.
Guns, revolvers, and findings.........	Free............	25 per cent.
Caps, cartridges, gunpowder	25 per cent......	Do.
Fuse, blasting powder, giant powder...	10 per cent......	10 per cent.
Hardware, agricultural implements and tools...........................	Free	Do.
Glue, lead, stove polish, corks.........	10 per cent......	Do.
Iron, steel, etc......................	Free............	Do.
Brass................................	10 per cent......	Do.
Railroad equipment...................	Free............	Do.
Jewelry....................... .. .	10 to 25 per cent.	10 to 25 per cent.

DUTIES ON IMPORTS.—Continued.

Articles.	From United States.	From other Countries.
Leather....................	Free.............	10 per cent.
Lumber............................	....do.........	Do.
Machinery........	....do.........	Do.
Coffee machinery	....do.........	Free.
Matches...........................	....do.........	10 per cent.
Musical instruments....................	....do.........	Do.
Naval stores..........................	....do.........	Do.
Oils................................	....do....	Do.
Cocoanut, neat's-foot, palm...........	10 per cent......	Do.
Paints	....do.........	Do.
Benzine and turpentine.................	Free.............	Do.
Toilet articles.................	10 to 25 per cent.	10 to 25 per cent.
Toilet soaps	Free..........	10 per cent.
Saddlery, carts, etc....................	....do.........	Do.
Axle grease, harness dressing, saddles..	10 per cent.....	Do.
Baby carriages and carriages...........	25 per cent......	25 per cent.
Sheathing metal.....................	Free..........	10 per cent.
Shooks and containers..................	....do.........	Do.
Alcohol............................	$10 per gal......	$10 per gal.
Stationery and books.................	Free.............	10 per cent.
Tea............................	10 per cent......	Do.
Tin and tinware.......................	....do....	Do.
Cigars :		
American......	Free.	
Foreign......................		$10 per M.
Cigarettes..........................	Free.............	25 per cent.
Snuff................................	....do.........	15 per cent.
Tobacco...........................	....do.........	Do.
Wines under 18 per cent trall...........	....do	Free.
Mineral waters...	10 per cent......	10 per cent.
Artists' materials.....................	Free.............	Do.
Birdseed.............................	....do.........	Do.
Boxes and cases.......................	....do...	Do.
Candy........................	25 per cent......	25 per cent.
Charcoal.............................	Free.............	10 per cent
Cotton waste..........................	....do......	Do.
Curiosities...........................	....do.........	Do.
Chewing gum.........................	10 per cent......	Do.
Dyes................................	....do.........	Do.
Electric and telephone instruments and materials........................	Free.............	Do.
Fertilizers...........................	....do.........	Free.
Lubricating compound.................	....do.........	10 per cent.
Plants and seeds......................	....do.........	Do.
Photographic supplies..................	10 per cent......	Do.
Pipes, tobacco........................	Free.............	25 per cent.
Cigar-holders..................	25 per cent......	Do.
Scientific instruments..................	....do.........	Do.
Shoe blacking........................	10 per cent.. ...	10 per cent.
Trunks	Free.	Do.
Travelling bags.......................	...do.........	Do.
Tombstones..........................	10 per cent......	Do.
Wicker and wicking...	Free..	Do.

EXPORTS FOR THE FIRST SIX MONTHS OF 1896 AND 1897.

| Whither exported. | 6 Months Ended June 30th. | | Increase. | Decrease. |
	1896.	1897.		
United States.. ...	$12,233,291.82	$11,260,705.87	....	$972,585.95
Australia and New Zealand.........	7,384.60	8,070.50	$685.90	....
Canada	15,938.61	12,922.76	....	3,015.85
China........	1,959.00	....	....	1,959.00
Pacific Islands.....	....	872.70	872.70	....
Total......... ...	$12,258,574.03	$11,282,572.83	$1,558.60	$977,560.80

Net decrease, $976,002.20.

IMPORTS FOR THE FIRST SIX MONTHS OF 1896 AND 1897.

| Whence imported. | 6 Months Ended June 30th. | | Increase. | Decrease. |
	1896.	1897.		
United States	$2,303,176.42	$3,058,380.92	$755,204.50	....
Great Britain	392,068.72	351,381.52	....	$40,687.20
Germany	31,122.74	52,878.70	21,755.96	....
China........	144,447.69	102,273.91	....	42,173.78
Japan...........	128,211.85	159,555.45	31,343.60	....
Australia and New Zealand	62,023.03	75,975.73	13,952.70	....
Canada...........	20,066.63	16,179.93	....	3,886.70
Pacific Islands. ...	4,391.91	3,003.16	....	1,388.75
France.....	5,929.36	18,385.70	12,456.34	....
Other countries....	24,388.34	70,474.23	46,085.89	....
Total...........	$3,115,826.59	$3,908,489.25	$880,798.99	$88,136.43

Net increase, $792,662.56.

The following tables may be interesting as show-ing the exports from the Hawaiian Islands. The tables give the articles, quantity, value, and the countries to which the articles are exported.

QUANTITY AND VALUE OF EXPORTS OF THE HAWAIIAN ISLANDS TO ALL PORTS FOR THE SIX MONTHS ENDED JUNE 30th, 1897.

Articles.	United States				Australia and New Zealand.	
	Pacific Ports.		Atlantic Ports.			
	Quantity.	Value.	Quantity.	Value.	Quantity.	Value.
Sugar..........pounds..	230,350,296	$6,668,595.37	145,612,711	$4,322,757.37	......	......
Rice.............do	2,168,600	87,378.30	......	......	......	......
Coffee...........do	218,489	31,756.52	......	......	8,975	$2,151.00
Bananas.......bunches..	43,457	43,334.50	......	......	......	......
Wool...........bales..	24	851.44	......	......	......	......
Do..........pounds..	10,024	......	......	......	......	......
Hides.........bundles..	1,170	......	......	......	......	......
Do...........pieces..	10,863	40,119.39	......	......	......	......
Pineapples.......do	64,874	7,429.70	......	......	1,150	100.00
Goatskins........do	3,163	930.00	......	......	......	......
Sheepskins.......do	4,914	1,140.45	......	......	......	......
Molasses.......gallons..	21,040	1,052.00	......	......	......	......
Betel leaves.....boxes..	70	350.00	......	......	......	......
Taro flour............	......	250.00	......	......	......	......
Watermelons.....pieces..	75	20.00	......	......	......	......
Plants and seeds.......	......	1,077.90	......	......	......	5.00
Sundry fruit..........	......	442.00	......	......	......	......
Bones and horns...pounds..	81,613	306.00	......	......	......	......
Curios...............	......	30.00	......	......	......	20.00
Canned fruits....dozens..	60	102.00	......	......	......	......
Sundries..............	......	555.16	......	......	......	738.20
Foreign..............	......	22,186.77	......	41.00	......	4,583.30
Honey...............	......	......	......	......	11,760	473.00
Total.........	......	$6,937,997.50	......	$4,322,798.37	......	$8,070.50

QUANTITY AND VALUE OF EXPORTS OF THE HAWAIIAN ISLANDS TO ALL PORTS, ETC.—Continued.

Articles.	Islands of the Pacific. Quantity.	Value.	Canada. Quantity.	Value.	Total. Quantity.	Value.
Sugar............pounds	....	....	....	....	375,963,007	$11,011,352.74
Rice..............do	....	....	11,754	$2,214.38	2,168,600	87,378.30
Coffee.............do	....	....	689	722.00	239,218	36,121.99
Bananas.......bunches	12	$6.00	....	....	44,158	44,062.50
Wool..............bales	....	....	....	....	24	....
Do..........pounds	....	....	44,480	3,558.40	54,504	4,409.84
Hides..........bundles	....	....	....	....	1,170	....
Do..........pieces	....	....	15,752	1,441.28	10,863	40,119.39
Pineapples.........do	....	....	....	....	81,776	8,970.98
Goatskins..........do	....	....	....	....	2,163	930.00
Sheepskins.........do	....	....	....	....	4,914	1,140.45
Molasses.......gallons	....	....	750	93.00	21,790	1,145.00
Betel leaves....boxes	....	....	....	....	70	350.00
Taro flour..........	....	....	....	....	....	20.00
Watermelons.....pieces	....	....	....	....	75	1,082.90
Plants and seeds......	....	....	....	....	....	442.00
Sundry fruit..........	....	....	....	....	....	306.00
Bones and horns...pounds	....	....	....	....	81,618	116.00
Curios..............	....	....	....	66.00	....	102.00
Canned fruits....dozens	....	....	....	30.00	60	....
Sundries............	....	6.00	....	....	....	1,339.36
Foreign.............	....	860.70	....	4,797.70	....	32,469.47
Honey...............	....	....	....	....	11,760	473.00
Total...............	....	$872.70	....	$12,922.76	....	$11,282,571.83

PERCENTAGE OF EXPORTS BY COUNTRIES.

	Per Cent.
United States:	
Pacific ports	61.49
Atlantic ports	38.31
Australia and New Zealand	.07
Canada	.11

The following table shows the value of merchandise imported, where from, and amount paying duties or entering free by treaty with the United States. It will be noticed that over half the imports come in free under the treaty.

VALUE OF MERCHANDISE IMPORTED AT ALL PORTS OF THE HAWAIIAN ISLANDS, AND COUNTRIES OF ORIGIN DURING THE SIX MONTHS ENDED JUNE 30th, 1897.

Country from which imported.	Goods free by treaty.	PAYING DUTY.		BONDED.	
		Goods.	Spirits.	Goods.	Spirits.
United States:					
Pacific ports..	$1,878,499.17	$291,443.14	$31,536.96	$1,776.65	$13,498.33
Atlantic ports	145,831.64	9,211.42	....	41.04	....
Great Britain...	... .	323,736.62	701.58	90.01	6,854.14
Germany.....	....	44,274.34	2,922.65	1.93	3,384.66
China	....	96,638.82	141.59	1,215.80	3,633.53
Japan...... ...	....	97,056.33	43,493.73	3,103.19	1,410.45
Australia and					
New Zealand.	....	10,995.33	....	2.29	206.97
Canada.........	....	5,118.93	36.90	15.20	1,748.90
Pacific islands..	....	199.91		....	....
France.........	....	8,321.01	42.50	....	2,954.55
Other countries.	....	13,557.64	1,105.49	19,956.62	54.28
Total...	$2,024,330.81	$900,553.49	$79,981.40	$26,202.73	$33,745.81

VALUE OF MERCHANDISE IMPORTED AT ALL PORTS OF THE HAWAIIAN ISLANDS, ETC.—Continued.

Country from which imported.	FREE BY CIVIL CODE.		Total.	Per cent.
	Goods.	Spirits.		
United States:				
Pacific ports........ ..	$651,843.78	$34,194.54	$2,902,792.57	74.27
Atlantic ports	488.25	16.00	155,588.35	3.98
Great Britain....... . .	19,999.17	....	351,381.52	8.99
Germany................	1,538.08	757.04	52,878.70	1.35
China................	644.17	....	102,273.91	2.62
Japan.............	14,486.75	5.00	159,555.45	4.08
Australia and New Zealand	64,771.14	....	75,975.73	1.94

VALUE OF MERCHANDISE IMPORTED AT ALL PORTS OF
THE HAWAIIAN ISLANDS, ETC.—Continued.

Country from which imported.	FREE BY CIVIL CODE.		Total.	Per cent.
	Goods.	Spirits.		
Canada................	$9,260.00	....	$16,179.93	.42
Pacific islands...........	2,803.25	....	3,003.16	.08
France.................	1,028.96	$6,038.68	18,385.70	.47
Other countries	35,800.20	....	70,474.23	1.80
Total................	$802,663.75	$41,011.26	$3,908,489.25	100.00

The above table includes specie ($423,550) imported for the last six months by civil code, all of which is from the United States.

The total value of exports to the United States, according to the records of this consulate-general, was $11,294,034.89, and for the same period in 1896 $12,205,778.55, while the Hawaiian custom-house figures give the values of said exports for the same periods as $11,282,571.83 and $12,258,-574.03, respectively. This discrepancy is explained by the fact that the total value of invoices presented at this office for certification includes commissions and insurance, whereas the Hawaiian custom-house, in stating values, deducts all charges.

DECLARED VALUE OF EXPORTS FROM THE DISTRICT OF HONOLULU AND THE AGENCIES CONNECTED TO THE UNITED STATES DURING THE SIX MONTHS ENDED JUNE 30th, 1896, AND ALSO FOR THE SIX MONTHS ENDED JUNE 30th, 1897.

FROM HONOLULU.

Articles.	SIX MONTHS ENDED JUNE 30th		Increase.	Decrease.
	1896.	1897.		
Awa root........	$396.42	....	....	$396.42
Bananas.........	49,601.48	$28,426.70	....	21,174.78
Betel leaves.. ...	268.80	292.57	$23.77	....
Coffee...	26,644.42	23,852.28	....	2,792.14
Hides and skins..	31,381.00	40,080.30	8,699.30	....
Household goods	3,600.75	2,399.00	....	1,201.75

DECLARED VALUE OF EXPORTS FROM THE DISTRICT OF HONOLULU, ETC.—Continued.

FROM HONOLULU.

Articles.	SIX MONTHS ENDRD JUNE 30th		Increase.	Decrease.
	1896.	1897.		
Returned American goods :				
Empty beer kegs	$5,817.30	$6,071.50	$254.20	....
Empty bottles..	435.42	291.75	....	$143.67
Miscellaneous...	10,294.24	3,365.32	....	6,928.92
Whiskey........	2,266.20	1,459.85	....	806.35
Pineapples.......	4,136.07	5,703.27	1,567.20	....
Rice....	68,912.89	77,691.56	8,778.67	....
Sugar...........	8,542,781.64	7,478,517.45	....	1,064,264.19
Sundries........	1,810.40	723.00	....	1,087.40
Wool...........	179.37	773.06	593.69	....
Total........	$8,748,526.40	$7,669,647.61	....	....

Total decrease in 1897, $1,078,878.79.

FROM HILO AGENCY.

Articles.	1896.	1897.	Increase.	Decrease.
Awa root........	$124.50	....	....	$124.50
Coffee....	276.28	$936.55	$660.27	....
Hides and skins..	1,014.78	1,382.98	368.20	... .
Returned American goods.....	94.50	1,628.00	1,533.50	....
Sugar......	1,499,457.00	1,609,733.99	110,276.99	....
Total........	$1,500,967.06	$1,613,681.52	....	....

Total increase in 1897, $112,714.46.

DECLARED EXPORTS, HAWAIIAN ISLANDS

Articles.	Quarter Ending—				Total.
	Sept. 30.	Dec. 31.	Mar. 31.	June 30.	
HILO.					
Coffee	$565.63	$832.26	$834.78	$336.55	$2,334.44
Hides and skins	914.62	432.96		548.20	2,730.56
Returned American goods	110.40		1,628.00		1,738.40
Sugar	396,882.72		634,435.11	975,298.88	2,006,616.71
Total	$398,473.37	$1,265.22	$636,897.89	$976,783.63	$2,013,420.11
HONOLULU.					
Awa		$464.26			$464.26
Bananas	$12,388.95	17,799.53	$15,294.00	$13,132.70	58,615.18
Betel leaves			292.57		292.57
Coffee	7,880.62	19,115.73	13,893.48	9,958.80	50,848.63
Household goods	3,141.50	1,852.00	431.00	1,968.00	7,392.50
Hides and skins	9,700.00	20,768.50	14,115.30	25,965.00	70,548.80
Pineapples	1,421.25	3,343.73	1,553.86	4,150.47	10,468.35
Pineapples, canned	3,845.00				3,845.00
Pineapple plants	620.00				620.00
Returned goods:					
Brandy	146.00				146.00
Empty beer kegs	1,059.55	2,217.00	2,313.75	3,757.75	9,348.05
Empty bottles		328.50		291.75	620.25
Miscellaneous	1,817.70	1,007.95	1,543.80	1,821.52	6,190.97
Wine			797.85	662.00	1,459.85
Whiskey		5,347.12			5,347.12
Rice	40,302.97	98,422.78	50,258.38	27,433.18	216,477.31
Sugar	1,634,656.31	830,169.27	3,468,070.39	4,010,447.06	9,943,343.03
Sundries	399.63	202.50	218.00	252.50	1,063.63
Taro flour			252.50		252.50
Whalebone		8,000.00			8,000.00
Wool	9,990.88	6,558.15	623.11	149.95	17,322.09
Total	$1,727,421.36	$1,015,597.02	$3,569,646.93	$4,099,990.68	$10,412,665.99

DECLARED EXPORTS, HAWAIIAN ISLANDS.—Continued.

Articles	Quarter Ending—				Total
	Sept. 30.	Dec. 31.	Mar. 31.	June 30.	
KAHULUI.					
Sugar	$147,891.98	$34,674.12	$777,144.74	$568,424.21	$1,528,435.05
Molasses		116.50	286.50	850.00	1,253.00
Hides	213.27	117.35	273.74	124.87	729.23
Lumber	216.85				216.85
Taro flour		4.25	3.00		61.75
Empty carboys	54.50	69.50			69.50
Returned goods		1,460.50	1,520.34	97.88	3,078.72
Household effects			162.03	25.50	187.53
Total	$148,376.60	$36,742.22	$779,390.35	$569,522.46	$1,534,931.63
MAHUKONA.					
Coffee		$1,577.30	$1,797.36		$3,374.66
Hides	$770.12	543.69	584.80	$567.33	2,465.94
Molasses		353.34			353.34
Returned goods		25.14			25.14
Sugar	152,278.58	127,438.01	319,164.29	339,679.20	938,560.02
Saddle trees		16.64			16.64
Total	$153,048.70	$129,954.12	$331,546.39	$340,246.53	$944,795.74

RECAPITULATION.

	Sept. 30.	Dec. 31.	Mar. 31.	June 30.	Total
Hilo	$398,473.37	$1,265.22	$696,897.89	$976,783.63	$2,013,420.11
Honolulu	1,727,421.36	1,015,597.02	3,569,656.93	4,099,990.68	10,412,665.99
Kahului	148,376.60	36,742.22	779,390.35	569,522.46	1,534,931.63
Mahukona	153,048.70	129,954.12	331,546.39	340,246.53	944,795.74
Total	$2,427,320.03	$1,183,558.58	$5,307,491.56	$5,986,543.30	$14,904,913.47

H.

STRATEGICAL POSITION.

THE STRATEGICAL POSITION OF HAWAII.

The main reason why Hawaii is a strategical point of value to the United States is that the Pacific is so wide that battleships cannot cross it from any foreign naval station to the Pacific coast without recoaling, and there is no place to recoal except Hawaii.

Exclusion of foreign countries from Hawaii will therefore practically protect the Pacific coast from trans-Pacific attack.

The following statements have been made by the leading experts of the United States army and navy directly upon the point at issue.

They are unanimously in support of the proposition that Hawaii strengthens the United States, and that control of Hawaii is essential to the safety of the Pacific coast and American commerce.

MAHAN ON HAWAII.

Captain Mahan's views on the importance of Hawaii as a military and naval stronghold are given in the following correspondence, which was read in the executive session of the Senate by Senator Teller:

QUESTIONS PUT TO MAHAN BY SENATOR KYLE.

WASHINGTON, D. C., February 3, 1898.

Capt. A. T. Mahan, U. S. N., 160 *West 86th Street, New York.*

DEAR SIR: Recent discussions in the Senate have

brought prominently to the front the question of the strategic features of the Hawaiian Islands, and in this connection many quotations have been made from your valuable and highly interesting contribution to literature in regard to these islands, and I am led to believe that you are as well qualified to give information relating to them as any man in the country.

I hand you herewith a list of four questions, and I shall be greatly pleased if you will kindly answer them. Thanking you in advance, I remain, very truly yours,

JAMES H. KYLE.

1. Would the possession of Hawaii strengthen or weaken the United States from a military standpoint?

2. In case of war, would it take a larger navy to defend the Pacific coast with or without the possession of Hawaii?

3. Is it practicable for any trans-Pacific country to attack the Pacific coast without occupying Hawaii as a base?

4. Could such attack be made by transporting coal in colliers and transferring coal at sea?

MAHAN'S REPLY.

160 WEST 86TH STREET, NEW YORK,
February 4, 1898.

Hon. James H. Kyle, U. S. Senate.

DEAR SIR: Your letter of the third is at hand. You appreciate, doubtless, that to give a categorical reply to questions such as you propose is very like giving a quotation apart from the context in which it stands. I shall try, however, to present such replies and their reasons as summarily as possible.

The Possession of Hawaii will Strengthen the United States.

1. From a military point of view the possession of Hawaii will strengthen the United States. Of course, as is constantly argued, every addition of territory is an additional exposed point; but Hawaii is now exposed to pass under foreign domination—notably Japan—by a peaceful process of overrunning and assimilation. This will inevitably involve its possession by a foreign power—a grave military danger to us—against which preoccupation by the United States is, in my judgment, the only security.

A Larger Navy necessary Without than With Hawaii.

2. In replying to the second question I must guard myself from being understood to think our present Pacific fleet great enough for probable contingencies. With this reservation a greater navy would not be needed for the defence of the Pacific coast than would be required with the islands unannexed. If we have the islands, and in the Pacific a fleet of proper force, the presence of the latter, or of an adequate detachment from it, at the Hawaiian Islands will materially weaken, if not wholly cripple, any attempted invasion of the Pacific coast (except from British Columbia), and consequently will proportionately strengthen us. With a fleet of the same size and Hawaii unoccupied by either party the enemy would at least be in a better position to attack us; while if he succeeded in establishing himself in any of our coast anchorages he would be far better off. For, in the latter case, the islands would not menace his communications with home; which they would if in our possession, because Hawaii flanks the communications.

It is obvious, also, that if we do not hold the

islands ourselves we cannot expect the neutrals in
the war to prevent the other belligerent from occupying them; nor can the inhabitants themselves
prevent such occupation.   The commercial value
is not great enough to provoke neutral interposi-
tion.   In short, in war we should need a larger
navy to defend the Pacific coast, because we should
have not only to defend our own coast, but to prevent, by naval force, an enemy from occupying the
islands; whereas, if we had preoccupied them, fortifications could preserve them to us.

Invasion of Pacific Coast Impracticable Without Hawaii as a Base.

3. In my opinion, it is not practicable for any
trans-Pacific country to invade our Pacific coast
without occupying Hawaii as a base.

Coaling at Sea Impracticable.

4. Coal can be transported in colliers, but as yet
it cannot be transshipped at sea with either rapid-
ity or certainty.   Even if it be occasionally practicable to coal at sea, the process is slow and un-
certain.   Reliance upon such means only is, in my
judgment, impossible.   A base must be had, and,
except the ports of our own coast, there is none to
be named alongside of Hawaii.

With much respect, I am, very truly yours,
   A. T. MAHAN.

The distances to the principal Pacific ports are
as follows:

	Miles.
Hawaii to San Francisco...	2,080
Hawaii to Nicaragua Canal..............	4,210
Hawaii to Tahiti...........................	2,389
Hawaii to Pagopago, Samoa...............	2,263
Hawaii to Auckland, New Zealand.........	3,850

	Miles.
Hawaii to Fiji.............................	2,736
Hawaii to Marshall Islands.................	2,098
Hawaii to Caroline Islands.................	2,602
Hawaii to Hong-Kong......................	4,917
Hawaii to Yokohama, Japan................	3,399
Hawaii to Unalaska, Aleutian Islands......	2,016
Hawaii to Sitka...........................	2,395
Hawaii to Vancouver......................	2,305

I.

COST OF LIVING, TRANSPORTATION, ETC.

San Francisco and Victoria are the two points of deportation for the Hawaiian Islands. The Oceanic Steamship Line has vessels sailing twice a month. One steamer sails for Honolulu, stays a few days, and returns to San Francisco. The other steamers touch at Honolulu and go on to the Australian colonies. Round-trip tickets can be obtained, and also lay-over tickets, at the company's offices on Montgomery Street, San Francisco. The Pacific Mail and O. & O. S. S. lines, running from China and Japan to San Francisco, also touch at Honolulu regularly. Arrangements can be made to lie over in Honolulu, visit the volcano, and proceed on the voyage by the next vessel.

From Victoria the C. & A. S. S. sail once a month.

The cost of round-trip passage is $125.

PRICE LIST OF PROVISIONS ON THE HAWAIIAN ISLANDS.

Fresh Hawaiian butter, from 25 to 50 cents per pound.

Hams, from 16½ to 30 cents per pound.

Bacon, from 16½ to 20 cents per pound.

Cheese, from 20 to 35 cents per pound.

Family pork, from 15 to 18 cents per pound.

Corned beef, 7 cents per pound.

Fresh meat, from 6 to 15 cents per pound.

Loin of porterhouse steaks, from 6 to 15 cents per pound.

Tinned fruits, per dozen, from $1.75 to $2.25.

Golden Gate flour, per 100 pounds, $2.50; lower grades, $2.20.

Hawaiian rice, $3.25 to $5 per 100 pounds.

Hawaiian bananas, per bunch, 25 to 55 cents.

Potatoes, from 1 to 2 cents per pound.

Eggs, per dozen, 25 to 50 cents.

Rolled oats, per case, $5.50.

Ice, in small quantities, 1½ cents per pound; 50 pounds and over, 1 cent per pound.

WAGES.

The following is an approximation of the wages paid to different classes of labor on the Hawaiian Islands:

Engineers on plantations, from $125 to $175 per month, house and firewood furnished.

Sugar-boilers, $125 to $175 per month, house and firewood furnished.

Blacksmiths, plantation, $50 to $100 per month, house and firewood furnished.

Carpenters, plantation, $50 to $100 per month, house and firewood furnished.

Locomotive-drivers, $40 to $75 per month, room and board furnished.

Head overseers, or head lunas, $100 to $150.

Under overseers, or lunas, $30 to $50, with room and board.

Bookkeepers, plantation, $100 to $175, house and firewood furnished.

Teamsters, white, $30 to $40, with room and board; Hawaiians, $25 to $30, with room; no board.

Field labor, Portuguese and Hawaiian, $16 to $18 per month; no board.

Field labor, Chinese and Japanese, $12.50 to $15 per month; no board.

In Honolulu bricklayers and masons receive from $5 to $6 per day; carpenters, $2.50 to $5; machinists, $3 to $5; painters, $2 to $5 per day of nine hours.

DOMESTIC LABOR.

The domestic labor in Honolulu, and in all parts of the islands, has for many years been performed by Chinese males, who undoubtedly make excellent house servants. During the last four or five years the Japanese have entered the field; the Japanese women are especially in demand as nurses for children.

The following are the prevailing rates of wages:

Cooks, Chinese and Japanese, $3 to $6 per week, with board and room.

Nurses and house servants, $8 to $12 per month, with board and room.

Gardeners or yard-men, $8 to $12 per month, with board and room.

Sewing-women, $1 per day and one meal.

Good substantial meals can be obtained at respectable Chinese restaurants and at the Sailors' Home for 25 cents, or board for $4.50 per week.

The market for all kinds of labor is overstocked, and it would be very unwise for any one to go to these islands with no capital on the mere chance of obtaining employment. The many steamships arriving at Honolulu bring numbers of people seeking employment who are obliged to return disappointed.

CURRENCY.

The currency of these islands is of the same unit of value as that of the United States. The gold is all of American mintage, and United States silver and paper money is in circulation and passes at par.

The Hawaiian money is paper, very little of which is seen in circulation, and silver. The paper money is secured by silver held in reserve.

The banks keep two accounts with their depositors, silver and gold.

23

The checks are so worded that the depositor may specify from which account the check is to be paid. If the check does not state in what currency it is to be paid, the law provides that the holder may demand gold if the amount is over $10.

The Hawaiian silver amounts to $1,000,000, $300,000 of which is held by the Government to secure a like amount of paper.

The minister of finance has estimated that there is $3,500,000 of money in circulation.

RATE OF EXCHANGE.

The rate of exchange is 1¼ per cent on Eastern cities of the United States, and 1 per cent on the Pacific coast. Gold is at a premium of 1 per cent.

J.

FREIGHT, PASSENGER, AND POSTAGE RATES.

The steamship lines plying between the coast of America and Honolulu are the Oceanic Steamship Company, the Oriental and Occidental Steamship Company, and the Pacific Mail.

One steamer of the Oceanic Line, the *Australia*, makes Honolulu her destination; the two other steamers of the line, after discharging passengers and freight, go on to Samoa and Australia. The steamers of the two other lines proceed to Japan and China.

The rates for passengers range from $75 to $100. The time from San Francisco to Honolulu by steamer is from six to seven days.

The Canadian-Australian Royal Mail Steamship Company's steamers, sailing from Vancouver and Victoria, stop at Honolulu and then proceed to Australia and New Zealand.

There are a number of fine sailing-vessels making regular trips between Port Townsend and San Francisco and Honolulu, with limited passenger accommodations. The price is $40 for cabin passage.

The bulk of the steam passenger and freight traffic between San Francisco and Honolulu is controlled by the Oceanic Steamship Company, their rates being $75 cabin and $25 steerage, while the two other lines charge $100 and $30, respectively.

FREIGHT RATES.

The rates of freight from here to San Francisco are: For steamers, $5 per ton and 5 per cent primage; sailing-vessels, $3 per ton and 5 per cent primage.

The rates to Atlantic ports range from $5 to $7 per ton, with 5 per cent primage.

The duration of the voyage between here and New York has been from 89 to 134 days.

RAILROADS.

There are three railroads on the islands. The Kahului Railroad, on the island of Maui, is 13 miles long; the Hawaiian Railroad, on the island of Hawaii, is about 20 miles long. These two roads are used principally to carry the products of the plantations to the various points of shipment. The principal road on these islands is the Oahu Railway and Land Company line, which runs from Honolulu to Waianae, the total length, including sidings, being 38.5 miles. This road was opened for traffic July 1, 1890, since which time its business has shown a steady increase, both in its passenger and freight traffic.

Last year the road carried 85,596 passengers, receiving a revenue of $30,993.50; 66,430.49 tons of freight were carried, earning $69,752.76.

The equipment consists of 5 locomotives, 14 passenger coaches, and 132 freight cars.

The road is bonded for $2,000,000, at 6 per cent, with $700,000 worth of stock, which is to be increased to $1,500,000.

RATES OF POSTAGE.

Domestic: Cents.

Letters to any part of the republic, for each one-half ounce................ 1

Drop or city letters or printed circulars, per one-half ounce or fraction .. 1

Domestic: Cents.

     Unsealed printed circulars to any part of the republic, per 4 ounces or fraction thereof.......................... 1

     Newspapers printed in the republic and sent from the office of publication to subscribers residing in the republic. Free

     Books, cards, photographs, etc., for each ounce.............................. 1

     Merchandise, samples of all kinds, for each ounce......................... 1

     Newspapers, pamphlets, almanacs, calendars, handbills, magazines, maps, occasional and other publications (not bound), for each 4 ounces or fraction thereof.............................. 1

     Registry fee, in addition to above charges............................. 10

Rates of foreign postage:

     To United States, Canada, Mexico, and colonies, letters, each one-half ounce or fraction.......................... 5

     Postal cards, each..................... 2

     Commercial papers, each 2 ounces or fraction (with a minimum charge of 5 cents).............................. 2

     Books, each 2 ounces.................. 1

     Photographs, each 2 ounces............ 1

     Newspapers, each 2 ounces............ 1

     Registration fee, in addition to above charges............................. 10

     Registration fee, with return receipts, in addition to above charges......... 15

Other countries of Postal Union:

     Letters, each one-half ounce........... 5

     Postal cards, each..................... 2

     Newspapers, each 2 ounces or fraction 2

     Photographs, each 2 ounces or fraction 2

     Samples (limit of weight 12 ounces, limit of size 12 by 8 by 4), each 2 ounces 2

INDEX.